XML for Data Architects

Designing for Reuse and Integration

XML for Data Architects

Designing for Reuse and Integration

James Bean

Relational Logistics Group and Global Web Architecture Group

MORGAN KAUFMANN PUBLISHERS

An imprint of Elsevier Science

Amsterdam   Boston   Heidelberg   London   New York   Oxford   Paris
San Diego   San Francisco   Singapore   Sydney   Tokyo

This book is printed on acid-free paper.

Senior Editor:	Lothlórien Homet
Publishing Services Manager:	Simon Crump
Senior Project Manager:	Angela G. Dooley
Editorial Coordinator:	Corina Derman
Project Management:	Graphic World
Composition:	SNP Best-set Typesetter Limited
Cover Design:	Frances Baca Design
Printer:	Maple-Vail

Morgan Kaufmann
An imprint of Elsevier Science
340 Pine Street, Sixth Floor, San Francisco, California 94104–3205, USA
http://www.mkp.com

Library of Congress Catalog Card Number: 2003104297
International Standard Book Number: 1-55860-907-5

Printed in the United States of America

This book is dedicated to my spouse and partner Sue.

Contents

Foreword

The challenges facing data architects in today's fast-paced environment are constantly growing and are a direct result of increasing complexity, interconnected systems, and new technologies. With the emergence of XML in 1998 and XML Schema in 2001, yet another architectural challenge has been added to this mix and it wasn't immediately obvious how this could be integrated into the mainstream since it introduced paradigms that radically differ from traditional relational data models.

Essentially, XML – the eXtensible Markup Language – is the first technology to provide a consistent, affordable, and extensible mechanism to describe both data and meta-data in the same document. While this seems like a simple enough extension on first glance, the consequences are quite profound, as this enables self-describing data, simplified interoperability, and the ability to store diverse kinds of data, such as textual documents, relational data, persistent object-oriented structures, and hierarchical information.

As a result, in only a few years XML has become the *lingua franca* of the Internet and is already used in such diverse applications as archaeology (e.g. *http://www-oi.uchicago.edu/OI/PROJ/XSTAR*), tax filing (e.g. *http://xml.coverpages.org/irs.html*), genomics (e.g. *www.fruitfly.org/sequence*), and many more domains. XML has thus quickly become an indispensable tool for describing, storing, and transforming data that cannot easily be made to fit into the relational model.

Due to its flexibility and hierarchical nature, XML calls for additional skills from the data architect. This book imparts the required knowledge and techniques. James Bean, a seasoned expert in database design, architecture, and all things XML takes you through the steps of getting acquainted with XML, learning about document types and XML schemas, and designing an XML architecture with a strong focus on reusability.

One of the major standards covered in this book is W3C XML Schema, which provides the essential capability to describe the structure of XML documents as well as to express restrictions on the data contained in the individual XML elements. This is done by means of so-called *simpleTypes* – which are similar to the datatypes used by relational databases, and this book devotes a chapter to the relationship between database types and XML Schema simpleTypes for various major relational databases – and *complexTypes* – which describe both the sequencing and nesting of XML elements inside each other.

In this function, XML Schema is a core technology for the data architect, and studied extensively in this book – especially with respect to taxonomy, reuse, and overall system design. This importance of XML Schema for data architects is also reflected in the positive feedback we constantly receive from our **xmlspy**® customers, many of which are now using the graphical XML Schema design tool in our product to design complex XML data models, just like they would use graphical tools to construct Entity-Relationship or UML diagrams for relational and object-oriented data models.

Another aspect to consider in this respect is the pervasive spread of XML through its wide adoption by major software vendors, such as Microsoft with its .NET framework and the Office 2003 products, as well as Oracle with the XML database functionality in Oracle 9i. As a result of this, XML becomes ubiquitous both on the desktop and in the data warehouse – and repurposing existing XML assets enables organizations to increase productivity and efficiency, provided that the data architect has a sound understanding of XML and its unique characteristics.

Which brings us to why you are holding this book in your hands...

Alexander Falk
President & CEO
Altova, Inc.

Acknowledgments

I would like to acknowledge Morgan Kaufmann publishers, and in particular I want to thank Lothlórien Homet for her enthusiasm, guidance, and patience and Corina Derman for her never-ending assistance. I would also like to thank Kelly Mabie and the Graphic World staff. I also acknowledge the many family members, business partners, clients, and friends who have been supportive of my work including: Sue Bean, Jack Bauer, David Bean, Lisa Bean ("SA"), Kimberly Bean ("Bug"), Beth Bauer, Norm Johnson, Sandy Johnson, Barb Wakefield, Dick Schreiber, Nick Torrez, Lara Tang, Gloria Michalak, Wally Sellman, Caren Shiozaki, Jerry Halterman, Mike Ruttledge, Deb Barra, Dennis Barra, Mike Nicewarner, Lori Gubernat, John Gubernat, Lorraine Cooper, Jerry Blidy, Dave Blidy, Renee Adams, Jackie Barkworth, Aprill Barnes, Tari Mattson, Kay Turner, Jarrod Reed, Bob Takoushian, John Sherrie, Patrick Vincent, Jorden Woods, Arka Mukherjee, Ph.D., Muralidhar Satyanarayana, and many others (you know who you are).

I would also like to acknowledge the contributions of the following individuals, technology companies, and technology standards organizations: Dr. Charles Goldfarb, Tim Burners-Lee, Alexander Falk, Altova, Microsoft, IBM, Sybase, Oracle, DAMA, and the W3C. The accomplishments of these people and organizations have resulted in tremendous business and technology advances and broad adoption of XML.

Introduction

The traditional enterprise is experiencing numerous technology challenges, the most recent of which are the results of new business paradigms (e.g., the Internet, the World Wide Web, economic pressures, and global e-commerce). Adding further complexity are traditional development practices, vertical system development, lack of support for data standards, acquisition of diverse businesses and technologies, and the implementation of software packages. These challenges beg for solutions that include cross-platform exchange and sharing of enterprise data.

Today's typical business enterprise is often composed of several autonomous business units. Often, each of these business units and their supporting systems has its own definition of mission-critical data. Regardless of the supporting technology, the business concept of a customer, vendor, or product processed by one system is of the same general context as that of the other systems. However, at a granular level the data characteristics of these business concepts tend to vary widely. These data characteristics are known as *metadata*. Perhaps the most often quoted definition for metadata is "data about data." Actually, metadata goes well beyond this simple definition to include the format, rules, and constraints that describe data.

eXtensible Markup Language (XML) has recently gained much notoriety as a technology solution. It can be used to advantage for many different types of applications such as moving data between different business systems or describing a business transaction, a request to persist or store data in a database, or a service request. By virtue of being platform agnostic, transactions and data exchanges are no longer relegated to custom or proprietary point-to-point interfaces. Rather than blatantly accepting the media hype surrounding XML, today's technologist must understand its strengths and weaknesses as well as determine when and how to apply it effectively. Although presenting tremendous capabilities, XML is not a singular solution or "silver bullet" to solve all problems. Use of XML still requires a defined process, rigorous application of standards, synergies with other technologies, and practical techniques.

XML is a relatively recent (circa 1997), yet stable, technology. Regardless of what you may have read, XML is in fact a form of descriptive metadata. On its own, XML is a syntax for implementing descriptive data containers within a document, transaction, or message. Schemas extend the metadata capabilities of XML by defining rules and constraints for the characteristics of data, such as structure, relationships, allowable values, and data types. When enterprise information is contained within an XML document or transaction and shared with other enterprise systems or possibly with external partners of the enterprise, we can quickly see the need for applying effective data architecture practices.

Although not a constraint, this book is developed from the perspective of those responsible for enterprise metadata. Specific responsibilities of metadata-related disciplines can vary, but most often professional titles include those of data architect, data analyst, data administrator, and data modeler. The world is rapidly changing and as data architects we should be "agents of change." As evidenced by the increasing demand for assistance with the definition of schemas, XML presents a tremendous opportunity for the data architect. To respond to the expectations of leadership and promote the value of data architecture, data architects need to have a firm grasp of XML and its capabilities and limitations. To exploit XML as a metadata technology, data architects must reform, adapt, and reapply aspects of their discipline to XML and related processes. If they do not, the use of XML will continue to proliferate across the enterprise, but with questionable result.

This book is intended to provide that much needed information. Simply put, those responsible for describing, defining, and designing data and data structures or those responsible for processing data-oriented transactions and messages will find value in this book. In Chapter 1 (Motivation and Rationale for Using XML), the reader will be introduced to XML as a metadata technology and to the rationale for its use. Interestingly, XML is not a "one size fits all" solution. The application of XML can vary widely and in some cases may not be the best technology choice. In many cases, XML is used to describe the content of simple documents. However, transaction- and message-oriented data present even greater opportunities for the application of XML. Chapter 2 (XML Document Types) describes the orientation and application of XML to different types of documents.

Also of importance is the distinction between XML for describing data content and a schema, which includes granular metadata rules that are applied to a referencing XML document. There are several types of schemas that can be used with XML. Each has a number of advantages and disadvantages. Often, the metadata practitioner is challenged with identifying which type of schema would provide the most value to an application of XML. Chapter 2 also provides guidance as to the capabilities, strengths, and weaknesses of the three types of schemas used most often. Although different schema types are described, my experience is that XML Schemas (W3C May 2001 Recommendation) are the most feature rich and advantageous for transaction- and message-oriented content. As a result, emphasis is placed on W3C XML Schemas for the other chapters.

Chapters 3 through 7 will help to guide the practitioner through the application and extension of critical metadata practices to XML and W3C XML Schemas. Chapter 3 (The Importance of Naming Standards [Taxonomy]) provides techniques for naming XML element and attribute containers in a manner that aligns with enterprise practices and that leverages the descriptive strengths of XML. Chapter 4 (W3C XML Schema vs Database Data Types) describes the "strong typing" capabilities of W3C XML Schemas as well as how supported types align with similar data types of the most common database products. As any data architect will recognize, data types alone are rarely specific enough to adequately describe a data value. Of additional importance are constraints such as the length, the number of decimal places, and allowable values. Chapter 5 (W3C XML Schema Data Type Facets) describes these and other constraints (known as "facets") that can be applied to a data type.

Data models such as entity relationship diagrams (ERD) are some of the data architect's most important deliverables. These models allow for the definition and visualization of data structures and relationships. Chapter 6 (Structure Models) describes the similarities between traditional data models and XML structures. Of significant importance is the development of "prototype" XML transactions as a form of modeling.

An architect of any discipline must consider flexibility and reuse. Both can be addressed by the identification and application of common patterns to a model. Chapter 7 (Architectural Container Forms) goes beyond modeling to apply an architectural pattern perspective to models.

Reuse presents one of the greatest potential benefits to application development. However, it is also the most misunderstood. Not only are enterprise reuse practices lacking in many development technologies, but the concept of reuse is also often inaccurately defined. Metadata reuse and the proliferation of metadata-based standards present tremendous opportunities for the data architect. Chapter 8 (W3C XML Schemas and Reuse) describes the reuse paradigm and presents techniques for effective reuse of W3C XML Schemas.

With the rapid acceptance and deployment of XML, the alignment of traditional roles, responsibilities, and expertise in technology have become convoluted. In their desire to leverage the strengths of XML, members of the development community often assume that XML should be their exclusive responsibility. However, in many cases these same development practitioners lack strong experience with metadata disciplines. Although they are gaining benefit in the short term, the proliferation of nonstandard XML transactions and schemas presents the potential for a costly long-term problem. Chapter 9 (Design and Engineering for the Data Architect) proposes a collaborative process in which the design of XML structures and engineering of schemas are a shared responsibility of both the development and metadata community. In addition, the reader is provided with practical design and engineering techniques.

Although the processes, practices, and techniques of previous chapters target transaction-oriented data, in many cases they can also be applied to document- and message-oriented content. XML has also gained visibility with recent industry emphasis on collaborative computing and in particular "Web Services." Chapter 10 (Web Services—An Introduction to the Future) introduces the concept of Web Services and describes the use of XML for describing messages.

XML and W3C XML Schema examples are presented throughout. The examples tend to revolve around important data concepts that are common to most industries. I have in several cases varied the applied naming techniques, structure, and form with the intent of demonstrating that there are few strictly enforced rules and each enterprise may desire to adapt and apply their own processes and standards to the use of XML.

To further assist the reader, the important concepts of each chapter are called out as the combination of Facts, Recommendations, Techniques, and Opportunities. *Facts* are based upon available reference or observation. Although subjective, *Recommendations* are the result of research and experience as a data architect. *Techniques* define specific practices that can be tactically applied. *Opportunities* allow the reader to decide whether to apply a particular technique to advantage or to avoid a potential pitfall.

In addition to other important reference sources, these concepts are summarized in Appendix A and cross-referenced to their original reference point in the chapter text. Appendix B presents syntactical examples of fundamental W3C XML Schemas syntax. These syntax fragments are provided to help the data architect with several of the most often used container, structure, and constraint declarations. Combined with the chapter content, this technique has resulted in a foundation reference that will assist data architects and metadata practitioners as well as those of other technical disciplines.

1

Motivation and Rationale for Using XML

Before embarking upon the journey to learn why *eXtensible Markup Language (XML)* is important or when it should be used in a technology application, you have to have some idea about how it came to be. XML has evolved to become a "conforming subset" of *Standard Generalized Markup Language (SGML)*. SGML has been in use for a number of years to describe and constrain the content of primarily text-oriented documents and files. Common examples of text-oriented content are the pages of a book, letters, notes, brochures, and presentations. As would be expected, the contents of these documents are strings of characters and words that are generally assembled to present a context (most often as collections of phrases, sentences, paragraphs, sections, and chapters). With this type of loosely structured information, rarely is there a need to describe granular pieces of information such as individual words or even more specific characteristics such as data types. SGML applications of this type include the use of descriptive tags to delineate sections of contained text and to describe text and document characteristics. Although the value of SGML for describing document-oriented data is undisputed, its application to other business and technology paradigms such as global e-commerce and enterprise data exchanges presents a few problems. First, SGML is implemented by a complex syntax that for many can be difficult to learn and apply. Also, there is a obvious lack of support for strongly typed data (e.g., data architects will recognize "strongly typed data" as the "data types" of a data element, column, field, or attribute).

Alternatives to text-oriented content are the data contained by e-business and enterprise data exchange transactions. For both global e-commerce and enterprise integration, the focus is on granular pieces of information that are processed and consumed in combination. Although there are exceptions, most e-commerce business transactions contain individual data elements rather than large strings of text such as sentences and paragraphs. Typical data contained in an e-commerce transaction include order numbers, product numbers, prices, monetary amounts, quantities, dates, names, and addresses. Whereas SGML could be used to describe an e-commerce transaction, it would be overly verbose and at the same time would not provide important metadata details such as the data types or data type facets for each element.

An XML *document* (e.g., a document, transaction, or message) is composed of named containers and their contained data values. An XML document is also known as an *instance* or XML document instance. Typically, these containers are represented as elements and attributes. *Element* containers may be defined to hold data, other elements, both data and other elements, or nothing at all. An *attribute* container is a bit different in that it may only hold data values or nothing. Unlike element containers, an attribute may not hold or contain another attribute. Externally, an XML document is generally a file. In the case of the Microsoft Windows operating system, the default file extension that terminates the file name is *.xml.*

The syntax for declaring attribute containers differs from that for an element. Element containers require both an open tag and a close tag (also known as a *begin tag* and an *end tag*). The combination of element open and close tags increases the verbosity and overall size of the XML transaction. Alternatively, the syntax for declaring attributes requires a single tag and a corresponding value (Fig. 1.1).

The internal structure of an XML document is roughly analogous to the hierarchical directory and file structure represented in Microsoft Windows Explorer (Fig. 1.2). The topmost element of the XML document is the *root element*, of which there is only one per document. This is similar to the topmost folder of Windows Explorer (i.e., the Desktop). As previously noted, elements may contain data values, other elements, combinations, or nothing at all. Elements contained by other elements are referred to as *nested elements*. The containing element is a *parent element*, and the nested element is a *child element*. A folder defined to Microsoft Windows Explorer can contain other folders, which may contain other folders, and so on. This is similar to nesting of XML elements in a document. Windows Explorer folders may also contain files,

Figure 1.1

Example of XML
element and attribute
syntax.

- The syntax for an element requires that the element name be enclosed by angle brackets ("<" and ">").
- Proper syntax requires that an "open" or "begin" tag is followed by an "end" or "close" tag.
- Alternative "shorthand" syntax allows that an element is defined by a single tag, with a trailing "/".

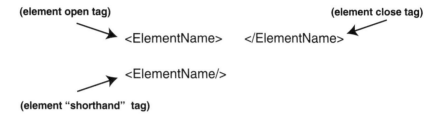

(element open tag)   **(element close tag)**

<ElementName>   </ElementName>

<ElementName/>

(element "shorthand" tag)

- The syntax for an attribute requires that the attribute name be in the form of an "attribute value pair."
- Attributes must be defined to an element.

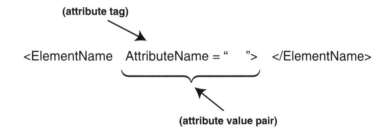

(attribute tag)

<ElementName   AttributeName = "   ">   </ElementName>

(attribute value pair)

documents, or programs, comparable to XML elements that contain data values. Attributes are similar to the "properties" of a Windows Explorer folder or file. What should be obvious is that the structure of XML exhibits similarities to structures of many other hierarchical, structural, and metadata technologies.

To process an XML document, an application program must be able to navigate the hierarchical structure and examine the contents of containers as necessary. A utility program known as a *parser* provides this functionality to the application program. As a simple explanation of the process, an application program invokes the parser, which navigates the XML document, identifies each container, and exposes the data values contained by each container to the application program. Some parsers can also compare a document to a set of metadata rules and notify the application program when an inconsistency or error has been encoun-

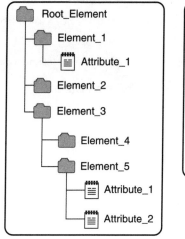

A Folder/File Hierarchy
(similar to Microsoft Windows Explorer, © Microsoft)   **XML Document Structure**

```
Root_Element
  Element_1
    Attribute_1
  Element_2
  Element_3
    Element_4
    Element_5
      Attribute_1
      Attribute_2
```

```
<Root_Element>
  <Element_1  Attribute_1=" " ></Element_1>
  <Element_2></Element_2>
  <Element_3>
    <Element_4></Element_4>
    <Element_5  Attribute_1=" "  Attribute_2=" "></Element_5>
  </Element_3>
</Root_Element>
```

Figure 1.2

Hierarchical similarities of a folder–file structure and XML.

tered. A schema defines a set of rules and constraints for the referencing XML document. This type of parsing is known as *validation*. As we will see in Chapter 4 (W3C XML Schema Data Types vs Database Data Types), the parsing and validation are processes that are required to check for data types and other metadata rules.

There are two primary types of parsers: the document object model (DOM) parser and the simple API for XML (SAX) parser. A *DOM parser* builds a hierarchical model of the parsed XML document (known as the "document object model"), with each of the important locations in the document, the various element and attribute containers, and characteristics of that model being represented as *nodes*. When the XML document is not particularly large and when sufficient memory is available (a DOM parser builds an in-memory model), a DOM parser tends to perform reasonably well. However, the greatest advantage of a DOM parser is that the structure of the XML document in its entirety is exposed to the processing application program. The application program can navigate and recurse through the document as needed.

Alternatively, a *SAX parser* is *event driven*. The hierarchical document structure and concept of nodes still apply, but each node of the structure is individually raised as an event to the processing application program, rather than the entire XML document as a complete structure. The application program (or associated logic) must then determine whether and how to process each event (i.e., each node). SAX parsers generally consume less memory than DOM parsers and typically perform well when "walking" the hierarchical structure (navigating top-down and left-to-right). However, SAX parsers place more processing burden on the application program for logic and navigation. Navigation such as recursion through a structure may require complex logic to reopen and parse the document several times. Processing an XML document with a SAX parser is roughly analogous to relational database processing from within a procedural language. With a relational database, an SQL query produces a *result set*. A *cursor* is opened on that result set, and the application program must navigate and *fetch* each row of the result set to process each data instance.

The hierarchical structure of a document is fundamental to XML. However, the motivation and rationale for using XML are based upon a number of important capabilities and strengths. The first of those is that XML is "self-describing."

Self-Describing

Although it leverages the descriptive and text-oriented strengths of SGML, XML goes well beyond. An XML document can include the rigorous use of descriptive element and attribute containers. The method for describing a container is to declare a named *tag*. In addition to identifying each element and attribute container by name, the tag can also be used to imply the type of contained data, as well as the container's location or position in the document. XML is therefore self-describing.

The data values contained within an XML document are known as *content*. When descriptive names have been applied to the elements and attributes that contain the data values, the content of the document becomes intuitive and self-explanatory to a person. That is, a person can follow the internal structure of the XML document and easily determine the type of information that each element or attribute is intended to contain. When the XML document represents data such as a delivery address, containers for address lines, city, country, and postal code become easily identified. Additionally, with the aid of a parser, auto-

```
<?xml version="1.0" encoding="UTF-8"?>
<ExampleCustomers>
 <Customer CustomerID="P123456" CustomerType="Customer-Prospect" Source="List 01-02-03">
  <CustomerAddresses>
   <Address AddressType="Residence-Primary" AddressNo="1">
    <AddressLines>
     <AddressLine LineNo="1">62789 N. Shadow Drive</AddressLine>
     <AddressLine LineNo="2">Building 23</AddressLine>
     <AddressLine LineNo="3">Apt. 236</AddressLine>
    </AddressLines>
    <AddressCity>Chicago</AddressCity>
    <AddressRegion>
     <StateUSAAbbrev StateName="Illinois">IL</StateUSAAbbrev>
    </AddressRegion>
    <AddressPostalCode>60699-0001</AddressPostalCode>
    <AddressCountry CountryCode="USA" CountryNo="840">USA</AddressCountry>
   </Address>
  </CustomerAddresses>
 </Customer>
</ExampleCustomers>
```

In this example, address lines, city, region, and other parts of an address are described by their element names (i.e., "tags").

Figure 1.3

XML is "self-describing."

mated applications can also navigate an XML document, locate elements and attributes of interest by their tag or name, and process the contained data. The result is that an XML document containing elements with descriptive names can be processed by an application program and read (or debugged) by a person (Fig. 1.3).

Fact:

XML is self-describing (supports descriptive element and attribute tags).

The use of XML to describe the contents of a transaction is a significant shift from more traditional transaction and interface file formats, for which only the raw data are carried, and either each data value has a fixed location within the file or some other method of separating one data value from another is present. Although fixed position and delimited files are functional, without a "map" of locations or a similar form of demarcation for contained data, the processing application has no method of navigating the file to identify, extract, and process the contained data. When the processes of application maintenance, enhancement, debugging, and problem resolution are considered, this can present a challenge for the application developer. Review of problem or error-prone transactions requires cross-referencing to a map of the file's structure. In addition, the lack of descriptive notation with a traditional interface file can limit the developer's ability to determine the context or intended use of a raw data value.

Of even greater value is the use of a *schema* as a method for further describing the content of the XML document. Depending on the capabilities of the parser, there are several different types of schemas that can be used to describe XML documents. As we will see in Chapter 2 (XML Document Types), schemas types have strengths and weaknesses. One of the more recent advances in this area is *XML schemas* (World Wide Web Consortium [W3C] Recommendation, May 2001). To avoid ambiguity with the term *schemas*, I will refer to the syntax and capabilities of the W3C XML Schema recommendation from here forward as "W3C XML Schemas." When I speak of schemas as a general concept for data or file structures and relationships and without regard to a single syntax or specific implementation, I will refer to "schemas" (in lowercase). W3C XML Schemas provide the ability to describe the data type of each container (e.g., elements and attributes) as well as other rules and constraints. Although there are several other types of schemas that can be used during validation, W3C XML Schemas are generally considered to be the most robust and widely accepted for transaction and message-oriented content and are the primary focus for this book.

W3C XML Schemas provide the ability to describe rules and constraints for the following:

- Base and derived data types (e.g., numeric, string, date, boolean, and others)

- Extended data types (e.g., custom data types derived by the data architect)

- Facets (e.g., additional constraints such as length, fractional digits, and others)

- Value limits (e.g., allowable minimum and maximum values)

- Enumeration (e.g., the defined set of allowable values for an element or attribute)

- Specific repeating element occurrences (e.g., cardinality and modality)

- Patterns (e.g., format and edit patterns)

As previously mentioned, a parser is a software utility that helps to navigate an XML document and extract data values. As an extension of this concept, a *validating parser* compares the rules and constraints of a schema to the XML document and informs the processing application of errors. To apply metadata constraints such as those supported by W3C XML Schemas, a validating parser that supports that particular schema type must be used.

Another important capability of XML is the ability to define element and attribute container names in a manner that supports enterprise naming standards or taxonomy rather than with a rigid syntax. Unlike *HyperText Markup Language (HTML)*, which has predefined elements that are not easily extended, the elements and attributes defined to an XML document are for the most part defined by the designer or implementer. There are relatively few predefined or reserved tags for an XML document (Fig. 1.4). Because XML tags are defined by the enterprise rather than predefined, an XML document is also extensible. That is, an XML document and referenced schema can be extended to incorporate new element and attribute containers as needed.

In part, a direct comparison between HTML and XML is not entirely fair. HTML is an excellent technology for presentation or *rendering* of content in a browser. That is, HTML elements and attributes are primarily for the visual formatting of document-oriented content. As an example, the HTML "<p>" element defines a paragraph. Similarly, when combined with attributes, the HTML "<font>" element instructs the browser to render content using the specified font style and size.

In addition to general presentation or rendering of content, HTML *forms* provide the ability to capture user-entered information from the browser and submit the captured data to a server. Intrinsic to an HTML form are elements and attributes that provide minimal support for descriptive metadata. As an example, the "<input>" element allows for an entry field to appear in the browser and to accept input of data. As a type of metadata validation, the input element also allows attributes for size and maxlength. The size attribute defines the size of the input field when rendered, and the maxlength attribute defines the maximum number of characters that may be entered in the field.

In contrast to HTML, XML is primarily used to describe and contain data. Although the most obvious and effective use of XML is to describe data, other technologies such as *eXtensible Stylesheet Language Transform (XSLT)* can also be used to format or transform XML content for presentation to a user. As an example, an XML stylesheet with font characteristics and headings can be applied to an XML document, with the data being rendered in a browser similar to that for HTML.

HTML Document

```
<html>
   <head>
      <title>Product Info</title>
   </head>
   <body>
      <p>
        <font face="Arial" size="2">
         <b>Product</b>
        </font>
       </p>
      <p>Product ID: 12345</p>
      <p>Product Description: Widget</p>
      <p>Product Dimensions:</p>
      <p>Weight: 2.5 LB</p>
      <p>Length: 14.3 IN</p>
      <p>Height: 6.1 IN</p>
      <p>Width: 21.7 IN</p>
   </body>
</html>
```

<html>, <head>, <body>, <p>, and other tags have specific meaning and are all predefined by the HTML syntax.

XML Document (Instance)

```
<?xml version="1.0" encoding="UTF-8"?>
<Product>
 <ProductID>12345</ProductID>
 <ProductDescription>Widget</ProductDescription>
 <ProductDimensions>
  <Weight Unit="LB">2.5</Weight>
  <Length Unit="IN">14.3</Length>
  <Height Unit="IN">6.1</Height>
  <Width Unit="IN">21.7</Width>
 </ProductDimensions>
</Product>
```

<Product>, <ProductID>, <ProductDescription>, and other tags are defined by the designer or implementer.

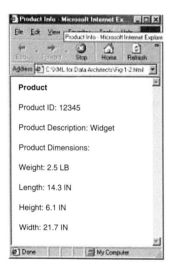

Figure 1.4

Predefined HTML tags vs. XML tags.

One of the most obvious differences between HTML and XML is the name applied to an element or attribute. As previously noted, most HTML elements and attributes are predefined and support specific presentation and rendering functions. For XML, element and attribute names are specific to the use and context of the document. Other than rare exceptions (such as the reserved XML attributes for language, version, and encoding), they do not have a predefined purpose. The advantage is that the designer or architect determines how the content of the document will be described. Rather than focusing on the font or presentation characteristics of the data, XML elements and attributes act as descriptive containers for the data. When the XML document is combined with a referenced schema, other metadata characteristics are also supported.

The most frequent opportunities to exploit the capabilities of XML are data-oriented. They include global e-commerce transactions and enterprise application data exchanges. However, the overall rationale for using XML is far broader in scope and potential than transaction exchanges. When the entire enterprise is considered rather than a single autonomous application, XML is also interoperable, reusable, flexible, and extensible.

Related to the self-describing characteristics of XML are the character encoding. Most XML documents are encoded using some form of Unicode, the common default for which is "UTF-8," which includes the ASCII character set. This allows the contents of an XML document to be viewed with most simple text editors. If the designer has also descriptively named the elements and attributes of the document, there is a potential to unintentionally expose sensitive data. An element container named <CreditCardNumber> would be obvious to an unauthorized viewer. As a result, some form of encryption or similar security may be necessary.

Interoperable

XML is an *interoperable* technology. Simply stated, if the sending and receiving platforms can read and write Unicode-encoded files (often using UTF-8 and ASCII) and an XML parser is available for those platforms, XML can be processed. Differences between operating systems or issues such as character set conversion become minimal concerns. Although many XML documents are encoded as simple ASCII, extensions for complex character sets and symbols are supported. This additional capability is supported by Unicode and can also be leveraged to data content described in languages other than English.

Considering that XML is in fact interoperable, it is also platform agnostic. It presents an opportunity to describe exchanges between autonomous technical environments and highly diverse enterprise applications. An XML transaction that is created and initially processed on a Windows platform with an SQL Server 2000 database could also be processed on a UNIX platform, using an Oracle database (obviously each platform and environment would need to support XML and Unicode). An obvious opportunity for interoperable processing is support of *enterprise integration* (also known as *enterprise application integration* or *EAI*).

Fact:

XML is generally interoperable (XML is by default encoded as Unicode and UTF-8, supporting basic ASCII characters).

A common form of enterprise integration is the sharing, exchange, or movement of data between autonomous enterprise systems that have been developed and maintained over a long period of time, on different technical platforms, and with different database architectures. As an example, product information maintained by a purchase order system might be shared and exchanged with the inventory management system and also with the order entry system. Each of these systems could be platformed on different hardware with different operating systems and different databases. As long as each platform supports the processing of Unicode character encoding and XML parsers are available, XML presents an effective method of describing interoperable data exchanges (Fig. 1.5).

As evidenced by leading technology journals, XML is rapidly becoming an important technology for interoperable and collaborative computing. Extended XML support and capabilities are being provided by most of the major technology vendors. At the time of publication, IBM, Microsoft, Oracle, Sybase, TIBCO, Altova, and numerous other technology providers are including XML support within many of their products and platforms. Although XML support can vary, the most common forms include XML parsers, XML software development kits, and database extensions to import, export, and persist data in XML format.

Another application of XML for which interest is growing is the definition of portable models for exchange between design and development tools. Many of these tools are providing XML import–export capabilities. It is envisioned that in the near future models engineered in

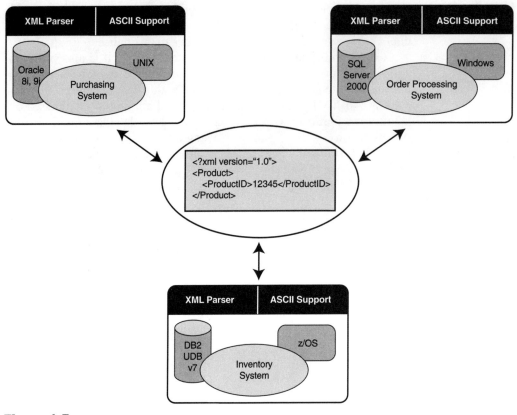

Figure 1.5

Use of XML for describing interoperable data exchanges.

one data modeling tool and exported using an XML described file format may be readily imported into other similar tools. The Object Management Group[1] is advancing this scenario by promoting the use of common XML-based toolset vocabularies to describe models and modeling objects with a standard XML structure.

[1] Object Management Group. OMG Modeling and Metadata Specifications. XML Metadata Interchange (XMI®). Available at http://www.omg.org/.

Reusable

Reuse presents one of the greatest opportunities for reducing application development costs, engineering costs, and ongoing maintenance costs as well as for promoting the use of enterprise data standards. In the simplest terms, *reuse* is the ability to develop something and use it more than once. Even more advantageous is *broad-scale reuse*, which extends this definition by promoting reuse outside the original purpose or context for which it was engineered.

A more formal definition of reuse includes two primary activities: *reuse engineering* (i.e., engineering something with the intent that it will be used more than once) and *reuse harvesting* (i.e., identifying something as being reusable, validating that it can be effectively reused, and then reusing it). Surprisingly, reuse is often misunderstood and is sometimes ignored in favor of other rapid development practices. Often the reason given for avoiding formalized reuse is difficulty in implementing practical reuse practices. However, with the advent of W3C XML Schemas, reuse can be implemented rapidly and leveraged in numerous ways.

Fact:

XML is reusable (W3C XML Schemas can be engineered as modular component schemas).

The World Wide Web Consortium "May 2001 Recommendation for XML Schemas"[2] has resulted in a metadata technology that can be structured to exhibit and support several types of reuse. Within a single W3C XML Schema, defined element containers, collections of element containers, and custom data types can all be defined and then reused by reference. As one example, a custom data type can be defined once (e.g., using a globally declared "simpleType" to represent the enterprise standard for monetary amounts) and can then be reused by reference throughout the schema (Fig. 1.6).

Of even greater value are modular external component W3C XML Schemas containing elements, custom data types, etc., that can be reused by inclusion and reference from within numerous other W3C XML Schemas. Consider the example of a postal address. An enterprise metadata standard for postal address allowing for flexibility such as that required to support highly diverse international postal address formats

---

[2] World Wide Web Consortium (W3C). XML Schemas. W3C Recommendation, May 2, 2001. Available at http://www.w3.org/TR/2001/REC-xmlschema-1-20010502/ (structures); http://www.w3.org/TR/2001/REC-xmlschema-2-20010502/ (data types).

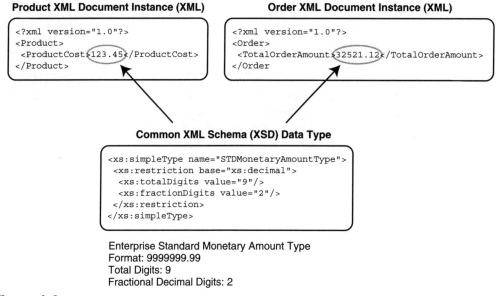

Figure 1.6

Example of reusable data type for monetary amount.

could be defined with a W3C XML Schema. The Address schema would then become a standard and could potentially be reused in different contexts (Fig. 1.7).

A component schema for an address can also be engineered in a manner that exhibits forms of transparency. Applications that do not require four or five street address lines, as would be required for many international addresses, can ignore those additional elements. The containers for these address lines are defined as "optional." As an enterprise standard, the W3C XML Schema for postal address can also be reused by other W3C XML Schemas to represent either a customer address, vendor address, or employee address. If the postal address structure requires future modifications, maintenance occurs within the component address schema rather than within all of the referencing schemas (Fig. 1.8).

When these standard schemas have been defined and published to the enterprise, initial development costs as well as ongoing maintenance costs (those specific to XML) can be reduced or avoided. Application-specific XML schemas can be engineered to reuse the component

```
<?xml version="1.0" encoding="UTF-8"?>
<ExampleCustomers>
 <Customer CustomerID="P123456" CustomerType="Customer-Prospect" Source="List 01-02-03">
  <CustomerAddresses>
   <Address AddressType="Residence-Primary" AddressNo="1">
    <AddressLines>
     <AddressLine LineNo="1">62789 N. Shadow Drive</AddressLine>
     <AddressLine LineNo="2">Building 23</AddressLine>
     <AddressLine LineNo="3">Apt. 236</AddressLine>
    </AddressLines>
    <AddressCity>Chicago</AddressCity>
    <AddressRegion>
     <StateUSAAbbrev StateName="Illinois">IL</StateUSAAbbrev>
    </AddressRegion>
    <AddressPostalCode>60699-0001</AddressPostalCode>
    <AddressCountry CountryCode="USA" CountryNo="840">USA</AddressCountry>
   </Address>
  </CustomerAddresses>
 </Customer>
</ExampleCustomers>
```

Address Schema (xsd)

Address
Address Lines (Lines 1–6)
Address City
Address Region
Address Postal Code
Address Country

Each of the examples of XML
documents could reference
the same W3C XML Schema
describing an address.

```
<?xml version="1.0" encoding="UTF-8"?>
<ExampleVendors>
 <Vendor VendorID="123457" VendorType="Vendor-Preferred">
  <VendorAddresses>
   <Address AddressType="Payment-Primary" AddressNo="1">
    <AddressLines>
     <AddressLine LineNo="1">Harcourt House</AddressLine>
     <AddressLine LineNo="2">50 Sheffield Place</AddressLine>
    </AddressLines>
    <AddressCity>London</AddressCity>
    <AddressPostalCode>EC3Y-9SY</AddressPostalCode>
    <AddressCountry CountryCode="GBR" CountryNo="826">England, U.K.</AddressCountry>
   </Address>
  </VendorAddresses>
 </Vendor>
</ExampleVendors>
```

Figure 1.7

Reuse of address schema in different contexts.

Figure 1.8

Standard address
schema referenced by
other schemas.

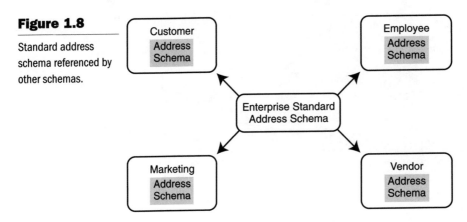

schemas by reference (similar to a conceptual form of "development by
assembly"), thereby avoiding "new" development or ongoing redevelopment of the same structures by other application development efforts.

Flexible

Database architectures and application-to-application interface files
are often engineered according to static structures. Consider the previous example of a postal address. Interface files that contain a North
American postal address are often defined with specifically named fields
for two street address lines, city, state, and postal code. However, as we
move toward a more global e-business paradigm, these traditional
address structures will be unable to support or describe international
postal address formats. To exchange highly variable global postal
address data with a static interface file, one of several traditional
approaches can be taken:

- Attempt to force global address data into existing interface
  files (prone to error).

- Reengineer and extend existing interface files to support
  international addresses.

- Develop new interface files.

- Ignore global address data (or portions thereof).

In addition to the interface files used for transactions and data exchanges, the source and target database architectures would also probably require modification. The cost of reengineering the existing database tables to accommodate structural changes can ripple through to data access functions and application logic. Something as simple as adding two or three additional street address lines can result in significant maintenance costs.

Fact:

XML is flexible (XML structures can be engineered to dynamically expand or contract).

Alternatively, XML presents a flexible transaction and data exchange solution. XML structures that are engineered according to vertical models and architectural forms are *flexible*. As we will see in Chapter 6 (Structure Models), a vertical model utilizes groups of similar elements. By using a flexible architectural form, the addition of new element containers to an XML document, such as the insertion of additional address lines, can be completed with minimal or no impact. Defining address line elements as optional adds another degree of flexibility. Only elements required to describe each type of address need to be present in the XML document. When properly architected, these XML structures can expand or contract to fit the context of the data content (Fig. 1.9).

Extensible

As we often hear, "the only thing that is constant is change." Business paradigms, technology platforms, and development practices undergo frequent modification. Consider the example of a business enterprise

Figure 1.9

Flexible architectural form (vertical).

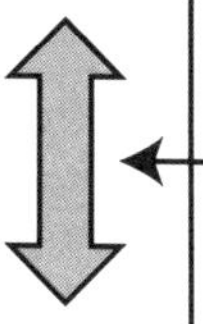

Address lines expand or contract as necessary.

```
<?xml version="1.0" encoding="UTF-8"?>
<Address AddressType="" AddressNo="">
 <AddressLines>
  <AddressLine LineNo="1"></AddressLine>
  <AddressLine LineNo="2"></AddressLine>
  <AddressLine LineNo="3"></AddressLine>
  <AddressLine LineNo="4"></AddressLine>
  <AddressLine LineNo="5"></AddressLine>
  <AddressLine LineNo="6"></AddressLine>
 </AddressLines>
 <AddressCity></AddressCity>
 <AddressPostalCode></AddressPostalCode>
 <AddressCountry CountryCode="" CountryNo=""></AddressCountry>
</Address>
```

Figure 1.10

Processing of an
extended XML
document.

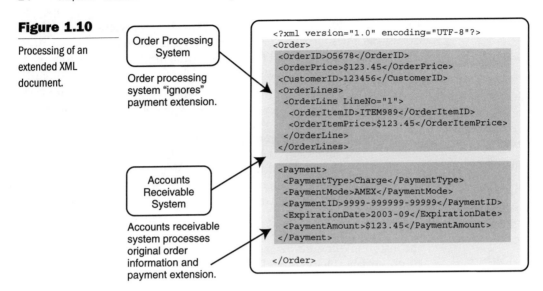

Order Processing
System

Order processing
system "ignores"
payment extension.

Accounts
Receivable
System

Accounts receivable
system processes
original order
information and
payment extension.

```
<?xml version="1.0" encoding="UTF-8"?>
<Order>
  <OrderID>O5678</OrderID>
  <OrderPrice>$123.45</OrderPrice>
  <CustomerID>123456</CustomerID>
  <OrderLines>
   <OrderLine LineNo="1">
    <OrderItemID>ITEM989</OrderItemID>
    <OrderItemPrice>$123.45</OrderItemPrice>
   </OrderLine>
  </OrderLines>

  <Payment>
   <PaymentType>Charge</PaymentType>
   <PaymentMode>AMEX</PaymentMode>
   <PaymentID>9999-999999-99999</PaymentID>
   <ExpirationDate>2003-09</ExpirationDate>
   <PaymentAmount>$123.45</PaymentAmount>
  </Payment>

</Order>
```

that sells products directly to the consumer but accepts payment through a third party. A simple order-processing transaction would contain basic customer, order, and order item information. However, payment information would be relegated to a third party, with settlement occurring outside the scope of the individual order transaction.

If the business later decides to directly offer a new payment medium (e.g., acceptance of credit cards), the order transaction might now require new fields for credit card number, expiration date, and authorization data. Transaction files would need to be extended with these new fields. If XML were used to define the transaction, it could be extended by appending or inserting the new elements and attributes into the base XML transaction and schema or by referencing these additional containers as a separate component schema (Fig. 1.10). Another benefit of this technique is that the additional elements and attributes do not have to be used by every application that processes the transaction.

Fact:

XML is extensible (XML structures and schemas can be extended or "added to").

As another example, consider a business enterprise that has embraced XML and is using a predefined industry schema that describes order transactions. These predefined schemas are sometimes referred to as a *vocabulary* (e.g., an XML "vocabulary" for orders). When the schema contains a comprehensive set of data elements supporting a particular function, that schema is a vocabulary. In this case the business would like to add their own alternative packaging units for each line item of the predefined schema.

If the schema were engineered using a W3C XML Schema, it could be extended by adding the additional elements with a unique qualifier (e.g., using a "namespace"). The resulting modifications would have minimal impact on the original XML schema and its continued use. A namespace provides the capability to uniquely identify a schema and its defined containers and avoid "collisions" with other similarly named containers. Namespaces can be a bit confusing to understand, but the concept is quite valuable. The namespace is usually described by a resource identifier (e.g., a universal resource identifier or URI). The intent of the namespace URI is to act as a unique pool or collection of participating things such as data elements. A prefix can be assigned to the namespace as a type of abbreviation. When this prefix is applied to XML elements or attributes, those containers are defined to and participate in the corresponding namespace.

Consider an XML element with a declared tag of "<title>." If the element were to contain data for a publication, the initial intent might be that this element would contain a book, magazine article, or similar title. However, if element containers for author data were also carried with the book data, the <title> element could mistakenly be populated with the title of the author (e.g., PhD., CEO, etc.). A creative data architect might resolve the issue by adding a second <title> element container to the book data. Although this solution is syntactically allowable, a processing application program might not know which of the <title> elements contained the publication's title or the author's title.

Namespaces, as supported by XML and W3C XML Schemas, allow the two example <title> element containers to be associated with and uniquely qualified by namespaces. A prefix can be associated with each unique namespace and then assigned to the elements. The first <title> element could be part of a "publication" namespace (e.g., "<publication:title>") and the second could be part of the "author" namespace (e.g., "<author:title>"). This technique helps to avoid named object collisions, where two element containers of the same name may contain data of different contexts. An industry vocabulary defined using W3C XML Schemas could be assigned to a namespace. If additional elements are required by the enterprise, they could be associated to a different namespace and then added to the schema. Collisions between like-named elements would be avoided, and the integrity of the original industry vocabulary would be retained.

As previously described, the advantages for using XML and W3C XML Schemas are many. However, effective use of XML as a metadata technology is not entirely "free." There are also requisite tasks and a few challenges. The first challenges are to align the data requirements and characteristics with a document type and to determine when XML can be used to advantage on a project.

2

XML Document Types

Although exhibiting many advantages and capabilities, XML may not always be the best metadata technology for a project. Determining whether XML should be applied requires careful evaluation of the project's data and functional requirements and the characteristics of the data that are to be described. When it has been determined that XML is advantageous, one of the initial architectural tasks is to ascertain whether a constraining schema should be applied (i.e., as the set of definitions, rules, and constraints applied during parsing and validation). Several types of XML schemas exist, resulting in one or more possible choices. However, each type of schema has distinct advantages and disadvantages. The three most common schema types include the following:

- Document type definitions (DTD or dtd)

- XML data reduced (XDR or xdr)

- W3C XML Schemas (XSD or xsd)

It is important to note that for some applications, an XML document (i.e., an XML file, document, transaction, or message) can be processed without any type of schema. When the XML document is clearly described, is represented as a simple structure, does not require the application of business rules and constraints, and is of limited size, parser validation to a schema may not be required (Fig. 2.1) However, XML

Figure 2.1

Simple XML document
instance.

```
<?xml version="1.0" encoding="UTF-8"?>
<ExampleHRTransaction>
 <EmployeeIdentifier>12345</EmployeeIdentifier>
 <EmployeeName>Sally M. Johnson</EmployeeName>
 <EmployeeHireDate>2002-05-27</EmployeeHireDate>
</ExampleHRTransaction>
```

documents without a referenced schema cannot be validated to ensure that contained data are of a particular data type or that the organization of the data elements in the document fits an expected or prescribed structure.

Schemas provide support for additional metadata characteristics such as structural relationships, cardinality, valid values, and in some cases data types. Each type of schema acts as a method of describing data characteristics and applying rules and constraints to a referencing XML document. Although there are several types of XML schemas that can be applied to advantage, one of the determining factors for selecting the appropriate schema type is the orientation and organization of the data content within an XML document instance. The internal structure of an XML document can be organized to represent different types of content, including document- or text-oriented, transaction-oriented, and message-oriented. There are also advantages and limitations of each type of XML schema.

A *document type definition (DTD)* type of schema is limited as to granularity and data typing support. Additionally, the syntax of a DTD is derived from SGML and therefore uses a syntax that is not as intuitive as other types of schemas (Fig. 2.2). A DTD used for validation of a typical e-commerce transaction can describe named element and attribute containers and the relationships between these containers as a structure. However, a DTD cannot describe whether the content of an element or attribute contains a date, a number, or any type of data other than a character. As a result, applying a DTD to a granular e-commerce transaction is not the most effective solution.

XML data reduced (XDR) types of schemas were an early attempt to provide much needed granularity and to describe data types for the content of an XML document that are not provided by DTDs. As noted earlier, XML is an excellent technology for describing the content of an e-commerce transaction or a data exchange. However, application of XML for these purposes also presents challenges in that DTDs do not describe granular metadata characteristics such as data types. To leverage the descriptive strengths of XML and overcome the type limita-

```
<?xml version="1.0" encoding="UTF-8"?>
<!ELEMENT ExampleHRTransaction (EmployeeIdentifier, EmployeeName, EmployeeHireDate)>
<!ELEMENT EmployeeIdentifier (#PCDATA)>
<!ELEMENT EmployeeName (#PCDATA)>
<!ELEMENT EmployeeHireDate (#PCDATA)>
```

Figure 2.2

Example of a document type definition.

tions of DTDs, XDRs were introduced. Initially, these types of schemas were supported by Microsoft and a few other technology companies. However, over time, support for XDR schemas slowed. A number of World Wide Web Consortium (W3C) participants proposed a more rigorous alternative that became known as the "XML Schemas Recommendation." W3C XML Schemas provided capabilities beyond those of XDR schemas and were also promoted and adopted by a more extensive number of technology providers. As a result, application of XDR schemas is dwindling, while alternative support for W3C XML Schemas grows. Given that the majority of technology vendors have pledged support for W3C XML Schemas in many of their products, our discussion of DTDs and XDRs will be limited.

W3C XML Schemas provide extensive metadata capabilities and are the recommended schema type for many applications. W3C XML Schemas provide a granular method of describing the content of an XML document. Like a DTD, a W3C XML Schema can descriptively identify or name the contents of a transaction. W3C XML Schemas also provide extensive capabilities in the areas of data types, customization, and reuse. Each element and attribute container of the XML document can be constrained by a specific data type as well as by additional characteristics such as minimum and maximum lengths, decimal positions, and other constraining facets. W3C XML Schemas also provide the capability of representing and including highly reusable structures, containers, and custom data types. Another added plus is that W3C XML Schemas are in the syntax of XML (they are self-describing and generally less cryptic than DTDs). Syntactically, a W3C XML Schema is a collection of elements and attributes, similar to an XML document. The placement, relationships, and values of these schema elements and attributes represent a series of rules that are described by the schema.

Like an XML document, a W3C XML Schema contains one "root" element (known as the "schema" element). If the schema is defined to a namespace, it may also contain a namespace reference. Although a namespace is generally applied to provide uniqueness and avoid named object collisions, the base or default namespace reference of a W3C XML Schema can also inform the parser of the schema version to apply. Like many technologies, W3C XML Schemas have evolved through a process of design, verification, and acceptance, and the schema version for each evolution is identified in part by the namespace. A prefix is assigned to this overall schema namespace, and all participating elements and attributes of the schema must include the prefix. The most common prefix applied to a W3C XML Schema is either "xs:" or "xsd:."

Following the root element of the schema are other elements, attributes, and constructs of various names and types. Each serves to describe a data container or characteristic of a referencing XML document instance. Elements can be defined to stand alone, or they can be grouped together to represent a set using a *complexType* or *group*. In contrast, attributes cannot stand alone and must be defined to an element. Both elements and attributes can have applied data types as well as other constraints and characteristics. As we will see in Chapters 4 (W3C XML Schema vs Database Data Types) and 5 (W3C XML Schema Data Type Facets), the ability to apply a data type and then further constrain the type with facets not only serves as a powerful metadata capability but also aligns well with the traditional practices of the data architect (Fig. 2.3).

Rather than choosing a single type of schema that should be applied to any and all forms of data contained in an XML document instance, a more effective approach is to identify the orientation, organization, and intended use of the data and then map to the most appropriate schema type. Most application programs (especially those of global e-commerce and enterprise application integration) will perform logic to present, export, import, read, write, update, share, or exchange data. The orientation of that data content will generally be one of three basic types:

- Document-oriented

- Transaction-oriented

- Message-oriented

Theoretically any schema type could be applied. However, the granularity, structure, and intended use of the contained data are the primary

Namespace prefix
applied to participating
elements, attributes, etc.

"Root" schema
element

Group of elements
referenced using a
"complexType"

Individual elements
defined "globally"
to the XML schema

Base namespace
in this example
describing the
version of
XML schemas
for the parser
to apply

Custom data
type constraints
using a base
type, simpleType,
and "facets"

Standard
data types

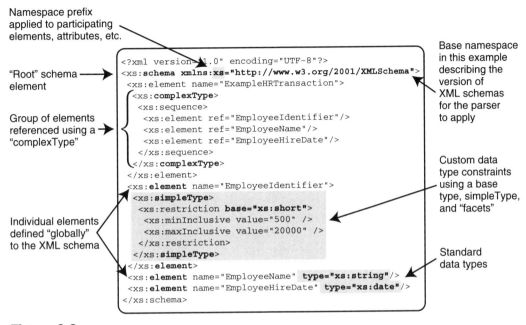

```xml
<?xml version="1.0" encoding="UTF-8"?>
<xs:schema xmlns:xs="http://www.w3.org/2001/XMLSchema">
 <xs:element name="ExampleHRTransaction">
 <xs:complexType>
  <xs:sequence>
   <xs:element ref="EmployeeIdentifier"/>
   <xs:element ref="EmployeeName"/>
   <xs:element ref="EmployeeHireDate"/>
  </xs:sequence>
 </xs:complexType>
 </xs:element>
 <xs:element name="EmployeeIdentifier">
 <xs:simpleType>
  <xs:restriction base="xs:short">
   <xs:minInclusive value="500" />
   <xs:maxInclusive value="20000" />
  </xs:restriction>
 </xs:simpleType>
 </xs:element>
 <xs:element name="EmployeeName" type="xs:string"/>
 <xs:element name="EmployeeHireDate" type="xs:date"/>
</xs:schema>
```

Figure 2.3

Example of a W3C XML Schema.

factors. Choosing a type of schema that matches the characteristics of the data and the requirements of the project are of significant value. Alternatively, mismatch or misapplication of a schema type can be an expensive proposition.

Document-Oriented Content

Document-oriented content has historically been the most common and recognizable type of data available for viewing on the Web. Simply stated, document-oriented content is a set of text strings that are often rendered in a browser as information, for reference, or for entertainment (i.e., targeted for visual and in some case audio consumption by a person).

Examples of document-oriented content include the following:

- Books, magazines, periodicals, and articles
- Newsletters, lists, and agendas
- Correspondence and documentation
- Brochures, advertising, and marketing materials
- Academic, education, or similar reference
- Product catalogs and descriptive product information

Document-oriented content is structured according to phrases, sentences, paragraphs, titles, table of contents, and the "flow" of information. Additionally, document-oriented content can also include formatting characteristics such as font type, font style, and font size. Although document-oriented content targeted for visual consumption can also be effectively expressed using XML, it is often contained within HTML (or similar) documents.

When XML is used to describe document-oriented content, a common practice is to organize the XML structure similar to that of a book with a table of contents and to reference a *stylesheet* for application of presentation and format characteristics. A stylesheet is another type of XML technology that references paths and locations within an XML document and represents rules for transforming the XML document into another form such as a different XML document or HTML (Fig. 2.4). The advantage of this approach is that the data values contained in the XML document are separate from the resulting form of presentation. As long as the structural integrity of the originating XML document is retained, the data can be modified or enhanced with minimal impact to the stylesheet. Regardless of changes to the data content, the format and presentation as rendered in a browser are consistent.

Another common use of this technique is to enable international Web sites with data content that is targeted for rendering with multiple languages. Language-specific content can defined to multiple XML documents and then rendered with a single XML stylesheet. Presentation is consistent regardless of the language being supported. An alternative approach is to describe the data content using a single base language and apply different language-specific XML stylesheets. Titles and headings would be described using different languages in each of the stylesheets and applied to the XML document content (Fig. 2.5). Although these techniques can be applied to advantage, neither is the "only" global or international XML solution.

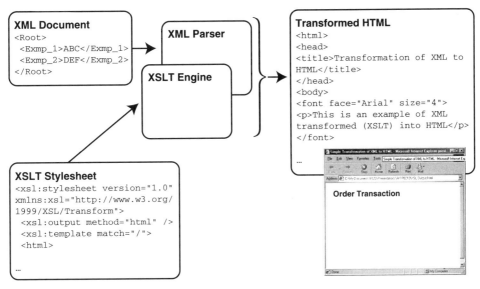

Figure 2.4

Application of an XML stylesheet to an XML document for rendering.

Recommendation:

XML Document Type Definitions (DTD) can be an effective method of describing and constraining simple document-oriented content. However, in many cases W3C XML Schemas can be applied equally well.

Document-oriented content can be described by most types of XML schemas. However, document-oriented content rarely requires granular metadata characteristics such as data types or allowable values. As a result, the use of W3C XML Schemas may be excessive. If the document-oriented content is primarily composed of simple text strings and the main intent is presentation or rendering in a browser, a DTD can be an acceptable choice. In rare cases a W3C XML Schema could also be applied to support complex document organization, navigation, and document structures that dynamically expand or contract (i.e., flexible).

Transaction-Oriented Content

XML is well suited as a method for describing transactions. Transaction-oriented content can serve a number of purposes but often repre-

Figure 2.5

MultiLanguage XML stylesheets applied to a single XML document.

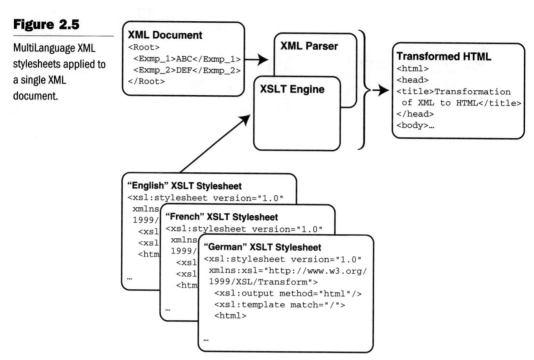

sents the content of an exchange between applications or the data captured from a Web form. The data contained within a transaction are generally composed of the information required to complete one or more enterprise application processes. Transactions tend to include very granular collections of data elements. As an example, a simple transaction representing a consumer goods order might include the following data elements:

- Order number

- Order date

- Customer number

- Payment method

- Order lines

  - Order line number

  - Order item or product number

- Order item quantity

- Order item unit of measure

- Order item price

- Order item price currency

As evidenced by the list of elements, the content of an order transaction is very granular rather than large strings of text as would be expected with document-oriented content. Although there are exceptions, transaction data are typically processed by automated programs rather than rendered in a browser for human consumption. When transaction content is targeted for processing by an application program, presentation and formatting such as that required for document-oriented content are rarely of significance. However, it is important to note that due to the self-describing nature of XML and with the assumption that descriptive element names have been applied, a person could potentially navigate the structure of the transaction and identify specific data elements for purposes such as design, testing, and debugging (Listing 2.1).

Listing 2.1

Example of an order as transaction-oriented content (XML).

```
<?xmlH version="1.0" encoding="UTF-8"?>
<Order>
     <OrderNumber>12345678</OrderNumber>
     <OrderDate>2003-02-15</OrderDate>
     <CustomerNumber>P1234567</CustomerNumber>
     <PaymentMethod>Cash</PaymentMethod>
     <OrderLines>
        <OrderLineNumber>1</OrderLineNumber>
        <OrderItem>GT-AL-1256</OrderItem>
        <OrderItemQuantity>10</OrderItemQuantity>
        <OrderItemUnitofMeasure>EA
        </OrderItemUnitofMeasure>
        <OrderItemPrice>123.45</OrderItemPrice>
        <OrderItemPriceCurrency>USD
        </OrderItemPriceCurrency>
     </OrderLines>
</Order>
```

Transaction-oriented content is most often consumed by one or more automated computer programs. The ability to interrogate, verify accuracy, and process transaction-oriented content relies heavily on metadata characteristics such as element names, element locations, and relationships. A typical processing application also needs to be aware of or check each data element for proper data types, lengths, number of occurrences of a data element, and allowable values (Fig. 2.6).

XML transactions that are targeted for direct viewing by a person will generally require an applied *XML stylesheet transformation (XSLT)* or some form of binding. The XSLT process can transform an XML structure into a presentation technology such as HTML (or into other forms and structures). As an alternative to transformation, *binding* is the association of XML elements with elements of a presentation technology such as HTML. There are other types of binding that include the association of database elements to XML elements or to presentation technologies.

W3C XML Schemas are an effective solution for describing the granular metadata characteristics of transaction-oriented content.

External to the Enterprise (Web)

XML transactions are often used to move or exchange data between the enterprise and external entities such as consumers, businesses, trading

Data element	Data type	Length	Integer digits	Decimal digits	Allowable values	No. of occurrences
Order Number	Numeric	8	8	0		1
Order Date	Date (ISO 8601)	10				1
Customer Number	String	8				1
Payment Method	String	20				1
Order Lines						1...n (repeating group)
Order Line Number	Integer	5	5	0	+1 to +32766	1
Order Item or Product Number	String	15				1
Order Item Quantity	Integer	5	5	0	+1 to +32766	1
Order Item Unit of Measure	String	2			EA, DZ, GR	1
Order Item Price	Decimal	11	8	3		1
Order Item Price Currency	String	3			USD, CAD, GBP	1

Figure 2.6

Example of order transaction metadata characteristics.

partners, and collaborative groups. The most common examples of external enterprise applications are e-commerce applications of two basic types:

- Business-to-Consumer (B2C)
- Business-to-Business (B2B)

Business-to-Consumer (B2C) applications are Internet- or Web-based applications used to conduct business between the enterprise and the consumer (generally a person). B2C applications are often referred to as "market facing." That is, a B2C application "presents" product and service information to a consumer-oriented market. Depending upon his or her level of interest, the consumer views the product and service information and makes choices to acquire additional information, purchase, or abandon the session. If the consumer elects to purchase a product, an application would collect the consumer's product selection, delivery, and payment information. Generally, these data would be structured as one or more transactions.

Often, HTML is used to present product and service data to a consumer. When combined with a stylesheet, XML can also be used for presentation. In this case, the product and service content of an XML document is transformed into a presentation form for rendering in a browser. With a B2C application, the information initially presented to the consumer (e.g., catalog, product, and service information) is often descriptive text that is document-oriented. As previously described, a DTD schema can be applied to advantage.

The order transaction generated from interaction of the consumer with the B2C Web site might use an HTML form (e.g., an HTML form to capture data entered and send it to the server as a form of transaction). The order transaction could also be described using XML. After the order transaction is received by the Web server, it must be processed to fill and ship the order and to collect payment. These processes may require several "back end" application programs. If the transaction from the server were formatted using XML, the order transaction could be easily moved and exchanged among the different programs and platforms (Fig. 2.7).

Transaction-oriented data will usually include individually defined data elements, each with specific characteristics and types. In this case, a W3C XML Schema is the preferred type of schema.

The alternative to a consumer application is a *Business-to-Business (B2B)* application, which targets other business enterprises as cus-

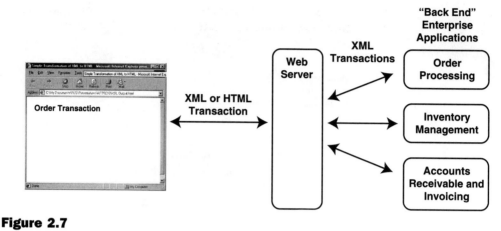

Figure 2.7

Example of a B2C transaction scenario using XML.

tomers. These applications will usually interact with other business programs to share and exchange transaction-oriented data. In some cases, a B2B application will also provide a user interface that allows human interaction with representatives of the target businesses. Often, a group of businesses within an industry will have agreed upon a common vocabulary to describe collaborative data exchanges. Historically, these industry vocabularies have been defined using electronic data interchange (EDI) or proprietary transactions. However, industry vocabularies defined by DTDs and W3C XML Schemas have recently become a preferred method (Fig. 2.8).

When an industry vocabulary is used, the transaction data are contained within one or more XML documents. These XML transactions are then described by corresponding schema vocabularies. This approach ensures that the sender and receiver of the exchange can effectively interpret and process the transaction data. At present there are many industry vocabularies in use. For some industries there are multiple schema vocabularies that define the same type of transaction data. Over time, the challenge for these industries will be to agree upon a common set and reduce the number of schema vocabularies.

Similar to that of a B2C transaction, B2B transaction-oriented content is a collection of granular data elements. Metadata characteristics for B2B data play a critical role. As businesses exchange transaction data, they need to ensure that each data element conforms to agreed

Figure 2.8

Example of a B2B
transaction scenario
using XML
vocabularies.

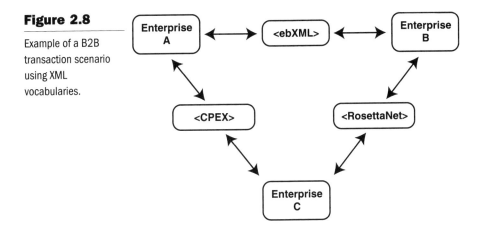

upon data types, lengths, and allowable values. Some industry vocabularies are currently defined using DTDs. However, in B2B scenarios it is suggested that DTD schemas are minimally effective. Given the data type capabilities, W3C XML Schemas are an obvious choice. This has also been recognized by many industry groups, and a noticeable effort to migrate vocabularies previously defined by DTDs to W3C XML Schemas is underway.

Internal to the Enterprise (EAI and Intranet)

In addition to external transactions and exchanges using XML, there are opportunities to apply XML to internally exchanged and processed transactions. The most common types of internal enterprise transactions are the following:

- Application-to-Consumer (A2C)
- Application-to-Application (A2A)

Application-to-Consumer (A2C) applications are roughly analogous to B2C applications, with the consumer being defined as an employee or representative of the enterprise. Like a B2C application, A2C applications present information for consumption by a person. However, the transaction is defined for processing "within the walls of the enterprise" rather than being ported over a public network such as the Web. A2C applications often support traditional enterprise systems such as inventory management, customer service, accounts payable, or finance.

One of the challenges faced by today's business enterprise is the ability to share and exchange between different types of systems and applications. For many traditional businesses, there is a long history of vertical application development and packaged software implementation that may have resulted in different technology platforms, operating systems, and databases. Some refer to these vertical systems as *autonomous* or *silo'ed.*

Generally, each of these systems has been engineered to support a specific business unit or business function. Often, these systems will retain parochial definitions of data and proprietary databases. Although the underlying technology and metadata may be different, at a conceptual level there are similarities between these systems, with information that would be valuable to share and exchange. Product data (e.g., product numbers, descriptions, and inventory amounts) are critical to inventory management and to order processing applications. The ability to link functionality of these two systems requires that the product data used by both are either defined in the same manner or can be translated into a common format. Both an inventory manager and a customer order processing representative should be able to view product data from within their respective systems (Fig. 2.9).

The challenge is that the order processing system and the inventory system may be supported by different technologies and environments. Both systems may have been developed with their own definitions of product data. Product numbers and similar data may be of different data types, lengths, and allowable values. Exchanging, sharing, or translating product data in a form that is common to and usable by both systems

Figure 2.9

Product data used by different systems.

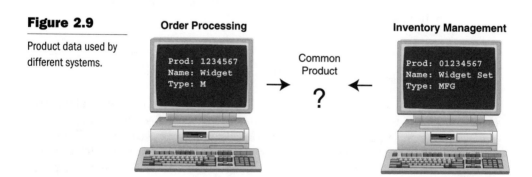

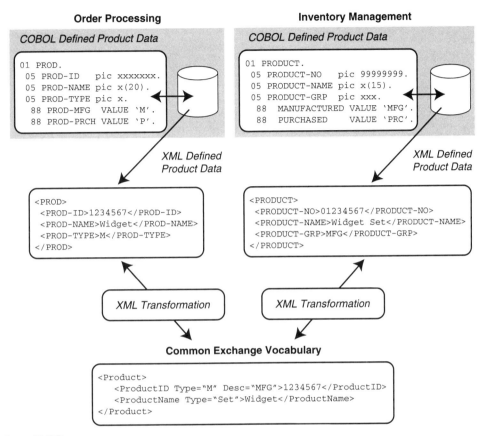

Figure 2.10

Product data converted to a common XML vocabulary.

can be difficult. XML can be used to describe the metadata characteristics of a product within each system and can also represent a common product vocabulary for exchanges (Fig. 2.10).

Different from A2C applications, *Application-to-Application (A2A)* processes are usually noninteractive. In addition to the lack of user interface as would be expected in an A2C scenario, the volume of transaction data can be higher. In some respects, an A2A process is analogous to a traditional interface file. Data from one system are moved to another system or exchanged with those of another system. As with the A2C scenario, the format and metadata characteristics of the data may be different from one system to another. The most common forms of metadata disparity among these systems include combinations of data type, length, decimalization, format, allowable values, and structure. When the transaction data are composed of granular data elements, the most appropriate schema type for describing either A2C or A2A transactions is W3C XML Schemas. The ability to define, constrain, and transform these internal enterprise transactions is critical to effective enterprise integration. In addition, standardized W3C XML Schemas can be used as internal vocabularies (roughly analogous to industry vocabularies) to help ensure that enterprise data are exchanged in a common and agreed upon manner.

Enterprise integration presents a significant opportunity to exploit the platform agnostic and metadata capabilities of W3C XML Schemas. However, the reader is cautioned that neither XML nor W3C XML Schemas are "silver bullet" solutions to integration. Enterprise integration requires a rigorous strategy that includes analysis, source-to-target mapping, assessment of metadata disparity, and development of transformation rules. Also, there may be examples for which data defined to different enterprise systems are so disparate that transformation and exchange are not advantageous or feasible.

Recommendation:

W3C XML Schemas are generally a very good fit for transaction-oriented content (both internal and external to the enterprise).

Message-Oriented Content

The client server model has a long history in the technology community including acceptance, adoption, evolution, and eventual maturity. It is the architectural foundation of many applications and in particular of Web-based applications. At a fundamental level, a client server application separates the interface, application logic, and data. As an example of client server processing, a client requests services of one or more servers in which they are processed, and a response is returned to the client (Fig. 2.11).

The most common processing model for messaging is a combination of service request, service resolution, and service response. In addition to a functional service response, this model can be extended to also include service failure or error messages. In the simplest scenario, messages are exchanged between clients (requesters) and servers (services) of the same technology and platform. With the advent of

Figure 2.11

Client server model.

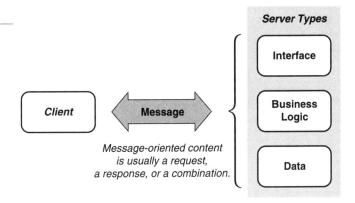

the Internet and World Wide Web, restrictions to use of the same processing technology and platform are of little value. Rather, Web applications and services are of many different types and technologies. As a result, there is a need to "hide" the underlying technology from the requester.

In a typical Web application scenario, service requesters and service providers are identified by a universal resource ID or an IP address that may be located anywhere in the world, and the platform may be almost any technology. In this case, the physical location, technology, and method by which a service request is resolved are often unknown to the requester. As services become more global, interoperability becomes an important characteristic. Also of importance are the semantics of a message. The client (i.e., the requester) must speak the interface language of the service. If a client request is structured in a manner that is not accepted or cannot be understood by the server (i.e., the service provider), the request will not be resolved.

Similar to transaction-oriented content, most messages are composed of granular data elements. Additionally, most messages tend to be specific to a defined function or activity and as a result are very compact (i.e., of limited size). Message-oriented content is the critical communication between clients and services. Web Services are an example of a service that is invoked by a message. More information on Web Services can be found in Chapter 10 (Web Services—An Introduction to the Future). Common examples of message-oriented Web Services include the following:

Figure 2.12

Simple example of Web service processing.

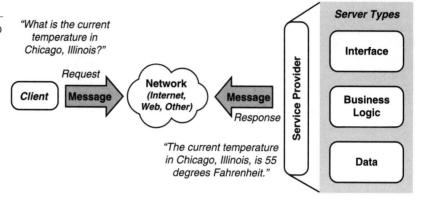

In each case, the client builds a message to include request data and parameters, sends the message to the Web Service where the request is resolved in some form, and acts upon a response. At a more technical level, the client requesting the service could wait for a response before continuing to process or may continue with other processes until the response is received. The Web Service receives the request, verifies the authenticity of the requester, validates the request, performs the requested service, and returns a response message. A simple example could be a request to a Web Service for the current temperature at a specific location (Fig. 2.12).

As with transaction-oriented content, XML is an effective solution for describing message-oriented content (in this case one or more messages). Because of the granularity of a message and the importance of validating the message content (e.g., data types or lengths), W3C XML Schemas are an effective solution for describing message-oriented content. In addition, XML is becoming the *lingua franca* for describing

- Requests for current product inventory levels
- Requests for current factory and assembly line status
- Requests for stock quotes
- Requests for weather conditions at various locations of the globe
- Requests for translation of amounts between different currencies

the content of a message between client requesters and Web Services. A form of XML-based protocol known as *simple object access protocol (SOAP)* is currently the common method for describing the content of a Web Services request message. Another form of XML known as *web services definition language (WSDL)* is also becoming the standard for describing the Web Services interface and structure of the message.

Recommendation:

W3C XML Schemas are generally a good fit for message-oriented content.

Choosing a Type of Schema

In addition to the orientation of the XML document, there are a several other characteristics that should be evaluated before a type of schema is selected. The first is the intended processing or use of the XML content. Data content that is intended to be processed in different ways or by different types of applications may warrant the selection and use of more than one schema type. For example, document-oriented content that is rendered in a browser and presented for consumption by a person may call for the use of a DTD schema. If the same document will also be used in a B2B scenario where the receiver of the data will decompose the document data to build an index of keywords, a more granular type of schema such as W3C XML Schemas may also be of value.

To determine the "best fit" type (or types) of schema, the architect should consider the following criteria:

- Data orientation (e.g., document, transaction, or message)

- Structural organization (e.g., hierarchical, relational, or free form)

- Granularity (e.g., discretely defined data elements or strings of text)

- Intended processing (e.g., presentation or application of business logic)

- Intended consumer (e.g., person or automated application)

- Interoperability (e.g., specific platforms or platform agnostic processing)

- Standardization and reuse (e.g., data types or reusable constructs)

- Considerations for performance

The orientation or type of data to be expressed using XML is critical to the identification of an applicable schema type. Data that are document-oriented rather than transaction- or message-oriented may fit one particular type of schema over another. Also of importance is the structural organization of the data. Data organization will most often be represented as either a hierarchy (e.g., parent–child–sibling structure such as the table of contents for a book), a set of related data (similar to relational tables, columns, and rows), or free form (unrelated or loosely related data elements, fragments, or strings of text).

Also of importance is the granularity of the data. If the data content comprises many individual data elements, a schema that supports data types (e.g., "strongly typed data") may be more appropriate than a more document-oriented schema type. In combination with granularity is the intended processing of the data. If the data are granular and will be processed by applications such as inventory management, order processing, or accounts payable, a schema that supports data types is probably warranted. Alternatively, if the data are targeted toward rendering in a browser or for presentation to a person a more document-oriented schema type may be warranted.

The consumer of the data also plays an important role. If the consumer of the data is a person, the need for strongly typed data or validation of valid values may or may not be of benefit. Alternatively, if the target consumer is an automated application, a W3C XML Schema may be of value. Whereas the XML document and data content are generally interoperable, validation with a particular type of schema can introduce challenges. Some schema types may not be supported by all technology products. XDR schemas are a good example. Support for XDR schemas is not widely available. Browser support for XDR schemas is generally limited to browsers that incorporate the Microsoft "MSXML" parser. If the provider or type of browser is unknown, it is possible that XML with a referenced XDR schema may not be supported. Alternatively, W3C XML Schemas are becoming more broadly accepted. In fact, Microsoft has stated that they will be supporting XML schemas (as evidenced by the recent Microsoft "MSXML4" parser).

Figure 2.13

Comparison of common XML schema types.

Data characteristics	DTD	XDR[a]	XSD
Data orientation			
Document-oriented support	X	X	X
Transaction-oriented support		X	X
Message-oriented support		X	X
Structural organization			
Hierarchical	X	X	X
Relational (indirect using by IDs, pointers, or structure)			X
Free form (primarily unstructured)	X		
Granularity			
Granular and discretely defined data elements		X	X
Large strings of text	X		X
Intended consumer			
Person	X	X	X
Automated application		X	X
Type of processing or consumption			
Visual (presentation or rendering)	X	X	X
Application of business logic		X	X
Interoperability			
Specific platform		—[b]	
Platform agnostic processing	X		X
Types, standardization, and reuse			
Strong data types		X	X
Custom or derived data types		X	X
Extensive support for data type facets			X
Reusable internal constructs		X	X
Reusable external constructs	X	—[c]	X
Ability to override reusable constructs			X

[a]It is suggested that when supported, XSD types of schemas are the much preferred replacement for XDR types of schemas.

[b]Support for XDR types of schemas is primarily found with Microsoft or Microsoft partner products. Additionally, Microsoft has included XML Schema (XSD) support in many of their products.

[c]Namespace reference to external schemas is described in the XML Data Reduced "Note." However, parser support varies.

Standardization and reuse are also important. Of the previously listed schema types, strongly typed data is supported only with XDR and W3C XML Schemas. XDR schemas allow limited data type customization, and parser support varies. Alternatively, W3C XML Schemas provide extensive capabilities in the area of custom and derived data types. To some degree, all three types of schemas support forms of reuse. However, W3C XML Schemas provide the most robust reuse support.

Fact:

Depending upon the characteristics of the data content, the intended use, and the number of processing applications, more than one type of schema may be required.

Recommendation:

If a single schema type must be used, consider using W3C XML Schemas as the default.

As a simple method of choosing a schema, consider a process for which characteristics of the contained data and the descriptive metadata are matched to the relative strengths of each type of schema. Some data characteristics are supported by more than one schema type, and the strengths of each schema can vary. A good fit is denoted when the characteristics of a particular use of XML are best addressed by the type of schema chosen (Fig. 2.13).

This technique can be easily applied but may not be definitive. However, it can provide general guidance to identify schemas that are good-fit candidates. If more than one schema type is found to be applicable, it is suggested that W3C XML Schemas are the best choice for describing transaction- and message-oriented content.

What should be obvious by now is that as a form of metadata, XML and especially W3C XML Schemas provide a significant opportunity for data architects to extend, enhance, and apply their skills. Use of XML as the method for describing the content of a document, transaction, or message will continue to grow, and the potential benefits are obvious. However, there are also risks. Without an effective XML design and engineering process and practical techniques, there is a significant risk of proliferation of nonstandard and largely disparate definitions of enterprise information assets. The most obvious areas of opportunity for applying data architecture practices to XML are naming (taxonomy), data types and facets, modeling, architecture, and reuse engineering.

3

The Importance of Naming Standards (Taxonomy)

The development of descriptive names for data elements, fields, and traditional data structures is historically a responsibility of the data architect. Data element names are a form of descriptive classification and identification that provide a context (i.e., a taxonomy). Given that XML is a self-describing metadata language, the responsibility for naming XML elements and attributes is an appropriate segue into the data architecture process. However, traditional techniques for data element naming have a long history that is often constrained by database technologies and products. The application of these traditional data element naming practices to XML elements and attributes can result in cryptic, complex, highly abbreviated, or, alternatively, overly verbose names.

To exploit the descriptive capabilities of XML and apply the benefits of a rigorous taxonomy, there are a number of guidelines that should be followed. Basically, all XML element and attribute names should be:

- Descriptive

- Concise

- Devoid of abbreviations or acronyms (unless easily recognized by a broad audience)

- Of "reasonable" length

Some data architects have adopted naming processes that are descriptive and intuitive and do not violate the basic syntax rules of XML.

When these processes are applied consistently and are well received by both the technology and business community, they can be adapted for application to XML data element and attribute names.

The process of naming and the parts of an element or attribute name may vary. However, as a general rule of thumb, an XML element or attribute name should be *intuitive*. A nontechnical person should be able to read a sample XML document and easily derive a reasonable understanding of the data contained in it. Many traditional approaches to data naming utilize a strictly enforced structure, and strict physical limitations (such as name length) that may present challenges for use with XML.

In addition to rigorous structural form, traditional data naming standards and processes often include the use of standard abbreviations, standard acronyms, and class words. For some naming standards, class words are also used as a method of describing the data type. When applied to databases and physical database components (e.g., columns, element, and fields), this approach can be advantageous. However, these techniques can also result in data element names with a very specific context that are restricted from broad scale reuse. The ability to share data between applications or to reuse standard data structures in different contexts is therefore limited.

Rather than forcing these same naming practices on XML, a better approach is to adopt techniques with specific value from those same naming standards and to avoid those that violate the intuitive rule. Before data architects can identify and adopt applicable naming techniques, they should have a basic knowledge of XML syntax, naming, and constraints.

Opportunity:

When existing enterprise data architecture naming standards and processes are descriptive, intuitive, and well received by the enterprise and do not violate XML syntax rules, they may be adapted for application to XML element and attribute names.

Recommendation:

An XML element or attribute name should be intuitive (the "intuitive rule").

Taxonomy Characteristics

A taxonomy is a form of naming or identification. The most common taxonomies also incorporate hierarchical classification and grouping. Names assigned with a specific taxonomy not only identify a particular object but also allow that thing to be classified or grouped with other objects that have similar characteristics. As an example, a person might have additional characteristics for gender, height, and weight and may also participate in other similar groups for mammals and bipeds.

Data architecture taxonomies classify, identify, and describe the content (e.g., data values) of a data element. A person who reads the data element name should be able to derive the intended content, as well as basic metadata characteristics. As a form of naming, some data architecture taxonomies will also describe data types, allowable values, and other metadata characteristics.

Similar to a data element, XML elements and attributes are described by a named tag. Syntactically, an XML element tag includes left and right angle brackets (e.g., "<ABC/>") that encapsulate the element name. XML attributes are similar in syntax to HTML attributes. They are specified in the form of an "attribute value pair" (e.g., xyz = " "). Other syntactical constraints for XML names are few. Basically, they include the following:

- An element or attribute name may be in uppercase, lowercase, or a combination (e.g., "<ABC/>," "<abc/>," and "<Abc/>" are all allowable element names).

- Element and attribute names are "case sensitive" (e.g., "<ABC/>" and "<abc/>" are entirely different elements).

- White space (e.g., a blank or space) is not allowed between name particles (e.g., "<ABC DEF GHI/>" is incorrect, whereas "<ABCDEFGHI/>" is correct).

- A name should not begin with a numeric digit (e.g., "<9ABC/>" is not allowed, but "<ABC9/>" is valid).

- There are a few reserved words that should not be used as part of a name (e.g., "XML," "xml," "LANG," and "lang" should not be part of an element or attribute name).

- There is no defined character length limit for a name (there may parser-specific constraints, and common sense should apply).

When these basic rules are applied in combination with a well-defined taxonomy process, the result is an element or attribute name that clearly describes intended content.

Name Particles

An XML element or attribute name is composed of one or more name particles. Name particles are words, abbreviations, or acronyms that in combination represent a complete name. Name particles may be nouns, adjectives, adverbs, or other descriptive modifiers (Fig. 3.1). Although there are exceptions, most traditional taxonomies will avoid name particles representing articles (e.g., "a," "an," or "the"), prepositions (e.g., "with," "to," "by," or "of"), pronouns (e.g., "I," "we," or "they"), and proper names (e.g., "James," "Sally," "Washington," or "Chicago"). Similarly, I recommend avoiding the use of articles, prepositions, pronouns, and proper names as part of an XML element or attribute name.

Recommendation:

Avoid the use of articles, prepositions, pronouns, and proper names as part of an XML tag name.

Recommendation:

Avoid the use of acronyms and abbreviations unless they are broadly recognized and accepted.

Evolution of business and advances in technology have resulted in a plethora of acronyms and abbreviations. Because of the sheer volume, many businesses have resorted to the publication of abbreviation and acronym lists. The problem with frequent use of abbreviations and acronyms as name particles is that unless they are broadly recognized and accepted (e.g., FBI, CIA, and UN), the data element name is no longer intuitive. To interpret the element name, you would need to consult an abbreviation list.

Many traditional data architecture taxonomy practices mandate the use of class words as an additional classifier. A *class word* describes the intended domain of data (e.g., allowable values, a data type, or a similar constraint). Although a class word that describes allowable values or

Figure 3.1

Name particles.

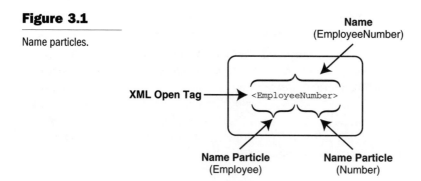

a data type may be applied to the name of a database element or column, there is no direct enforcement of those constraints from the name. The addition of class words to an XML element or attribute name presents a similar challenge. Constraints specific to allowable values and data types are implemented by a supporting schema. Validation of an XML document to a W3C XML Schema allows data type, enumeration values, and other constraints to be applied, regardless of the element or attribute name. If a representative class word were added to an element name and the content of that element were exchanged with another system, the constraints (e.g., allowable values or data type) might not be supported. As a result, the class word would be of little value to the XML element name, and in some examples could actually mislead an application developer.

Consider a data element that contains a data value of "2003-03-15." On one database platform, this data value may be described as a "Date" data type and on another by a "Character" data type. Including a class word for "Character" in the element name could introduce a potential for misinterpretation.

Additionally, many class words are applied in an abstract manner. A class word for "Number" is often incorrectly applied to represent the concept of an identifier (e.g., "CustomerNumber"), but in fact the allowable content of that element might be character or mixed character and numeric values. As an example, many organizations have applied a data element name for "Part Number," yet the data contained by that element might include values such as "A-123456."

Also considered ambiguous is the difference between ordinal and nominal numbers. Ordinal numbers are of a defined order or sequence and usually are not subject to business logic (e.g., logic to multiply two ordinal numbers is most likely of no value). Nominal values are subject to derivation and the application of business logic. A class word that implies a numeric data type but does not distinguish between ordinal and nominal numbers could also be misleading to an application developer.

Recommendation:

Use class words only when they are concise and representative of a recognized and clearly defined constraint.

If a class word is descriptive, concise, and unambiguous, it may be of value to include in an XML element name. In the example of an element named "<EmployeeBirthDate/>," the use of class word "Date" is beneficial. In viewing the element, it would be obvious to the reader that the intended content of the element container is temporal. However, beware that a class word such as "Date" does not imply, specify, or constraint the format of a data value. Although the content of the example element is assumed to be a date, it could also be of several possible formats:

- YYYY-MM-DD
- MM-DD-YYYY
- Month DD, YYYY
- DD Month YYYY
- Other formats and derivations

As a side note, to comply with the "Date" data types supported by W3C XML Schemas,[1] all Date data defined to XML should adhere to the ISO 8601 Date and Time standard[2] or should be described in a manner that clearly informs the reader of the intended format. However, there is no specific or syntactical restriction guaranteed by the use of a "Date" class word.

Name Character Case

Another fundamental characteristic of a data element name and more specifically an XML name is character case. For our discussion, we will assume that English is the language applied to the XML tags (it is possible that other languages could be used as well). With XML, there are a number of character case options. The character case applied to traditional data element names is often restricted by a metadata repository, data modeling tool, or database infrastructure. For some database products, uppercase may be required for data element names. For others, only lowercase characters are allowed. XML is not constrained by character case, and any of the forms shown in Table 3.1 may be applied.

Each of the previous character case examples is supported by XML. However, the data architect needs to consider the self-describing

---

[1] World Wide Web Consortium (W3C). XML Schemas. W3C Recommendation May 2, 2001. Available at http://www.w3.org/TR/2001/REC-xmlschema-1-20010502/ (structures); http://www.w3.org/TR/2001/REC-xmlschema-2-20010502/ (data types).
[2] International Standards Organization (ISO). ISO 8601, Date and Time, TC154 Technical Committee. http://www.iso.ch/iso/en/stdsdevelopment/tc/tclist/ TechnicalCommitteeDetailPage.TechnicalCommitteeDetail?COMMID=3827.

Table 3.1   Character Case in XML Tag Names

XML element name	Character case
<EMPLOYEENUMBER/>	All uppercase characters
<employeenumber/>	All lowercase characters
<EmployeeNumber/>	Mixed character case, all leading uppercase
<employeeNumber/>	Mixed character case, first leading lowercase, other leading uppercase

strength of XML and to determine whether the resulting name is intuitive. As exhibited by the previous examples, applying a single consistent character case to a data element without any other form of name particle separation (e.g., using all upper case or all lowercase characters) results in names that can be difficult to interpret (remember that spaces are not allowed between name particles for an XML tag). It is therefore suggested that unless some other existing enterprise naming standard or constraint prevails, XML names of all uppercase characters or all lowercase characters should be avoided.

Recommendation:

Unless there is an obvious constraint or limitation (e.g., existing technologies and tools only support a specific character case), consider using mixed character case for XML element and attribute names.

Of particular interest and value is a mixed character case format, in which the leading character of each name particle is uppercase and all remaining characters are in lowercase (e.g., <EmployeeNumber/>). This application of mixed character case is intuitive and provides a simple form of implied separation between most name particles of a data element name.

Name Particle Separators

Of significant importance to a data element name is the ability to visually derive and logically assemble the individual name particles (as if reading a phrase or sentence). English and many other scripts utilize a space or blank (e.g., "white space") between the words of a sentence as a form of separation. However, white space is prohibited within the name of an XML data element or attribute. Without some form of visual separation between name particles, interpreting a long data element name that is composed of several name particles and acronyms can be difficult. Without some form of separation between name particles, it appears as if the data element name is "run together." In the example in Figure 3.2, the individual name particles of "EMPLOYEE" and "NAME" are easy to identify but are separated by a space, which is not allowed by XML.

Recommendation:

Name particle separators should only be used to improve readability of element and attribute names.

Some traditional data element naming practices include some form of separator character between name particles. For physical database naming such as that applied to the columns of a database table, an underscore ("_") is often used. Procedural programming languages such as COBOL use a dash as a separator ("-"). Other programming languages such as Visual Basic use a period ("."). In addition to an underscore, dash, and period, XML allows colons (":") as separator characters for element and attribute names. Although a colon may be applied, it is strongly suggested that use of a colon be avoided because it has other meaning when used with a namespace prefix. In each case, the intent of the character is to provide a method of separating name particles and to ease the interpretation of the data element name.

A disadvantage to using an underscore, dash, or period to separate name particles is that each character occurrence also consumes one additional position of the entire name. Although not directly applicable to XML, many technology platforms have maximum limits for the length of a column or data element name. The challenge is to offset the visual complexity of a data element name with the constraints of the technology. It may be of greater value to apply uppercase to the leading

Figure 3.2

Example of an invalid name particle separator.

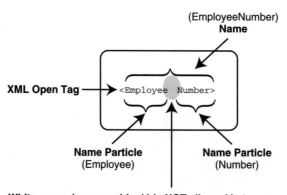

White space (space or blank) is NOT allowed between name parts.

characters of a data element name as separators rather than inserting additional characters.

Fact:

Name particle separators such as an underscore ("_"), dash ("-"), and period (".") can be used in an XML element or attribute name. However, such use will consume a character position with each occurrence.

As mentioned, an alternative solution to name particle separators is related to character case. When mixed character case can be applied to XML element and attribute names, there may be an opportunity to avoid using name particle separators, yet provide the same benefit. Use of a technique known as "camel case" (i.e., where the leading character of each name particle is uppercase, whereas all remaining characters are lowercase) can imply separation between name particles. Although the name particles are concatenated to represent the entire XML element or attribute name, visual separation is readily evident.

As an example, a data element of "EMPLOYEE NAME" could be described using XML syntax by any of the forms shown in Table 3.2.

If XML is used, each of the previous employee name element examples would be syntactically correct. The first example presents a challenge in that name particles are not easily determined. Other examples exhibit an effective form of visual separation between name particles. However, in those examples in which a character is used as the separator, an extra position is consumed, which increases the element name

Table 3.2   Examples of Data Element Names and Separators

XML element name	Name particle separator types used
<EMPLOYEENAME/>	None
<EMPLOYEE_NAME/>	An underscore
<EMPLOYEE-NAME/>	A dash
<EMPLOYEE.NAME/>	A period
<employeename/>	None
<employee_name/>	An underscore
<employee-name/>	A dash
<employee.name/>	A period
<EmployeeName/>	Implied with camel case

length as well as the overall size of the XML document. If the element name length were significant or an implied length guideline were imposed for XML element names, the data architect might be forced to apply some form of abbreviation or other limiting technique.

Additionally, if the XML file were a transaction that included many elements with names of significant length, the overall size of the transaction would be increased. As an example, if the XML transaction contained "<employee_name>" elements for all employees of the enterprise, the result might be that several thousand characters of the total document size were used only to separate data element names. Although there is no direct correlation, depending upon the total document size, network performance of a transaction exchange might be adversely impacted. Note that this example should not be used as an excuse to enforce cryptic element names. Rather it should serve as additional justification for deriving effective element and attribute names and using each character of the name wisely.

The example of "<EmployeeName/>" used camel case in which the leading character of each name particle is uppercase and all remaining characters are lowercase. The result is an obvious visual separation of name particles. Also, the lack of a separator character results in fewer name characters being consumed.

Recommendation:

If the applied character case is camel case, the use of a leading character of upper case for name particles will result in an implied name particle separator. Additional name particle separators such as an underscore ("_"), dash ("-"), and period (".") can then be avoided.

Name Length

The XML specification does not include an explicit maximum limit for element or attribute name lengths. In theory, an XML element could be hundreds of characters in length. However, be aware that extremely long XML element and attribute names can also introduce inefficient processing. Although extremely verbose names are not recommended, highly abbreviated XML element and attribute names also cause inefficient use of XML. Names that are highly abbreviated can be as difficult to read and interpret as those that are overly verbose. A number of important characteristics should be considered in the length of an XML element or attribute name. An XML element or attribute name should:

- Be of reasonable length
- Not be overly verbose
- Not be highly abbreviated or cryptic

Recommendation:

XML element and attribute names should be of reasonable length (not overly verbose and not highly abbreviated).

Recommendation:

XML element and attribute name lengths should be rationalized and aligned with the most common data sources and targets.

One important assumption that can assist in determining the most effective approach to XML element and attribute naming is knowledge of how XML will be used or processed. If we assume that XML will be used as a method of transaction or message exchange, we can also assume that there will usually be one or more target processes. Although not always the case, the data content for each of these targets will often be extracted from the XML document and inserted into a database. This is not to say that all XML transactions should be directly persisted in a database. Yet these activities are not unusual. A common technique for determining the maximum allowable length of an XML element or attribute name is to compare, rationalize, and align the naming constraints of source and target database platforms. One recent U.S. government document stated that XML element names should not exceed 30 characters in length.[3]

Name Specificity

Another important aspect of XML element and attribute taxonomy is the specificity of a name. Most traditional data element naming techniques result in very explicit names. Often, these names reflect a specific implementation rather than a descriptive context. Consider the following representative examples:

- CORPORATE_EMPLOYEE_IDENTIFIER_NUMBER
- PAYROLL_EMPLOYEE_IDENTIFIER_NUMBER

---

[3] Crawford M, Egan D, Jackson A. Federal Tag Standards for Extensible Markup Language. GS018T1, p 27. Logistics Management Institute (LMI), June 2001. Available at http://xml.gov/.

- VEHICLE_PARKING_TAG_EMPLOYEE_
  IDENTIFIER_NUMBER

If each of the previous examples were representative of the same "EMPLOYEE IDENTIFIER" data and were described by the same metadata (e.g., data type and length), we could assume that each instance would contain the same type of data. However, each data element name describes a specific application or use of the "EMPLOYEE IDENTIFIER." This level of specificity may have resulted from the underlying database that requires unique column names within the same table, or it may result from the applied taxonomy practices. In either case, the potential for reuse of the employee identifier data in other contexts is significantly limited.

Considering that an XML transaction may be exchanged across the enterprise and may contain data of the same general definition, a more effective approach is to apply a more abstract element name. An element for "EMPLOYEE IDENTIFIER" could be defined to represent an enterprise standard and then applied in different contexts. If a single XML transaction containing Employee Data were exchanged among many systems, it might contain and reference "EMPLOYEE IDENTIFIER" as an element, contained as a child within different parent elements. The parent elements provide a context for the use of the employee identifier data by acting as "roles" (Listing 3.1).

There are several different approaches to application of parent elements as roles or classifications, and each has advantages and disadvantages, as we will see in Chapter 8 (W3C XML Schemas and Reuse). When a role type has been defined (either by an owning or parent element or as a classification attribute), the child element can be named in the abstract. Rather than defining uniquely named XML elements for each of the potential applications (e.g., corporate, payroll, and vehicle), a single common element for "EMPLOYEE IDENTIFIER" could be defined and then reused in different contexts.

As exhibited by the previous employee transaction example, abstract XML element names can be of value. This technique can be applied in a manner to support enterprise metadata standards and reuse. However, caution is advised. One of the strengths of XML is its self-describing nature. We should still apply the intuitive rule. If the element name is so abstract as to be ambiguous or nonintuitive, there are significant dangers. Extremely

Opportunity:

Abstract XML elements and attributes that exclude internal "roles" or "classifications" from the name and apply the roles as parent elements or descriptive attributes are highly reusable.

Listing 3.1

Example of an employee transaction with multiple uses of "employee identifier."

```xml
<?xml version = "1.0" encoding = "UTF-8"?>
<ExampleTransaction>

    <CorporateHumanResourcesData>
        <EmployeeIdentifier>12345</EmployeeIdentifier>
    </CorporateHumanResourcesData>

    <PayrollData>
        <EmployeeIdentifier>12345</EmployeeIdentifier>
    </PayrollData>

    <VehicleParkingTagData>
        <EmployeeIdentifier>12345</EmployeeIdentifier>
    </VehicleParkingTagData>

</ExampleTransaction>
```

abstract element names could be misinterpreted or applied in a context that has no logical meaning.

Fact:

XML element and attribute names that are overly abstract can introduce unnecessary complexity and even the potential for misinterpretation.

Extending the previous example, we could name the element as "Identifier" (e.g. "<Identifier />"), and further describe a new parent role element to include "Employee." In this case, the "Identifier" element is intended to be an enterprise standard potentially used in different contexts. The problem is that "Identifier" is highly abstract and its definition and use are questionable. Even when the element is applied correctly, it requires excessive levels of element nesting to provide sufficient context for use (Listing 3.2).

Strengths of a taxonomy lie in both specificity and abstraction. A reasonable balance must be applied. As a rule of thumb, the following list of taxonomy characteristics may help to determine when it would be of value to consider naming an element in the abstract:

- The element represents a common and easily recognized data concept.

- The element is a candidate for broad scale reuse.

- The resulting element name clearly defines intended content.

Listing 3.2

Additional levels of
parent element nesting
required for an overly
abstract element.

```xml
<?xml version = "1.0" encoding = "UTF-8"?>
<ExampleTransaction>

    <CorporateHumanResourcesData>
        <Employee>
            <Identifier>12345</Identifier>
        </Employee>
    </CorporateHumanResourcesData>

    <PayrollData>
        <Employee>
            <Identifier>12345</Identifier>
        </Employee>
    </PayrollData>

    <VehicleParkingTagData>
        <Employee>
            <Identifier>12345</Identifier>
        </Employee>
    </VehicleParkingTagData>

</ExampleTransaction>
```

Opportunity:

The data architect is generally well versed in taxonomy and naming processes and has a tremendous knowledge of enterprise information assets (definition and use). Regardless of the level of abstraction, specificity, or other taxonomy processes applied to XML, there is an obvious opportunity for data architects to participate and apply their skills.

- The resulting element name is intuitive.

- The resulting element name is unambiguous.

- The resulting element name cannot be misinterpreted to represent data of a different form or meaning.

Rather than abstractly named elements, XML elements that are specifically named can also be used to advantage. However, specifically named elements are not prone to broad-scale reuse (there may be valid reasons why an element is excluded as a reuse candidate). It may be that the element is restricted to a specific context or process. There may also be some characteristic of the data that demands a unique name. Regardless of the level of specificity or abstraction that is applied to an XML element name, the data architect is often well versed in taxonomy practices. The ability to define and apply a descriptive and rigorous taxonomy to XML elements and attributes presents a valuable opportunity for the enterprise.

Traditional Approaches to Data Element Naming

Traditional approaches to data element naming are many. Most were developed with obvious value and benefit to the technology community. However, several of these approaches were constrained by dependencies or limitations resulting from targeted database implementations of that time. As an example, some database products have a stringent limit on the maximum number of characters allowed for an element or column name and are constrained to using only uppercase characters. As a result, many physical data element and database column names are highly abbreviated and often appear cryptic to the uninitiated.

As the process of information engineering evolved to become a predominate method for identifying, describing, and classifying information assets of the enterprise, other forms of data element naming were derived and applied to the attributes of logical data models. Because a logical data model is intended to be devoid of any underlying implementation, it is also somewhat more abstract. Data architects were provided with more freedom to apply descriptive names to the information assets of the enterprise. As part of the forward engineering process, these attributes would later be translated to a more physical adaptation and the constraints of the database again came into play. In an attempt to apply a rigorous taxonomy and structure to a name, several naming techniques were born.

One of the most well known is based upon the Data Entity Naming Conventions component of the Information Resource Dictionary System (IRDS) standard.[4] Techniques adapted from this standard are broadly used across the industry and promote a highly structured approach to data element naming. The obvious benefits are data element

---

[4] American National Standards Institute (ANSI), X3 Working Group. X3.138 Information Resource Dictionary System. Data Entity Naming Conventions, Special Publication 500-149; Manual for Data Administration, Special Publication 500-208 [InterNational Committee for Information Technology Standards (INCITS)]. Available at http://www.x3.org/incits/.

names that all follow a consistent structure and form and that in a limited manner also describe intended allowable values (as inferred from the domain or class word). The most common application of this technique has resulted in a data element name being constructed of the following name components:

- Prime word

- Modifier (or modifiers)

- Class word

A prime word is most often a noun and may represent a role or classification. The data element name "PAYROLL EMPLOYEE IDENTIFIER NUMBER" is perhaps an extreme example of traditional data element naming (some may argue that the naming technique has not been applied as would be in their enterprise, but let us stay with the example for the sake of argument). In this example, "Payroll" is the prime word. The prime word would be followed by one or more modifiers. In this case, both "Employee" and "Identifier" are modifiers. Ambiguity is often seen in the area of modifiers because they may be adjectives (which bode well as modifiers of a noun) or they may be other nouns, verbs, or adverbs. Also, as additional modifiers are applied, the name becomes more specific. In some cases, this specificity is of value. Specificity can also constrain the ability to reuse the data element in other contexts. If the sample data element were actually representative of a common employee identifier for the enterprise that is being used in the context of a payroll system, name specificity for this same element would restrict the potential for reuse in another context (e.g., Vehicle Parking Tag Employee Identifier Number).

Completing the data element name is the class word, in this case, "Number." The challenge with class words is that in some scenarios they can be misleading. When data elements that act as some form of identifier are considered, many data architects name or describe them as a "number." However, the reality is that often these identifiers are composed alpha characters or combinations of alpha characters and numeric digits. In this case (and there are many similar examples), the value of the class word is limited. Consider common and well-known examples such as an automobile operator's license number, a license plate number, a customer account number, and so on. The physical data type for each of the examples could vary widely, yet the class word implies a numeric value.

Long-time data architects are often familiar with this challenge to naming and more specifically to class words. In fairness, there are also many examples for which a class word is indeed accurate and of use to the technology practitioner reading the data element name. The problem is knowing when such applications of class words are factual and concise and when they are not. The rigorous application of class words similar to IRDS naming approaches can become a de facto rule that forces the use of a class word, whether or not it is concise and accurate.

As noted previously, another challenge with traditional taxonomy practices is that physical element and database column names are either translated or derived from similar forms of naming. Again, consider the scenario of an Employee Payroll Identifier Number for a new human resources system. Although abbreviated to conform to database name length constraints, the following physical data element name appears to be reasonably descriptive: "PAY-EMP-IDENT-NO."

The example of the physical data element name is also based upon a prime word, modifier, and class word based taxonomy and is composed of four name particles (i.e., PAY, EMP, IDENT, and NO). It may be assumed that the first particle is an abbreviation for "Payroll," the second particle is an abbreviation for "Employee," the third is an abbreviation for "Identifier," and the last is the terminating class word for "Number." Although the intent is that a data value held by this element will represent an "Payroll Employee Identifier Number," there are a number of obvious questions:

- Is the Employee Identifier actually numeric?

- Is the Employee Identifier unique across all occurrences?

- Is the Employee Identifier generated as a nonintelligent number, or is there some form of internal intelligence?

- Is there a minimum or maximum length or value?

- Is an Employee Identifier data value common across the enterprise, but in this case applied to a payroll system?

- Is the Employee Identifier based upon or derived from another form of identifier (e.g., tax identifier or Social Security Number)?

- Is it possible that the context is misaligned (e.g., Employee Identifier for Payroll is actually another form of identification issued outside the enterprise, but captured within the human resources system as a form of validating citizenship)?

The reality is that the example of the data element name is subject to potential misinterpretation. Depending upon the answers to the listed questions, associated business rules and application logic may vary. Incorrect assumptions based upon the name could result in processing errors and potential rework of an application program. Also, the example violates the intuitive rule. An uninitiated user might or might not determine that the highly abbreviated physical data element name was intended to represent a Payroll Employee Identifier Number. Beyond these concerns is the architectural perspective. The example of the data element name is far too specific to support reuse in other contexts. An architectural alternative might be a standard element defined for an Employee Identifier that is common across the enterprise. The assumption is that the definition and metadata characteristics of this identifier would be common regardless of context.

Although traditional data naming practices can be applied to XML element and attribute names, the data architect should carefully consider an adaptation that extends traditional practices to also leverage the strengths of XML.

Alternative Taxonomies for XML

Alternative methods of XML naming can be many. Unfortunately, the numerous industry XML publications and vocabularies do not provide guidance or insight into a common approach. By virtue of its flexibility, self-descriptive capabilities, and the lack of a length limitation, XML element and attribute naming presents a challenge to industry naming standards. Allowing different names for the same data element can introduce a similar form of data disparity as may already exist in the enterprise.

Consider the fact that XML can be used to describe the content of a transaction to exchange, share, or move data between different systems. An obvious advantage would be an element name that is common to both the source and target system. However, in the case of autonomous enterprise systems with parochial definitions of data, this may be a rarity. Another advantageous approach would be to derive a

Figure 3.3

Traditional element
name revised to
leverage the strengths
of XML.

```
<?xml version="1.0" encoding="UTF-8"?>
<ExampleTransaction>

  <PayrollEmployeeIdentifierNumber>12345</PayrollEmployeeIdentifierNumber>

</ExampleTransaction>
```

```
<?xml version="1.0" encoding="UTF-8"?>
<ExampleTransaction>

 <PayrollData>
  <EmployeeIdentifier>12345</EmployeeIdentifier>
 </PayrollData>

</ExampleTransaction>
```

common vocabulary for the exchange that includes standard names and definitions for contained data elements. If either the source or target systems did not recognize these names, a transformation would need to take place.

Application of a rigorous XML taxonomy should also limit the number of transformations and, over time, promote the use of a common vocabulary for all sources and targets. This is a noble goal, and applying an effective approach to XML element and attribute naming can provide a much needed foundation. However, as a general rule of thumb, always assume that a transaction exchange between autonomous systems will require at least one transformation. The goal should be to reduce the number of unnecessary transformations, which would be the result if all of the systems began to apply a rigorous taxonomy and utilized a common exchange vocabulary. Other uses of XML, such as display or rendering of content for consumption by a user, provide even more motivation for descriptive naming. The design of a stylesheet is far more effective when the source data are intuitively named.

An effective approach to XML taxonomy combines the aspects described previously with a method of assembling name particles that is simple and intuitive. Rather than using a highly structured and ordered prime word, modifier, and class word system, another approach is to form names according to natural language (and in the case of English, left-to-right order). Additionally, the use of abbreviations should be avoided, and class words would optionally be applied when (and only when) they are concise, accurate, and add value to the name. Name specificity to a degree that prohibits reuse would be acceptable only when those elements are intentionally limited to use in a defined context. Alternatively, the element names would be named to a degree of abstraction that allowed for accurate, concise, unambiguous, and intuitive, yet reusable, names (Fig. 3.3).

As a note of caution, data architects should not cast their traditional naming standards or taxonomy practices aside. In many cases, these same practices can be leveraged or adapted to take advantage of the strengths of XML. Also, class words should not be abandoned in their entirety. Many class words can be applied accurately and with resulting value. The challenge for the data architect is to identify and apply taxonomy practices and techniques of benefit and avoid others. The development of rigorous taxonomy practices are a fundamental data architecture practice. As we will see in Chapter 4 (W3C XML Schema vs Database Data Types), alignment of supported data types is another important function.

4

W3C XML Schema vs Database Data Types

As previously noted, W3C XML Schemas (W3C Recommendation, May 2001) provide a rigorous and highly standardized method for describing strongly typed data. Syntactically, this is accomplished through the use of data types and data type facets. W3C XML Schemas also provide the ability to define custom data types as extensions and derivations of supported types. As one example, rather than defining numerous monetary amount data elements with different formats, the data architect can define a set of standard monetary data types that could then be applied as necessary to referencing XML elements and attributes. As the use of XML transactions to exchange, share, and move data among enterprise systems grows, this technique also acts as a method to proliferate and enforce data standards.

The application of a schema data type is actually a form of edit checking. When an XML document references a corresponding W3C XML Schema and that schema has applied data types to element and attribute definitions, the parser validation process will compare the data values contained by those elements and attributes to the data types defined in the schema. If the data values do not conform to the constraints of the data types defined in the W3C XML Schema, an error will be raised to the processing application. It is important to note that the parser will not apply corrections or modifications to the data contained in the XML document. Rather, resolution and action are left to the processing application. As an example, if the data type violation is critical, the processing application may be designed to reject processing the content of that element, or it may abandon the entire process.

Also of importance is the varied support for data types among database platforms and related technologies. Interestingly, there are few database data types that are defined with identical characteristics across all database products. Variations between database data types can include minimum and maximum supported values, maximum length, fractional digit support, internal encoding, and external format (e.g., date and time data type formats). It might initially appear that a data type of "integer" or "date" would describe the same allowable content, number of digits, character length, and format, regardless of the database platform. However, this is rarely the case. Many database systems support different implementations of these as well as other data types. The differences between data types are similar to the many product-specific dialects and extensions of SQL. Although SQL is based upon well-defined industry standards and the core functions are common across most relational database platforms, there are many syntactical derivations and extensions that also make each implementation unique (e.g., an SQL query coded for a Sybase Transact-SQL database might not operate on an IBM DB2 product).

Similar to the SQL example, the data types used to describe the content of a database column or data element can also vary from product to product. It is my opinion that W3C XML Schemas provide a far more robust and exact representation of data typing than is currently supported by most database platforms and programming languages. In one sense, the support of W3C XML Schemas for strongly typed data is extremely powerful. In another sense, the use of W3C XML Schemas is mistakenly assumed to be able to "magically" resolve data disparity between autonomous systems. The reality is that participation of the data architect for mapping of metadata characteristics and capabilities between source and target data stores is invaluable.

Fact:

Data types are not always implemented or supported among database products in the same manner regardless of the data type name.

Some technologists might question the need to research and align W3C XML Schema data types with database data types. The reality is that the data contained within most XML transactions will probably have originated from one of two possible sources. The data content of consumer-oriented e-commerce transactions (e.g., B2C), either will have originated as key-entered data or will have been derived from the user's Web session (Fig. 4.1). An enterprise application data exchange will usually originate from a database extraction (Fig. 4.2). In either case, the ultimate target of this transaction data is often an enterprise database.

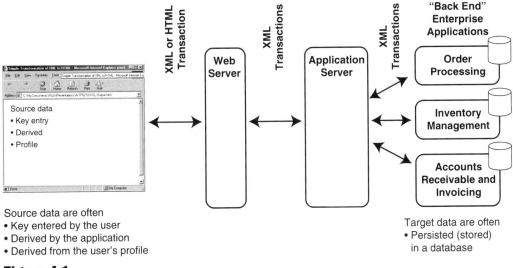

Figure 4.1

Consumer-oriented web transaction.

Figure 4.2

Enterprise application integration transaction.

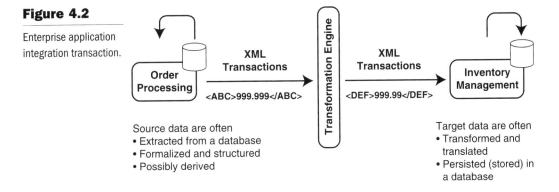

Fact:

The most common examples of data carried in a transaction or interface file will have in some form originated from a database and will in some form be persisted in a target database.

Given these examples, it becomes obvious that mapping and alignment of transaction data types and database data types become critical activities. This would be true whether the method of interface were a traditional flat file, comma-separated variable file, XML-formatted transaction, or another format. The data typing strengths of W3C XML Schemas can provide a significant advantage when data between autonomous systems are exchanged and shared.

Basic W3C XML Schema Data Types

The May 2001 W3C XML Schemas Recommendation[1] describes extensive support for strongly typed data. Three general categories of data types are supported:

- Built-in primitive types

- Built-in derived types

- Custom types

Built-in primitive types are foundation data types that can be referenced and applied to XML elements and attributes in their native form (generally using a "type" or "base" attribute reference and a corresponding W3C XML Schema "simpleType"). Many of the built-in primitive types also support facets as methods of constraining allowable content beyond the basic scope of the data type (e.g., length, minimum length, or maximum length, and many others). Many of the supported W3C XML Schema data types are based upon or aligned with recognized international and industry standards. As examples, the date, time, and dateTime types are all aligned with the ISO 8601 "extended format" (i.e., ccyy-mm-dd and ccyy-mm-ddThh:mm:ss).

Custom data types can be derived from built-in primitive types and derived types by using constraining facets. As an example, a custom data type could be defined to represent a whole number that would be restricted to containing data values between 1000 and 2000. An integer data type would be used as the base type, and constraining facets for a minimum value and a maximum value would also be applied. The list of built-in primitive types defined to the W3C XML Schemas Recommendation is extensive. When transaction and message-oriented data are considered, types of particular interest to the data architect are listed in Table 4.1.

Fact:

W3C XML Schemas provide extensive date and time data type support (e.g., date, time, duration, time zone, and fractional date particles). However, other than basic date and time data types, database platforms may not provide corresponding ISO 8601 data types. Use of some W3C XML Schema date and time types can require use of character or numeric database types to contain date data and the application of derivation logic.

---

[1] World Wide Web Consortium (W3C). XML Schemas. W3C Recommendation, May 2, 2001. Available at http://www.w3.org/TR/2001/REC-xmlschema-1-20010502/ (structures); http://www.w3.org/TR/2001/REC-xmlschema-2-20010502/ (data types).

Fact:

W3C XML Schema decimal data types and several of the integer data types are by default not constrained by a minimum or maximum value (i.e., they are "infinite"). However, most database decimal and integer data types have specific minimum and maximum limits. Caution is advised when one exchanges numeric data that have the potential to exceed database minimum and maximum limits.

In addition to primitive built-in data types, W3C XML Schemas also support derived types. The most frequently used derived types originate as variations of two built-in primitive types (i.e., string and decimal). Although there are several derived string types, a single derived type is directly derived from the decimal type (e.g., "integer"). There are several residual types derived from that integer type and still others derived from those residual types. With an emphasis on transaction-oriented data elements, only derived types of significant interest are listed in Table 4.2.

As described, W3C XML Schemas support a wide variety of built-in data types (those that are intrinsically supported), as well as additional derived data types. W3C XML Schemas also provide the ability to create custom data types by applying constraining facets. Custom data type support is a powerful capability when the numerous formats, patterns, lengths, and decimalization required by most businesses are considered. We will learn more about constraining facets in Chapter 5 (W3C XML Schema Data Type Facets).

Alignment with Relational Database Product Data Types

Many businesses have acquired and implemented various database technologies. Although XML extensions are available for many relational database products, XML is not in itself a database. However, XML is often used to describe data extracts from, insertions into, and exchanges between application systems and their respective databases. A frequent challenge encountered by the data architect when data are exchanged between different systems is variation in database data type support. A data type supported by one database product could be vastly different from the same data type defined to another database. Often, the solution to disparate data type support includes a process of mapping source data types to target data types and the resulting transformation.

Tables 4.3 through 4.7 describe the most common data types supported by several database products and mapped to data types supported by frequently used W3C XML Schemas. In some cases, a

W3C XML Schema data type may not have a direct relationship to a corresponding database data type. In other cases the W3C XML Schema data type may be supported by the database, but minimum and maximum values and default format may differ.

When using these tables to compare the data types, note that internal database formats can vary from external formats for extracted data (date, time, and timestamp data types are a few examples). Similarly, some examples of numeric values are "signed" to portray the allowable range of values (e.g., non-negative or negative only). Also, although some of the numeric examples are expressed as signed data to imply the allowable range of values, some numeric data types do not allow a sign character or annotation as part of a stored data value (similar to an "absolute" number). Consult your database or SQL programming documentation to determine whether a sign is required or allowed for numeric values.

When a W3C XML Schema data type is not directly supported, some form of transformation may be required. The type and complexity of transformation logic can vary based on the level of disparity between the data types. It is assumed that, over time, the listed database products will continue to evolve with resulting changes in support for both XML and data types.

W3C XML Schema Data Types to IBM DB2 UDB 7 Data Types

DB2 Universal Database (UDB) (versions 7 and 7.2) are database product offerings from IBM that were founded upon the relational model. The DB2 product has a long history in information technology and is widely used. DB2 UDB provides extensive support for enterprise application data, distributed application data, and e-commerce transaction data. The DB2 UDB products also provide support for XML. However, extensions or additional database components may be required. The DB2 UDB line of products is also available for several different hardware and operating system platforms.

Although many basic data types are supported by the DB2 UDB product, when these are compared with W3C XML Schema data types, there are several differences and constraints. Also, variations in data type support may be evident between versions and supported operating systems. Version-specific information regarding data type and XML support is available from IBM.[2] Table 4.3 compares the most frequently used W3C XML Schema data types with those supported by DB2 UDB.

W3C XML Schema Data Types to Oracle 9*i* Data Types

The Oracle database product (version 9*i*) is a relational database offering from Oracle Corporation. Like DB2, Oracle relational database products have foundations in the relational model and are widely implemented. Oracle database products are often used to support enterprise application data, distributed application data, and persistence of e-commerce transactions. Oracle 8*i* and 9*i* also provide support for XML. Again, extensions or additional database components may be required.

The Oracle line of database products is available for several different hardware and operating system platforms. Basic data types are supported by Oracle 8*i* and 9*i* products. However, there may be differences between data type characteristics and support compared with those for W3C XML Schema data types. Conversion functions for some XML data and data types may be available. It is also important to note that some variation in data type support may be evident between versions and supported operating systems. Additional information regarding data type and XML support is available from Oracle Corporation.[3] Table 4.4 compares the most frequently used W3C XML Schema data types with those supported by Oracle database products.

W3C XML Schema Data Types to Sybase ASE 12.5 Data Types

The Sybase Adaptive Server Enterprise (ASE) database product (version 12) also provides support for XML (product extensions or additional components may be required). The Sybase ASE line of products is also available for several different hardware and operating system platforms.

---

[2] IBM DB2 Universal Database, SQL Reference, Version 7.1, SC09-2974-01. IBM, 1993, 2001. DB2 Universal Database for OS/390, z/OS, SQL Reference, Version 7, SC26-9944-01. IBM, 1982, 2001. Available at http://www.ibm.com/.

[3] Oracle 9*i* Applications Developer Guide, release 1 (9.0.1), part A88876-02. Oracle Corporation, 1996–2001. Available at http://www.oracle.com/.

Several basic data types are supported by the ASE product. However, when compared to W3C XML Schema data types, there are also several differences and constraints. It is important to note that some variation in data type support may be evident between database versions and supported operating systems. Sybase also provides the Adaptive Server Anywhere (ASA) product, which supports many of the same data types as those supported by the ASE database product. However, be aware that there are also many differences. Additional information is available from Sybase.[4] Table 4.5 compares the most frequently used W3C XML Schema data types with those supported by Sybase ASE products.

W3C XML Schema Data Types to SQL Server Data Types

Completing this section on popular database products is Microsoft SQL Server. SQL Server is also founded on the relational model and provides extensive support for both enterprise and e-commerce applications. As with several other database products, SQL Server provides support for XML (depending upon the version). Again, extensions or additional database components may be required. Most basic data types are supported by SQL Server, although variations may exist when compared with W3C XML Schema data types. Additionally, some variations in data types and characteristics may be evident between versions and supported operating systems. Additional information may be available from Microsoft.[5] Table 4.6 compares the most frequently used W3C XML Schema data types with those supported by SQL Server.

Applying a Data Type using W3C XML Schema Syntax

When data are exchanged between platforms, application systems, and database products, mapping of data types is a critical activity. Use of XML and W3C XML Schemas to describe an exchange or integration

---

[4] Sybase Adaptive Server Enterprise 12.5. Transact-SQL, Content ID 1009196, revised Feb. 1, 2002. Sybase Inc., 2002. Available at http://www.sybase.com/.
[5] Microsoft SQL Server, Transact-SQL Reference (on-line), Data Types, Updated September 2001. Available at http://msdn.microsoft.com/library/default.asp?url= /library/en-us/tsqlref/ts_da-db_7msw.asp.

transaction can provide much needed support. As we have learned, the XML document instance contains data values. A schema describes metadata characteristics, rules, and constraints that are applied to the XML document during the parser validation process. One of the checks completed during the parser validation process is to compare the data values in the XML document with the data type declarations found in the schema.

The method of applying a W3C XML Schema data type differs from more traditional metadata declarations such as Data Definition Language (DDL). The basic syntax for applying a W3C XML Schema data type to an XML element or attribute is "type="datatype"," where "datatype" is one of the supported W3C XML Schema types (e.g., "integer," "date," "dateTime," "decimal," "boolean," or other). This basic form can also be extended to apply other related metadata constraints such as length limitations. Simply applying an intrinsically supported data type to an XML element or attribute is but one possible technique. A custom data type declared within a W3C XML Schema applies one or more restrictions to a built-in or derived data type. Additional restrictions or constraints are applied using data type facets such as a length, minimum or maximum value, list of allowable values, or pattern (Listing 4.1).

Technique:

The syntactical form for applying W3C XML Schema data types is "type="datatype"" where "datatype" is a supported W3C XML Schema type such as "integer," "date," "dateTime," "decimal," or "boolean."

Specific responsibility for engineering of W3C XML Schemas can vary by enterprise and technology organization. As we will see in Chapter 9 (Design and Engineering for the Data Architect), enterprise metadata definitions and characteristics are generally the responsibility of the data architect. However, the syntactical application of metadata constraints to a W3C XML Schema can be assigned to the data architect, developer, or other technology personnel. Regardless of specific responsibility, the data architect should have a solid foundation of knowledge in relation to W3C XML Schema data types and syntax.

Listing 4.1

Custom data type using W3C XML Schema simpleType syntax.

```
<xs:simpleType name="STDMonetaryType">
    <xs:restriction base="xs:decimal">
        <xs:totalDigits value="9"/>
        <xs:fractionDigits value="2"/>
    </xs:restriction>
</xs:simpleType>
```

The following examples include simple XML elements as they might be defined to an XML document and fragments of W3C XML Schema syntax describing the application of data types. The examples are organized by logical groupings of data types (e.g., date and time, integer, decimal, boolean, URI, and string).

W3C XML Schema Basic Date and Time Data Types

```
<!-  =========================================  ->
<!- XML Document Fragment - Date and Time Elements ->
<!-  =========================================  ->
<date>
    <dateyyyy-mm-dd>2001-12-21</dateyyyy-mm-dd>
    <dateyyyy-mm>2001-12</dateyyyy-mm>
    <datemm-dd>12-21</datemm-dd>
    <dateyyyy>2001</dateyyyy>
    <datemm>12</datemm>
    <datedd>21</datedd>
    <datetime>2001-12-21T00:00:00</datetime>
    <duration>P1Y2M3DT02H03M04S</duration>
</date>

<time>
    <timebase>23:01:01</timebase>
    <timezone-offset>23:01:01-01:00</timezone-offset>
</time>

<!-  =========================================  ->
<!- W3C XML Schema Fragment - Date Elements ->
<!-  =========================================  ->
    <xs:element name="date">
      <xs:complexType>
        <xs:sequence>
          <xs:element ref="dateyyyy-mm-dd"/>
          <xs:element ref="dateyyyy-mm"/>
          <xs:element ref="datemm-dd"/>
          <xs:element ref="dateyyyy"/>
          <xs:element ref="datemm"/>
          <xs:element ref="datedd"/>
          <xs:element ref="datetime"/>
          <xs:element ref="duration"/>
        </xs:sequence>
```

```
      </xs:complexType>
   </xs:element>

   <xs:element name="dateyyyy-mm-dd" type="xs:date"/>
   <xs:element name="dateyyyy-mm" type="xs:gYearMonth"/>
   <xs:element name="datemm-dd" type="xs:gMonthDay"/>
   <xs:element name="dateyyyy" type="xs:gYear"/>
   <xs:element name="datemm" type="xs:gMonth"/>
   <xs:element name="datedd" type="xs:gDay"/>
   <xs:element name="duration" type="xs:duration"/>
   <xs:element name="datetime" type="xs:dateTime"/>


<!-- ============================================ -->
<!-- W3C XML Schema Fragment - Time Elements -->
<!-- ============================================ -->
<xs:element name="time">
   <xs:complexType>
      <xs:sequence>
         <xs:element ref="timebase"/>
         <xs:element ref="timezone-offset"/>
      </xs:sequence>
   </xs:complexType>
</xs:element>

<xs:element name="timebase" type="xs:time"/>
<xs:element name="timezone-offset" type="xs:time"/>
```

W3C XML Schema Basic Integer Types

```
<!-- ============================================ -->
<!-- XML Document Fragment - Integer Elements -->
<!-- ============================================ -->
<integer>
   <integerbase>99999999999999999</integerbase>

   <integerlongmin>-9223372036854775808</integerlongmin>
   <integerlongmax>+9223372036854775807</integerlongmax>

   <integerintmin>-2147483648</integerintmin>
   <integerintmax>+2147483647</integerintmax>

   <integershortmin>-32768</integershortmin>
   <integershortmax>+32767</integershortmax>
```

```
      <integerbytemin>-128</integerbytemin>
      <integerbytemax>+127</integerbytemax>
</integer>

<!-   =============================================   ->
<!- W3C XML Schema Fragment - Integer Elements ->
<!-   =============================================   ->
<xs:element name="integer">
   <xs:complexType>
     <xs:sequence>
       <xs:element ref="integerbase"/>
       <xs:element ref="integerlongmin"/>
       <xs:element ref="integerlongmax"/>
       <xs:element ref="integerintmin"/>
       <xs:element ref="integerintmax"/>
       <xs:element ref="integershortmin"/>
       <xs:element ref="integershortmax"/>
       <xs:element ref="integerbytemin"/>
       <xs:element ref="integerbytemax"/>
     </xs:sequence>
   </xs:complexType>
</xs:element>

<xs:element name="integerbase" type="xs:integer"/>
<xs:element name="integerlongmin" type="xs:long"/>
<xs:element name="integerlongmax" type="xs:long"/>
<xs:element name="integerintmin" type="xs:int"/>
<xs:element name="integerintmax" type="xs:int"/>
<xs:element name="integershortmin" type="xs:short"/>
<xs:element name="integershortmax" type="xs:short"/>
<xs:element name="integerbytemin" type="xs:byte"/>
<xs:element name="integerbytemax" type="xs:byte"/>
```

W3C XML Schema Basic Decimal Data Types

```
<!-   =============================================   ->
<!- XML Document Fragment - Decimal Element->
<!-   =============================================   ->
<decimal>
   <decimalbase>9999999999999999999999999999.99999999
   </decimalbase>
</decimal>
```

```
<!— ========================================  —>
<!— W3C XML Schema Fragment - Decimal Element —>
<!— ========================================  —>
<xs:element name="decimal">
   <xs:complexType>
     <xs:sequence>
       <xs:element ref="decimalbase"/>
     </xs:sequence>
   </xs:complexType>
</xs:element>

<xs:element name="decimalbase" type="xs:decimal"/>
```

W3C XML Schema Basic Boolean Data Types

```
<!— ========================================  —>
<!— XML Document Fragment - Boolean Elements —>
<!— ========================================  —>
<boolean>
  <booleantrueliteral>true</booleantrueliteral>
  <booleanfalseliteral>false</booleanfalseliteral>
  <booleantrue>1</booleantrue>
  <booleanfalse>0</booleanfalse>
</boolean>

<!— ========================================  —>
<!— XML Schema Fragment - Boolean Elements —>
<!— ========================================  —>
<xs:element name="boolean">
  <xs:complexType>
      <xs:sequence>
          <xs:element ref="booleantrueliteral"/>
          <xs:element ref="booleanfalseliteral"/>
          <xs:element ref="booleantrue"/>
          <xs:element ref="booleanfalse"/>
      </xs:sequence>
  </xs:complexType>
</xs:element>

<xs:element name="booleantrueliteral" type="xs:boolean"/>
<xs:element name="booleanfalseliteral"
type="xs:boolean"/>
```

```
<xs:element name="booleantrue" type="xs:boolean"/>
<xs:element name="booleanfalse" type="xs:boolean"/>
```

W3C XML Schema Basic URI Data Types

```
<!— ============================================= —>
<!— XML Document Fragment - URI Element —>
<!— ============================================= —>
<URL>
   <anyURI>www.xyz-abc.com</anyURI>
</URL>


<!— ============================================= —>
<!— XML Schema Fragment - URI Element —>
<!— ============================================= —>
<xs:element name="URL">
  <xs:complexType>
     <xs:sequence>
          <xs:element ref="anyURI"/>
       </xs:sequence>
  </xs:complexType>
</xs:element>

<xs:element name="anyURI" type="xs:anyURI"/>
```

W3C XML Schema Basic String Data Types

```
<!— ============================================= —>
<!— XML Document Fragment - String Elements —>
<!— ============================================= —>
<string>
  <stringbase>abcdefg 12345678 CR LF TAB</stringbase>
  <stringnormalized>abcdefg</stringnormalized>
  <stringtoken>abcdefg</stringtoken>
</string>


<!— ============================================= —>
<!— XML Schema Fragment - String Elements —>
<!— ============================================= —>
<xs:element name="string">
```

```
<xs:complexType>
    <xs:sequence>
        <xs:element ref="stringbase"/>
        <xs:element ref="stringnormalized"/>
        <xs:element ref="stringtoken"/>
    </xs:sequence>
</xs:complexType>
</xs:element>

<xs:element name="stringbase" type="xs:string"/>
<xs:element name="stringnormalized"
type="xs:normalizedString"/>
<xs:element name="stringtoken" type="xs:token"/>
```

As we will see in Chapter 5 (W3C XML Schema Data Type Facets), in addition to basic W3C XML Schema data types (both primitive and derived), each type can be further constrained by applying data type facets. The result is a custom data type derivation.

Using Identifiers

Although not directly addressed in the previous section on data types, W3C XML Schemas (as well as several other types of schemas) provide support for an "ID" type. Depending upon the use and definition of identifying data, application and enforcement of a unique identifier assigned to elements or attributes of an XML document can be of value. This concept is not unlike the unique identifier of a logical model entity or the primary key of a database table. In the case of an XML ID type, there are also limitations.

A unique identifier can be defined as one or more data elements that uniquely identify one set of data from another of the same context. As found in most enterprise business systems, unique identifiers are often applied to customers, prospects, vendors, products, items, parts, assemblies, physical assets, human resources, and many other foundation data concepts. The data elements that identify this information are often named something like "Customer Number," "Vendor ID," or "Part Number." When identifying data are stored in a database (i.e., "persisted"), unique identifiers are sometimes implemented as primary keys or as a form of unique index.

The business rules used to construct and assign an identifier data value can vary from system to system. Some systems will sequentially assign a number from a register when a new data instance is created (e.g., addition of a new customer record). Other systems may construct an identifier value as the combination of other data values, as the result of an algorithm, or by using a timestamp. Identifiers can also be intelligent or non-intelligent. An intelligent identifier includes one or more recognizable characteristics that have meaning or context for either a person or application program. A non-intelligent identifier does not portray any intentional meaning and is often a set of nondescript digits or characters.

Recommendation:

Identifying data that are critical to the processing of an XML transaction or message should be included as an element or attribute and be clearly described by name or location in the document.

Similar to a data model entity or a database table, unique identifiers may also be of value to an XML transaction. This is especially true when the XML transaction contains more than one set of similar data (e.g., a single XML document contains many occurrences of customers, orders, and products). The ability to distinguish one set of data from another is often critical to application processing. Even in cases in which the XML document contains a single occurrence of data (e.g., a single customer, order, or product), the inclusion of identifiers derived from the source of the data is also valuable. Identifying data will help to avoid potential ambiguity, duplication, or collision of enterprise data when the transaction is processed.

There are several methods for defining an identifier to an XML transaction. An identifier can be defined as an XML element. Often this element is a child element of a group of similar or related elements. Another technique is to define an identifier as an attribute of a specific element (Fig. 4.3).

Some identifiers are combinations of multiple data values. When an identifier is the aggregate of separately defined data values (known as a composite identifier or composite key), these separate values should also be described to the XML document as separate elements or attributes. To simplify navigation and processing, identifier elements that in combination represent a single identifier should also be located together (possibly as elements within a parent or group element). They should also be specified in the correct sequence (Fig. 4.4).

In some cases, the data values of a composite key are processed as a single combined data value. If the identifier value is processed both as a set of individual identifier data values and as a single combined identifier data value, it may be advantageous to also carry an additional

Implementing an Identifier as an XML Element

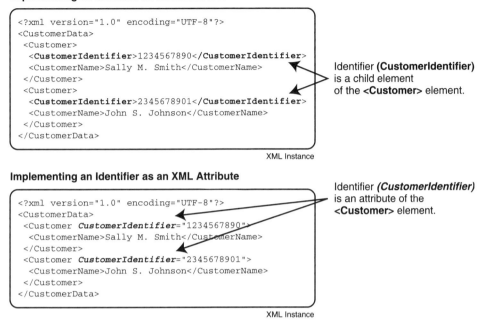

```
<?xml version="1.0" encoding="UTF-8"?>
<CustomerData>
 <Customer>
  <CustomerIdentifier>1234567890</CustomerIdentifier>
  <CustomerName>Sally M. Smith</CustomerName>
 </Customer>
 <Customer>
  <CustomerIdentifier>2345678901</CustomerIdentifier>
  <CustomerName>John S. Johnson</CustomerName>
 </Customer>
</CustomerData>
```

Identifier **(CustomerIdentifier)** is a child element of the **<Customer>** element.

XML Instance

Implementing an Identifier as an XML Attribute

```
<?xml version="1.0" encoding="UTF-8"?>
<CustomerData>
 <Customer CustomerIdentifier="1234567890">
  <CustomerName>Sally M. Smith</CustomerName>
 </Customer>
 <Customer CustomerIdentifier="2345678901">
  <CustomerName>John S. Johnson</CustomerName>
 </Customer>
</CustomerData>
```

Identifier *(CustomerIdentifier)* is an attribute of the **<Customer>** element.

XML Instance

Figure 4.3

Identifier techniques for an XML transaction.

Recommendation:

The same level of granularity and composition of unique identifiers as defined by the data source or data target should be used in the XML transaction. If the identifier is a combination of separate data elements (e.g., a composite key), similar containers should be defined.

element or attribute to contain the concatenated identifier data value. This is a less desirable technique because the component data values become ambiguous and non-decomposable. Also, the aggregate or concatenated identifier data value must be derivable (e.g., XML and W3C XML Schemas do not provide intrinsic logic capability to derive data values). Regardless of the method used for implementation, the same level of granularity and composition of unique identifiers should be applied to the XML transaction.

Although providing an identifier as part of an XML transaction is important, application processing of identifiers does not necessarily ensure uniqueness. W3C XML Schemas provide a unique identifier data type (ID) that

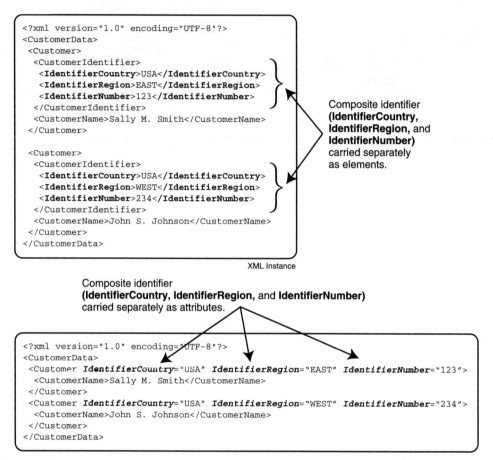

```
<?xml version="1.0" encoding="UTF-8"?>
<CustomerData>
 <Customer>
  <CustomerIdentifier>
   <IdentifierCountry>USA</IdentifierCountry>
   <IdentifierRegion>EAST</IdentifierRegion>
   <IdentifierNumber>123</IdentifierNumber>
  </CustomerIdentifier>
  <CustomerName>Sally M. Smith</CustomerName>
 </Customer>

 <Customer>
  <CustomerIdentifier>
   <IdentifierCountry>USA</IdentifierCountry>
   <IdentifierRegion>WEST</IdentifierRegion>
   <IdentifierNumber>234</IdentifierNumber>
  </CustomerIdentifier>
  <CustomerName>John S. Johnson</CustomerName>
 </Customer>
</CustomerData>
```

Composite identifier **(IdentifierCountry, IdentifierRegion,** and **IdentifierNumber)** carried separately as elements.

XML Instance

Composite identifier **(IdentifierCountry, IdentifierRegion,** and **IdentifierNumber)** carried separately as attributes.

```
<?xml version="1.0" encoding="UTF-8"?>
<CustomerData>
 <Customer IdentifierCountry="USA" IdentifierRegion="EAST" IdentifierNumber="123">
  <CustomerName>Sally M. Smith</CustomerName>
 </Customer>
 <Customer IdentifierCountry="USA" IdentifierRegion="WEST" IdentifierNumber="234">
  <CustomerName>John S. Johnson</CustomerName>
 </Customer>
</CustomerData>
```

Figure 4.4

Composite identifiers.

can be applied to any defined XML element or attribute (Fig. 4.5). When the XML transaction is validated to the corresponding W3C XML Schema, the parser will check for duplicate data values within that XML document and notify the parsing application of a uniqueness violation or error.

There are limitations to identifier data types (e.g., ID). First, the W3C XML Schema ID data type is only checked for uniqueness during the parser validation process. Second, data values held by element or attribute containers defined as ID will only be checked for uniqueness

Recommendation:

Use of the W3C XML Schema identifier data type (ID) should be limited to data elements and attributes for which uniqueness within a single XML document is required. Owing to limitations of allowable data values, the "ID" data type should not be used to describe database primary keys or similar unique identifiers. Ensuring uniqueness of database identifiers (i.e., primary keys) should be left to the originating database systems.

across repetitions of the same containers within a single XML document or transaction. There is no capability in XML or W3C XML Schemas to verify or ensure that identifiers are in fact unique for an external data source such as a database. Third, the ID data type is derived from a string data type and data values must conform to syntax used to define XML element and attribute names (e.g., no embedded white space, no leading numeric digit, and no colon within an identifier data value). Data values defined by an ID data type must be string and may not contain a leading numeric digit.

In addition to data type support of W3C XML Schemas, there are a number of additional constraints that can be applied. As an example, an element defined by a "string" type can be further constrained as to minimum and maximum length or to a set of allowable values. These additional constraints are defined by data type facets.

Figure 4.5

W3C XML Schema syntax for "ID" data type.

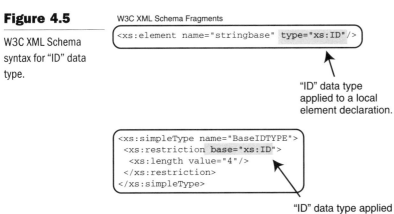

W3C XML Schema Fragments

```
<xs:element name="stringbase" type="xs:ID"/>
```

"ID" data type applied to a local element declaration.

```
<xs:simpleType name="BaseIDTYPE">
 <xs:restriction base="xs:ID">
  <xs:length value="4"/>
 </xs:restriction>
</xs:simpleType>
```

"ID" data type applied as part of a globally declared simpleType.

Note that this simple type also constrains the length of the ID to a fixed length of four characters.

Table 4.1   W3C XML Schema Built-In Primitive Types (Frequently Used) (subset derived from the May 2001 W3C XML Schemas Recommendation)

W3C XML Schema built-in primitive type	Examples of values and format
duration	Example value: P1Y2M3DT1H2M3S Format: P9Y9M9DT9H9M9S Legend: P = literal (implied as "period") Y = literal (years) M = literal (months) D = literal (days) T = literal (implied "time") H = literal (hours) M = literal (minutes) S = literal (seconds)
dateTime	Example value: 2003-03-15T11:37:02.123 Format: CCYY-MM-DDTHH:MM:SS.sss Legend: CCYY = year (including century) MM = month DD = day T = literal (implied "time") HH = hour MM = minute SS = second sss = fractional seconds sss...n (where applicable)
date	Example value: 2003-03-15 Format: CCYY-MM-DD Legend: CCYY = year (including century) MM = month DD = day

Table 4.1 *Continued*

W3C XML Schema built-in primitive type	Examples of values and format
time	Example value: 11:37:02.123 Format: HH:MM:SS.sss HH:MM:SSZ (implied time zone of UTC) HH:MM:SS+HH:MM (positive offset from UTC) HH:MM:SS-HH:MM (negative offset from UTC) Legend: HH = hour MM = minute SS = second sss = fractional seconds sss...n (where applicable) Z = literal (implied time zone of UTC)
gYearMonth	Example value: 2003-03 Format: CCYY-MM Legend: CCYY = year (including century) MM = month
gYear	Example value: 2003 Format: CCYY Legend: CCYY = year (including century)
gMonthDay	Example value: 03-15 Format: MM-DD Legend: MM = month DD = day

Continued

Table 4.1   *Continued*

W3C XML Schema built-in primitive type	Examples of values and format
gMonth	Example value: 03 Format: MM Legend: MM = month
gDay	Example value: 15 Format: DD Legend: DD = day
string	Example value: AbcdefgABCDEFG123456 # $ % * Format: X (any characters allowable by XML, unspecified length)
boolean	Example values: "0" (value for false) "1" (value for true) "false" (literal value for false) "true" (literal value for true)
base64Binary	Format: Base 64 encoded data (e.g., RFC 2045)
hexBinary	Example value: 3FA8 Format: X (unspecified number of digits) Legend: Each digit must be a value of "0" through "9" or "A" through "F" (supporting hexadecimal digits)

Table 4.1 *Continued*

W3C XML Schema built-in primitive type	Examples of values and format
float	Example value: 15E31 Format: s9Es9 (floating point) Legend: s = sign (+, −, absolute, undeclared) 9 = mantissa (in the range of −2E24 to 2E24) E = literal (implied notation for exponent) 9 = exponent (in the range of −149 to 104)
decimal	Example value: 12345678.12345678 Format: s9.9 (unspecified number of digits) Legend: s = sign (+, −, absolute, undeclared) The W3C XML Schema Recommendation states that a minimum of 18 digits must be supported.
double	Example value: 100E231 Format: s9Es9 (floating point, double precision) Legend: s = sign (+, −, absolute, undeclared) 9 = mantissa (in the range of −2E53 to 2E53) E = literal (implied notation for exponent) 9 = exponent (in the range of −1075 to 970)
anyURI	Example value: www.abcdefgXXX123.com Format: URI string (e.g., RFC 2396, RFC 2732)

Table 4.2   W3C XML Schema Built-in Derived Types (Frequently Used) (subset derived from the May 2001 W3C XML Schemas Recommendation)

W3C XML Schema built-in derived type		Examples of values and format
Derived from	**Derived type**	
string	normalizedString	Example value: AbcdefgABCDEFG123456 # $ % *
		Format: X (any characters allowable by XML, excluding carriage return, line feed, and tab, of unspecified length)
string	token	Example value: AbcdefgABCDEFG123456 # $ % *
		Format: X (any characters allowable by XML, excluding carriage return, line feed, tab, and leading or trailing white space, of unspecified length)
decimal	integer	Example value: 123456789
		Format: s9(n) Value thresholds Min value: −infinite Max value: infinite
		Legend: s = sign (+, −, absolute, undeclared) n = unlimited length
integer	nonPositiveInteger	Example value: −12345
		Format: s9(n) Value thresholds Min value: −infinite Max value: 0
		Legend: s = sign (+, −, absolute, undeclared) n = limited length re value thresholds

Table 4.2 *Continued*

W3C XML Schema built-in derived type		Examples of values and format
Derived from	**Derived type**	
integer	long	Example value: 123456789
		Format: s9(n) Value thresholds Min value: −9223372036854775808 Max value: +9223372036854775807
		Legend: s = sign (+, −, absolute, undeclared) n = limited length re value thresholds
integer	nonNegativeInteger	Example value: 12345
		Format: s9(n) Value thresholds Min value: 0 Max value: infinite
		Legend: s = sign (+, −, absolute, undeclared) n = limited length re value thresholds
nonPositiveInteger	negativeInteger	Example value: −12345
		Format: s9(n) Value thresholds Min value: −infinite Max value: −1
		Legend: s = sign (+, −, absolute, undeclared) n = limited length re value thresholds

Continued

Table 4.2 *Continued*

W3C XML Schema built-in derived type		
Derived from	**Derived type**	**Examples of values and format**
long	int	Example value: 123456789
		Format: s9(n) Value thresholds Min value: −2147483648 Max value: +2147483647
		Legend: s = sign (+, −, absolute, undeclared) n = limited length re value thresholds
long	short	Example value: 12345
		Format: s9(n) Value thresholds Min value: −32768 Max value: +32767
		Legend: s = sign (+, −, absolute, undeclared) n = limited length re value thresholds
long	byte	Example value: 127
		Format: s9(n) Value thresholds Min value: −128 Max value: +127
		Legend: s = sign (+, −, absolute, undeclared) n = limited length re value thresholds

Table 4.2 *Continued*

W3C XML Schema built-in derived type		Examples of values and format
Derived from	**Derived type**	
nonNegativeInteger	positiveInteger	Example value: 12345
		Format: s9(n) Value thresholds Min value: +1 Max value: +infinite
		Legend: s = sign (+, −, absolute, undeclared) n = limited length re value thresholds
nonNegativeInteger	unsignedLong	Example value: 12345
		Format: 9(n) Value thresholds Min value: 0 Max value: 18446744073709551615
		Legend: n = limited length re value thresholds
nonNegativeInteger	unsignedInt	Example value: 12345
		Format: 9(n) Value thresholds Min value: 0 Max value: 4294967295
		Legend: n = limited length re value thresholds
nonNegativeInteger	unsignedShort	Example value: 12345
		Format: 9(n)

Continued

Table 4.2   *Continued*

W3C XML Schema built-in derived type		
Derived from	**Derived type**	**Examples of values and format**
		Value thresholds Min value: 0 Max value: 65535
		Legend: n = limited length re value thresholds
nonNegativeInteger	unsignedByte	Example value: 127
		Format: 9(n) Value thresholds Min value: 0 Max value: 255
		Legend: n = limited length re value thresholds

Table 4.3   Comparison of Frequently Used W3C XML Schema Data Types with IBM DB2 UDB 7 Data Types

Frequently used W3C XML Schema types	IBM DB2 UDB 7 and 7.2
duration	The "duration" type is not directly supported. It may be possible to format, convert, and derive duration values using a string type such as "CHAR." However, such techniques may require custom application logic.
dateTime	The "dateTime" type is not directly supported. The DB2 "TIMESTAMP" type may provide similar support. However, both the internal storage and format of TIMESTAMP data vary from W3C XML Schema "dateTime" types. An obvious variation is that the TIMESTAMP type does not include a literal of "T" to denote separation of date from time.
date	The "date" type is supported as the DB2 "DATE" type. However, the internal storage of DATE data may vary from the W3C XML Schema "date." Also, DB2 supports an installation parameter that may introduce variations in format.
time	The "time" type is supported as the DB2 "TIME" type. However, the internal storage of TIME data may vary from "time" in W3C XML Schema. In particular, the W3C XML Schema format for time is "HH:MM:SS," whereas the DB2 format for time is "HH.MM.SS." In some cases, the display format for time can be set as an implementation or user option. Additionally, the DB2 representation of time does not include a time zone designator and fractional seconds are not supported (fractional second support is provided by DB2 "TIMESTAMP").
gYearMonth gYear gMonthDay gMonth gDay	The W3C XML Schema "date" types of: gYearMonth, gYear, gMonthDay, gMonth, and gDay are not directly supported. It may be possible to format, convert, and derive these date values using a string type such as "CHAR." However, such techniques may require custom application logic.
string	The "string" type is supported by DB2 UDB as one of several "CHARACTER" types. However, the W3C XML Schema "string" type does not specify a specific or maximum length as a number of character positions. The DB2 UDB CHARACTER types have implied maximum lengths and may provide varying support depending upon the character type (e.g., double byte).

Continued

Table 4.3   *Continued*

Frequently used W3C XML Schema types	IBM DB2 UDB 7 and 7.2
	Also, consideration should be given to internal storage of string or character data when persisted in the database. Encoding of internally stored data may vary (i.e., Unicode, UTF-8, ASCII, or EBCDIC).

DB2 UDB type	Approximate Maximum character length
CHAR	254
VARCHAR	32672
LONGVARCHAR	32700
CLOB	2147483647
NCLOB	4294967295
LONG	2147483647

boolean	The "boolean" type is not directly supported. DB2 types of either SMALLINT or CHAR may be used to contain similar boolean data values (e.g., "0," "1," "false", or "true"). However, use of DB2 SMALLINT or CHAR types may require custom application logic.
base64Binary	The "base64Binary" type is not directly supported. However, depending upon the type, application, and encoding of the data values, it may be possible to use other graphic and double byte DB2 types. However, a common use of hex64Binary type is to describe document MIME type data of graphic, picture, artwork, or similar, which may or may not be supported by DB2. Use of other DB2 types may require custom application logic.

DB2 UDB type	Approximate maximum character length
GRAPHIC	127
VARGRAPHIC	16336
LONGVARGRAPHIC	16350
BLOB	2147483647

hexBinary	The "hexBinary" type is not directly supported. It may be possible to format, convert, and derive duration values using a string type such as "CHAR." However, such techniques may require custom application logic.

Table 4.3 *Continued*

Frequently used W3C XML Schema types	IBM DB2 UDB 7 and 7.2
float	The "float" type is supported to some degree by DB2 REAL, FLOAT, and DOUBLE types. However, the minimum and maximum values (both mantissa and exponent) may vary from the allowable values of the W3C XML Schema "float" type.
decimal	The "decimal" type is directly supported by DB2 DECIMAL and NUMERIC types. However, the minimum and maximum values (both total digits and fractional digits) may vary from the allowable values of the W3C XML Schema "decimal" type.
integer long	The "integer" and "long" types are not directly supported. However, the BIGINT, INTEGER, or SMALL INT DB2 types may be used in some applications. It is important to note that the W3C XML Schema "integer" type does not specify a minimum or maximum value (i.e., infinite). The "long" type corresponds to the DB2 BIGINT type and allowable values. The DB2 types have specific minimum and maximum limits. DB2 UDB type — Approximate value thresholds BIGINT (min) — −9223372036854775808 BIGINT (max) — +9223372036854775807 INTEGER (min) — −2147483648 INTEGER (max) — +2147483647 SMALLINT (min) — −32768 SMALLINT (max) — +32767
int	The "int" type is directly supported by the DB2 INTEGER type.
short	The "short" type is directly supported by the DB2 SMALLINT type.
byte	The "byte" type is not directly supported. However, the BIGINT, INTEGER, or SMALLINT DB2 types may in some applications be used. It is important to note that the W3C XML Schema "byte" type specifies a minimum value of "−128" and a maximum value of "+127." The DB2 types have other minimum and maximum limits.

Continued

Table 4.3   *Continued*

Frequently used W3C XML Schema types	IBM DB2 UDB 7 and 7.2	
	DB2 UDB Type	Approximate value thresholds
	BIGINT (min)	−9223372036854775808
	BIGINT (max)	+9223372036854775807
	INTEGER (min)	−2147483648
	INTEGER (max)	+2147483647
	SMALLINT (min)	−32768
	SMALLINT (max)	+32767
double	The "double" type is supported to some degree by DB2 REAL, FLOAT, and DOUBLE types. However, the minimum and maximum values (both mantissa and exponent) may vary from the allowable values of the W3C XML Schema "double" type.	
anyURI	The "anyURI" type is not directly supported. However, depending upon the type, application, and encoding of the data values, it may be possible to use other DB2 types. Use of other DB2 types may require custom application logic. Possible DB2 UDB types: DATALINK (external file or object reference) CHAR (simple string value)	

Table 4.4   Comparison of Frequently Used W3C XML Schema Data Types with Oracle 9*i* Data Types

Frequently used W3C XML Schema types	Oracle 9*i*
Duration	The "duration" type may be indirectly supported by the Oracle INTERVAL YEAR TO MONTH and INTERVAL DAY TO SECOND types. However, use of these types may depend on Oracle installation parameters, format, and allowable values. Transformation or custom application coding may be required.
dateTime	The "dateTime" type may be indirectly supported by the Oracle TIMESTAMP, TIMESTAMP WITH TIMEZONE, and TIMESTAMP WITH LOCAL TIMEZONE types. However, use of these types may depend on Oracle installation parameters, format, and allowable values. Transformation or custom application coding may be required. Also, the "default" format for Oracle date values is "DD-mmm-YYYY."
date	The "date" type may be indirectly supported by the Oracle DATE type. However, use of this type may depend on Oracle installation parameters, format, and allowable values. Transformation or custom application coding may be required. The Oracle "TO_DATE" function may provide some added capabilities. Also, the "default" format for Oracle date values is "DD-mmm-YYYY."
time	The "time" type may be indirectly supported by the Oracle TIMESTAMP, TIMESTAMP WITH TIMEZONE, and TIMESTAMP WITH LOCAL TIMEZONE types. However, use of these types may depend on Oracle installation parameters, format, and allowable values. Transformation or custom application coding may be required. The Oracle "TO_DATE" and "TRUNC" functions may provide some added capabilities. Also, the "default" format for Oracle date values is "DD-mmm-YYYY". Fractional seconds support is undocumented and unknown.
gYearMonth gYear gMonthDay gMonth gDay	The W3C XML Schema "date" types of: gYearMonth, gYear, gMonthDay, gMonth, and gDay are not directly supported. It may be possible to format, convert, and derive these date values using a string type such as "CHAR." However, such techniques may require custom application logic.

Continued

Table 4.4   *Continued*

Frequently used W3C XML Schema types	Oracle 9*i*
string	The "string" type is supported by Oracle as one of several "CHARACTER" types.
	However, the W3C XML Schema "string" type does not specify a specific or maximum length as a number of character positions. The Oracle 9*i* CHAR types have implied maximum lengths and may provide varying support depending on the character type (e.g., double byte).
	Also, consideration should be given to internal storage of string or character data when persisted in the database. Encoding of internally stored data may vary.

Oracle 9*i* type	Approximate maximum character length
CHAR	2000
VARCHAR2	4000
NCHAR	2000
NVCHAR2	4000
CLOB	4294967295
NCLOB	4294967295
LONG	2147483647

boolean	The "boolean" type is not directly supported.
	Oracle types of either NUMBER or CHAR may be used to contain similar boolean data values (e.g., "0," "1," "false," and "true").
	However, use of Oracle NUMBER or CHAR types may require custom application logic.
base64Binary	The "base64Binary" type is not directly supported.
	However, depending upon the type, application, and encoding of the data values, it may be possible to use other graphic Oracle types. However, a common use of hex64Binary type is to describe document MIME type data of graphic, picture, artwork, or similar, which may or may not be supported by Oracle.
	Use of other Oracle types may require custom application logic.

Oracle 9*i* type	Approximate maximum character length
BLOB	4 gb
BFILE	4 gb (external reference)
RAW	2000
LONG RAW	2 gb

Table 4.4   *Continued*

Frequently used W3C XML Schema types	Oracle 9*i*
hexBinary	The "hexBinary" type is not directly supported. It may be possible to format, convert, and derive duration values using a string type such as "CHAR." However, such techniques may require custom application logic.
float	The "float" type is not directly supported. It may be possible to format, convert, and derive single precision floating point values using a string type such as "CHAR" or the "NUMBER" type. However, such techniques may require custom application logic.
decimal	The "decimal" type is directly supported by the Oracle NUMBER type. However, the minimum and maximum values (both total digits and fractional digits) may vary from the allowable values of the W3C XML Schema "decimal" type.
integer long	The "integer" and "long" types are indirectly supported by the Oracle NUMBER type for some applications. It is important to note that the W3C XML Schema "integer" type does not specify a minimum or maximum value (i.e., infinite). The Oracle NUMBER type has specific minimum and maximum limits. Oracle 9*i* type Approximate value thresholds NUMBER (min) -1×10^{-130} NUMBER (max) $+9.99 \times 10^{125}$
int	The "int" type is not directly supported. However, the NUMBER type may be used in some applications. It is important to note that the W3C XML Schema "int" type specifies a minimum value of "–2147483648" and a maximum value of "+2147483647." The Oracle number type also has specific minimum and maximum limits. Oracle 9*i* type Approximate value thresholds NUMBER (min) -1×10^{-130} NUMBER (max) $+9.99 \times 10^{125}$
short	The "short" type is not directly supported. However, the NUMBER type may in some applications be used. It is important to note that the W3C XML Schema "short" type specifies a minimum value of "–32768"and a maximum value of "+32767." The Oracle number type also has specific minimum and maximum limits.

Continued

Table 4.4 *Continued*

Frequently used W3C XML Schema types	Oracle 9*i*	
	Oracle 9*i* type	Approximate value thresholds
	NUMBER (min)	-1×10^{-130}
	NUMBER (max)	$+9.99 \times 10^{125}$
byte	The "byte" type is not directly supported.	
	However, the NUMBER type may be used in some applications. It is important to note that the W3C XML Schema "byte" type specifies a minimum value of "−128" and a maximum value of "+127." The Oracle number type also has specific minimum and maximum limits.	
	Oracle 9*i* type	Approximate value thresholds
	NUMBER (min)	-1×10^{-130}
	NUMBER (max)	$+9.99 \times 10^{125}$
double	The "double" type is not directly supported.	
	It may be possible to format, convert, and derive double precision floating point values using a string type such as "CHAR" or the "NUMBER" type. However, such techniques may require custom application logic.	
anyURI	The "anyURI" type is not directly supported.	
	However, depending upon the type, application, and encoding of the data values, it may be possible to use other Oracle types.	
	Use of other Oracle types may require custom application logic.	
	Oracle 9*i* type:	
	BFILE (external file or object reference)	
	CHAR (simple string value)	

Table 4.5   Comparison of Frequently Used W3C XML Schema Data Types with Sybase ASE 12.5 Data Types

Frequently used W3C XML Schema types	Sybase ASE 12.5
duration	The "duration" type is not directly supported. It may be possible to format, convert, and derive these date values using a string type such as "char." However, such techniques may require custom application logic.
dateTime	The "dateTime" type may be indirectly supported by the Sybase datetime and smalldatetime types. However, the minimum and maximum allowable values may not match the W3C XML Schema "date" type. Also, the literal of "T" to designate the separation of date data from time data is not evident.
date	The "date" type may be indirectly supported by the Sybase datetime and smalldatetime types. However, the minimum and maximum allowable values may not match the W3C XML Schema "date" type. Additionally, the format and allowable values may depend on installation parameters (set dateformat and set date first). Also, the default format for date is "MMM DD YYYY."
time	The "time" type may be indirectly supported by the Sybase datetime and smalldatetime types. However, there is no documented support for time zone or a time zone designator. Additionally, support for fractional seconds varies between the two types.
gYearMonth gYear gMonthDay gMonth gDay	The W3C XML Schema "date" types of: gYearMonth, gYear, gMonthDay, gMonth, and gDay are not directly supported. It may be possible to format, convert, and derive these date values using a string type such as "char," "datetime," and "smalldatetime." However, such techniques may require custom application logic.
string	The "string" type is supported by Sybase as one of several "Character" types. However, the W3C XML Schema "string" type does not specify a specific or maximum length as a number of character positions. The Sybase character types have implied maximum lengths and may provide varying support depending upon the character type (e.g., double byte).

Continued

Table 4.5 *Continued*

Frequently used W3C XML Schema types	Sybase ASE 12.5
	Also, consideration should be given to internal storage of string or character data, when persisted in the database. Encoding of internally stored data may vary.

Sybase ASE 12.5 type	Approximate maximum character length
char	255
varchar	255
nchar	255
nvarchar	255
text	214748647

Frequently used W3C XML Schema types	Sybase ASE 12.5
boolean	The "boolean" type is not directly supported. Sybase types of either bit or char may be used to contain similar boolean data values (e.g. "0," "1," "false," and "true"). However, use of Sybase bit or char types may require custom application logic.
base64Binary	The "base64Binary" type is not directly supported. However, depending upon the type, application, and encoding of the data values, it may be possible to use other graphic Sybase types. However, a common use of hex64Binary type is to describe document MIME type data of graphic, picture, artwork, or similar, which may or may not be supported by Sybase. Use of other Sybase types may require custom application logic.

Sybase ASE 12.5 type	Approximate maximum character length
binary	255
varbinary	255
image	2147483647

Frequently used W3C XML Schema types	Sybase ASE 12.5
hexBinary	The "hexBinary" type is not directly supported. It may be possible to format, convert, and derive duration values using a string type such as "char." However, such techniques may require custom application logic.
float	The "float" type is supported to some degree by Sybase float, double, and real types. However, the format and minimum and maximum values (both mantissa and exponent) may vary from the allowable values of the W3C XML Schema "float" type.

Table 4.5   *Continued*

Frequently used W3C XML Schema types	Sybase ASE 12.5
decimal	The "decimal" type is directly supported by the Sybase decimal, numeric, and dec (synonym) types. However, the minimum and maximum values (both total digits and fractional digits) may vary from the allowable values of the W3C XML Schema "decimal" type.
integer long	The "integer" and "long" types are indirectly supported by the decimal, numeric, int, and integer (synonym) types for some applications. It is important to note that the W3C XML Schema "integer" type does not specify a minimum or maximum value (i.e., infinite). The Sybase types have specific minimum and maximum limits.

Sybase ASE 12.5 type	Approximate maximum character length
numeric (min)	-10^{38}
numeric (min)	$+10^{38}(-1)$
decimal (min)	-10^{38}
decimal (max)	$+10^{38}(-1)$
int (min)	-2147483648
int (max)	$+2147483647$

int	The "int" type is directly supported.
short	The "short" type is directly supported as the Sybase smallint type.
byte	The "byte" type is indirectly supported by the Sybase smallint and possibly by the tinyint types. However, the smallint type has minimum and maximum value limits that are greater than the W3C XML Schema byte type. The W3C XML Schema byte type has a minimum value of "−128" and a maximum value of "+127." Also, the Sybase tinyint type is limited to non-negative integer numbers (with values from 0 to 255).

Sybase ASE 12.5 type	Approximate maximum character length
smallint (min)	-32768
smallint (max)	$+32767$
tinyint (min)	0
tinyint (min)	255

Continued

Table 4.5   *Continued*

Frequently used W3C XML Schema types	Sybase ASE 12.5	
double	The "double" type is supported to some degree by Sybase float, double, and real types. However, the format and minimum and maximum values (both mantissa and exponent) may vary from the allowable values of the W3C XML Schema "double" type.	
anyURI	The "anyURI" type is not directly supported. However, depending upon the type, application, and encoding of the data values, it may be possible to use other Sybase character types. Use of other Sybase types may require custom application logic.	
	Sybase ASE 12.5 type	Approximate maximum character length
	char	255
	varchar	255
	nchar	255
	nvarchar	255
	text	214748647

Table 4.6 Comparison of Frequently Used W3C XML Schema Data Types with SQL Server Data Types

Frequently used W3C XML Schema types	SQL Server
duration	The "duration" type is not directly supported. It may be possible to format, convert, and derive these date values using a string type such as "char." However, such techniques may require custom application logic.
dateTime	The "dateTime" type may be indirectly supported by the SQL Server datetime and smalldatetime types. Depending upon the application some indirect support may be available from the "timestamp" type. However, the minimum and maximum allowable values may not match the W3C XML Schemas "date" type. Also, the literal of "T" to designate the separation of date data from time data is not evident.
date	The "date" type may be indirectly supported by the SQL Server datetime and smalldatetime types. However, the minimum and maximum allowable values may not match the W3C XML Schema "date" type. Also, the format and allowable values may depend on installation parameters (set dateformat and set date first).
time	The "time" type may be indirectly supported by the SQL Server datetime and smalldatetime types. However, there is no documented support for time zone or a time zone designator.
gYearMonth gYear gMonthDay gMonth gDay	The W3C XML Schema "date" types of: gYearMonth, gYear, gMonthDay, gMonth, and gDay are not directly supported. It may be possible to format, convert, and derive these date values using a string type such as "char," "datetime," and "smalldatetime." However, such techniques may require custom application logic.
string	The "string" type is supported by SQL Server as one of several "Character" types. However, the W3C XML Schema "string" type does not specify a specific or maximum length as a number of character positions. The SQL Server character types have implied maximum lengths and may provide varying support depending upon the character type (e.g., double byte).

Continued

Table 4.6 *Continued*

Frequently used W3C XML Schema types	SQL Server
	Also, consideration should be given to internal storage of string or character data when persisted in the database. Encoding of internally stored data may vary.

SQL Server type	Approximate maximum character length
char	8000
varchar	8000
text	2147483647
nchar (Unicode support)	4000
nvarchar (Unicode support)	4000
ntext (Unicode support)	1073741823

Frequently used W3C XML Schema types	SQL Server
boolean	The "boolean" type is not directly supported. SQL Server types of either bit or char may be used to contain similar boolean data values (e.g., "0," "1," "false," and "true"). However, use of SQL Server bit or char types may require custom application logic.
base64Binary	The "base64Binary" type is not directly supported. However, depending upon the type, application, and encoding of the data values, it may be possible to use other graphic SQL Server types. However, a common use of hex64Binary type is to describe document MIME type data of graphic, picture, artwork, or similar, which may or may not be supported by SQL Server. Use of other SQL Server types may require custom application logic.

SQL Server type	Approximate maximum character length
binary	8000
varbinary	8000
image	2147483647

Frequently used W3C XML Schema types	SQL Server
hexBinary	The "hexBinary" type is not directly supported. It may be possible to format, convert, and derive duration values using a string type such as "char." However, such techniques may require custom application logic.
float	The "float" type is supported to some degree by SQL Server float and real types. However, the format, minimum, and maximum values (both mantissa and exponent) may vary from the allowable values of the W3C XML Schema "float" type.

Table 4.6 *Continued*

Frequently used W3C XML Schema types	SQL Server
decimal	The "decimal" type is directly supported by the SQL Server decimal and numeric types. However, the minimum and maximum values (both total digits and fractional digits) may vary from the allowable values of the XML Schema "decimal" type.
integer long	The "integer" and "long" types are indirectly supported by the decimal, numeric, bigint, and int types for some applications. It is important to note that the W3C XML Schema "integer" type does not specify a minimum or maximum value (i.e., infinite). The SQL Server types have specific minimum and maximum limits.

SQL Server type	Approximate value thresholds
numeric (min)	-10^{38}
numeric (max)	$+10^{38}(-1)$
decimal (min)	-10^{38}
decimal (min)	$+10^{38}(-1)$
bigint (min)	$-9,223,372,036,854,775,808$
bigint (max)	$+9,223,372,036,854,775,807$
int (min)	-2147483648
int (max)	$+2147483647$

int	The "int" type is directly supported.
short	The "short" type is directly supported as the SQL Server smallint type.
byte	The "byte" type is indirectly supported by the SQL Server smallint and possibly by the tinyint types. However, the smallint type has a minimum and maximum value limit that is greater than the W3C XML Schema byte type. The W3C XML Schema byte type has a minimum value of "−128" and a maximum value of "+127." Also, the SQL Server tinyint type is limited to non-negative integer numbers (with values from 0 to 255).

SQL Server type	Approximate value thresholds
smallint (min)	-32768
smallint (max)	$+32767$
tinyint (min)	0
tinyint (max)	255

Continued

Table 4.6   *Continued*

Frequently used W3C XML Schema types	SQL Server
double	The "double" type is supported to some degree by SQL Server float and real types. However, the format, minimum, and maximum values (both mantissa and exponent) may vary from the allowable values of the W3C XML Schema "double" type.
anyURI	The "anyURI" type is not directly supported. However, depending upon the type, application, and encoding of the data values, it may be possible to use other SQL Server character types. Use of other SQL Server types may require custom application logic.

SQL Server type	Approximate maximum character length
char	8000
varchar	8000
text	2147483647
nchar (Unicode support)	4000
nvarchar (Unicode support)	4000
ntext (Unicode support)	1073741823

5

W3C XML Schema Data Type Facets

Data type *facets* are additional metadata constraints that may be applied to a W3C XML Schema data type. From a metadata perspective, facets are metadata rules or limitations for a data type. Data architects will quickly recognize that facets provide extended data type support. The most familiar are those that support lengths and fractional decimal digits. Similar constraints are often defined for the attributes of logical data model entities, for the elements of physical model objects, and for the columns of relational database tables. In addition, most procedural and object-oriented programming languages provide support for constraints that are similar to facets.

Commonly applied facets include the following:

- Length (as the number of character positions)
- Value limits (minimum and maximum values as a range or threshold)
- Decimal digits (both total and fractional)
- Enumeration (a list of allowable values)
- Patterns (edit patterns including literals and allowable digits)
- White space (applied to string or character data)

Length is perhaps the constraint used most often to define the maximum possible length for a data element. Character or string types supported by a database are often defined with a maximum possible number of character positions. Similarly, if the data type is decimal, there may be a defined limit for the total number of digits (often referred to as the "precision") and the number of fractional decimal digits (often referred to as decimal "scale"). W3C XML Schemas provide support for length (in several forms), including total digit, and fractional digit facets.

A string data value can be constrained by several different length facets. W3C XML Schemas support a fixed length facet, a minimum length facet, and a maximum length facet. Other supported string facets include enumeration (e.g., a list of allowable data values) and facets to control whether carriage returns, line feeds, or tabs will be retained after validation.

Decimal data types can also be constrained by length, by fractional decimal digits, and by allowable values. Interestingly, a numeric data type such as "integer" can have its length constrained by the same syntactical length facets as those applied to string data. Decimal data types can also have their length constrained by the "totalDigits" facet.

An even more powerful type of facet is a pattern. A pattern can specify the allowable characters within a string, as well as expected literals. Consider a Social Security Number (SSN) as used in the United States. A common presentation format for a SSN is "999-99-9999." This format specifies that three numeric characters are followed by two numeric characters, which are followed by four terminating numeric characters. Additionally, an embedded dash (as a literal "-" character) is used to separate the three segments. With W3C XML Schemas, a pattern can be defined to check for and enforce formats similar to the SSN example.

Fact:

Facets further limit, constrain, or describe a data type. In some cases and depending upon the data type, facets may be combined.

W3C XML Schemas provide extensive support for facets. Depending upon the data type to which they are applied and the context in which they are used, facets can also be combined. As an example, an XML element defined by a decimal data type might be further constrained by several facets including the total number of digits, the number of fractional decimal digits, and a range of allowable values.

Character Length

Most relational database products support several data types for character or string data. One such data type is known as "character" or "char" and another is known as "variable character" or "varchar." As implied by the name, a character data type is intended to describe or contain character (e.g., string) data. A variable character data type is also of variable length (i.e., the number of character positions can vary depending upon the characteristics of the data). Length is perhaps the facet used most often for character data types.

Although described as "variable," most variable character data types have a maximum possible number of characters for the type. The content of a variable character database column can be a data value of up to "n" number of character positions. Conceptually, content of less than the maximum possible character positions will consume less space in the database table. Physical implementations can vary and the actual amount of required disk storage can also include additional data used by the database for internal pointers and similar constraints. Similar to a variable character data type, a "character" database column can also store a data value of up to the specified maximum number of character positions. Character data types are generally of a fixed length (taking up a fixed amount of disk space regardless of the length of the contained data).

Technique:

Character length facets can be used to help resolve differences between metadata characteristics of disparate data sources and targets by constraining the number of character positions to the lowest common denominator.

W3C XML Schemas support a length facet that is somewhat similar to the length constraint supported by most database products. However, W3C XML Schemas go well beyond describing a maximum or fixed length. Supported facets include length, minLength, and maxLength (Fig. 5.1). The *length* facet specifies a fixed number of characters for a contained data value. When applied to an XML element or attribute, the contained data values must always be of the specified length (neither less than or greater than). If a *minLength* facet has been applied, the contained data value must be of at least the specified length but may also be greater. Alternatively, a *maxLength* facet constrains a data value that must not exceed the specified number of character positions.

As noted previously, some facets may be combined for the same data type as applied to an element or attribute. Both the minLength and maxLength facets could be applied to the same XML element, resulting in a range of allowable character positions (e.g., a minimum length of 8 positions and a maximum length of 20 positions). Combining length facets can be a powerful technique for resolving disparate data sources and targets, when that disparity is length related and the limitations of the source and target are not in direct conflict. However, the reader is

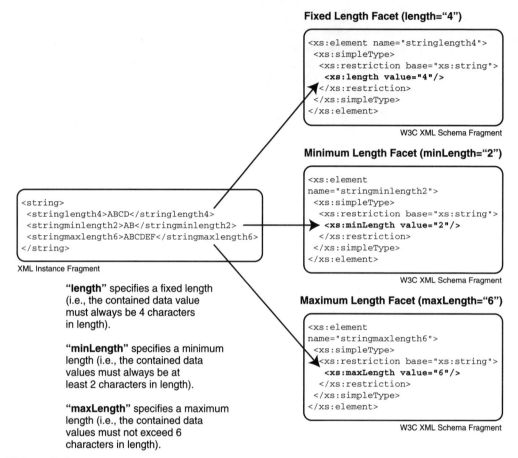

Fixed Length Facet (length="4")

```
<xs:element name="stringlength4">
 <xs:simpleType>
  <xs:restriction base="xs:string">
   <xs:length value="4"/>
  </xs:restriction>
 </xs:simpleType>
</xs:element>
```
W3C XML Schema Fragment

Minimum Length Facet (minLength="2")

```
<xs:element
name="stringminlength2">
 <xs:simpleType>
  <xs:restriction base="xs:string">
   <xs:minLength value="2"/>
  </xs:restriction>
 </xs:simpleType>
</xs:element>
```
W3C XML Schema Fragment

Maximum Length Facet (maxLength="6")

```
<xs:element
name="stringmaxlength6">
 <xs:simpleType>
  <xs:restriction base="xs:string">
   <xs:maxLength value="6"/>
  </xs:restriction>
 </xs:simpleType>
</xs:element>
```
W3C XML Schema Fragment

```
<string>
 <stringlength4>ABCD</stringlength4>
 <stringminlength2>AB</stringminlength2>
 <stringmaxlength6>ABCDEF</stringmaxlength6>
</string>
```
XML Instance Fragment

"length" specifies a fixed length (i.e., the contained data value must always be 4 characters in length).

"minLength" specifies a minimum length (i.e., the contained data values must always be at least 2 characters in length).

"maxLength" specifies a maximum length (i.e., the contained data values must not exceed 6 characters in length).

Figure 5.1

Character length facets.

cautioned that length constraints will not resolve all forms of data disparity and may in fact introduce other complications (e.g., truncation of data values). The data architect still needs to identify the type of disparity and determine how length facets might be applied.

Modality is a term that describes the concept of optional or mandatory. An XML element can be defined as mandatory with a *minOccurs* value of "1," and an XML attribute is defined as mandatory with a *use* value of "required." Alternatively, an element defined with a *minOccurs* value of "0" and an attribute defined with a *use* value of

Technique:

The minLength facet can be used to check for a mandatory data value being present for an XML element or attribute. If a minLength value of "1" is defined, a validating parser will check to ensure that the data value contained in the XML document is of at least one character position. If no data value is specified (i.e., similar to a "null"), a validation error will be raised.

"optional" are optional. However, this declaration of modality (e.g., optional or mandatory) is specific to whether the referenced XML element or attribute container is present within the referencing XML document but does not declare whether that container holds a data value or remains empty. Although an XML element may have been defined as being mandatory (i.e., *minOccurs* value of "1"), it can be present in the XML document without containing any data.

Specifying a *minLength* facet with a value of "1" in the W3C XML Schema can provide a method of checking for a mandatory data value. Be aware that although present, the data value might be invalid. As an example, a single blank space might be included as the data value of the element, which would pass a *minLength* validation check. However, a data value of a blank space might not be valid for that element.

Value Limits (Minimum and Maximum Thresholds)

Value limits are similar to a range of minimum and maximum allowable data values. When minimum and maximum value facets have been applied during the parser validation process, the data value of the container must be between the specified minimum and maximum. When a data value falls outside the specified range, an error will be raised.

Technique:

In some cases, value limit facets (minInclusive, maxInclusive, minExclusive, and maxExclusive) can be used to help resolve differences between metadata characteristics of disparate data sources and targets by limiting the range of allowable values to an agreed upon range between systems.

W3C XML Schemas support for value limits goes beyond a simple range (Fig. 5.2). The data architect or schema designer could specify an inclusive group (i.e., a group in which the range of data values must be between or include the specified minimum and maximum) or an exclusive group of data values (i.e., a group in which the range of data values must be between but not include the specified minimum and maximum). Value thresholds that are of an inclusive group are specified using *minInclusive* and *maxInclusive* values. Value thresholds that are of an exclusive group are specified using *minExclusive* and *maxExclusive* values. The data architect could also specify a minimum without a maximum and a maximum without a

**Minimum and Maximum Inclusive Facets
(minInclusive="10", maxInclusive="100")**

```
<xs:element name="Min-MaxInclusive">
 <xs:simpleType>
  <xs:restriction base="xs:integer">
   <xs:minInclusive value="10"/>
   <xs:maxInclusive value="100"/>
  </xs:restriction>
 </xs:simpleType>
</xs:element>
```
W3C XML Schema Fragment

```
<ValueLimits>
 <Min-MaxInclusive>10</Min-MaxInclusive>
 <Min-MaxExclusive>11</Min-MaxExclusive>
</ValueLimits>
```
XML Instance Fragment

**Minimum and Maximum Exclusive Facets
(minExclusive="10", maxExclusive="100")**

```
<xs:element name="Min-MaxExclusive">
 <xs:simpleType>
  <xs:restriction base="xs:integer">
   <xs:minExclusive value="10"/>
   <xs:maxExclusive value="100"/>
  </xs:restriction>
 </xs:simpleType>
</xs:element>
</xs:element>
```
W3C XML Schema Fragment

"minInclusive" specifies a minimum allowable data value.

"maxInclusive" specifies a maximum allowable data value.

"minExclusive" specifies a minimum value that must be exceeded by the contained data value.

"maxExclusive" specifies a maximum value that must not be exceeded by the contained data value.

Figure 5.2

Value limit (threshold) facets.

minimum. Depending upon the data type to which the facets were defined, this allows for an infinite value.

Digits (Number of and Type)

As defined to numeric data types (e.g., decimal and derived data types of integer, long, int, short, and byte), digit facets are roughly analogous to the length facets of a string data type. Although the syntax is different, similar constraints are also common among most relational database products. W3C XML Schemas support facets for constraining the number of total numeric digits and fractional digits (Fig. 5.3).

Figure 5.3

Digits facets.

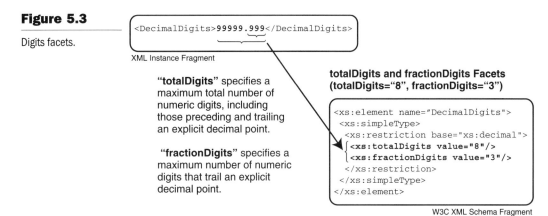

XML Instance Fragment

"totalDigits" specifies a maximum total number of numeric digits, including those preceding and trailing an explicit decimal point.

"fractionDigits" specifies a maximum number of numeric digits that trail an explicit decimal point.

totalDigits and fractionDigits Facets (totalDigits="8", fractionDigits="3")

```
<xs:element name="DecimalDigits">
 <xs:simpleType>
  <xs:restriction base="xs:decimal">
   <xs:totalDigits value="8"/>
   <xs:fractionDigits value="3"/>
  </xs:restriction>
 </xs:simpleType>
</xs:element>
```

W3C XML Schema Fragment

When applied to string or character data, length facets constrain or limit the number of data value character positions. Similarly, digit facets constrain the total number of digits (precision) and also the fractional decimal digits of a numeric data type (scale or decimal scale). The *totalDigits* facet describes the total number of digits for a numeric data type (including both whole numbers and fractional digits). The *fractionDigits* facet specifies the number of fractional decimal digits that trail an explicit decimal point (i.e., to the right of the decimal point). The decimal point and an optional sign are not included in the number of digits specified by either totalDigits or fractionDigits facets.

Technique:

Digit facets can be used to help resolve differences between metadata characteristics of disparate data sources and targets by limiting the number of digits and character positions to the lowest common denominator.

One frequently observed form of disparity between autonomous enterprise systems is the metadata definition of monetary amounts. Differences in the maximum number of digits and the number of fractional decimal digits are often found between financial reporting, pricing, order processing, inventory, and invoicing systems. As an example, product unit cost might be defined to the purchasing system as a decimal data type with seven total digits and two fractional digits (e.g., a COBOL "picture" of "S99999v99"). However, the product unit cost might be defined to the inventory management system as a decimal data type with seven total digits and three fractional digits (e.g., a COBOL "picture of: "S9999v999"). Exchanging data values between these two systems could result in truncation, rounding, and potential error.

Most validating parsers will interpret the W3C XML Schema digits facets as a "maximum" number of allowed numeric digits. Using the previous example of disparate product unit cost amount definitions, it is possible to define a data type that would contain data values from either system without causing an error. A new custom data type could be defined as a decimal data type, allowing for the greatest number of whole number digits and fractional digits. Combining the total number of digits would define the value required for the totalDigits facet. The resulting data type could then be used to describe the content of a product unit code amount exchanged between differing enterprise applications. However, this technique is not "free" and not without potential for error. Data values that exceed the constraints of the target or receiving system would need to be resolved by truncation, rounding, or the application of business logic.

Of even greater advantage is the ability to define several standard monetary amount data types using the totalDigits and fractionDigits facets. With this technique, the data architect would rationalize the many financial and monetary data elements of enterprise and determine what specific metadata characteristics were common. A custom data type (using a "simpleType") could be defined with totalDigits and fractionDigits specified for each. The resulting custom data types would represent enterprise metadata standards for describing monetary amounts. As new XML documents, transactions, and messages are designed, monetary amount type could be applied accordingly.

Another justification for use of totalDigits and fractionDigits facets is global e-commerce. In North America, most monetary amounts are defined to include two fractional decimal positions. When varied currencies of the world are considered, this technique is often ineffective. Some currencies are defined without any fractional decimal positions, whereas others require two or three. As examples, the Bahraini dinar, Iraqi dinar, Jordanian dinar, and Kuwaiti dinar may require three digits of decimal scale. The Andorran peseta, Belarus ruble, Comoros franc, Guinea franc, Italian lira, and others require zero digits of decimal scale.[1] To support their respective divisional units, custom data types could be developed with varying fractionDigits facets. The obvious advantage of W3C XML Schemas is their ability to define or extend data types with fractional decimal digits facets to address these global currency needs.

---

[1] Currency Data Concept, Web Globalization Guide Framework. James Bean © 1996–2002. Available at http://www.globalwebarch.com/.

Enumeration (Allowable and Valid Values)

Technique:

Enumeration facets (a list of allowable values) can be used to help enforce standards and in some cases to resolve differences between metadata characteristics of disparate data sources and targets by limiting the allowable values to an agreed upon set for both systems.

Some data elements are constrained by business rules such as a rule that all data values must be from a defined set. From a data architecture perspective, this concept is also known as a "domain of valid values" or data elements that represent standard "code sets." A few of the more common industry and international code set standards include U.S. state abbreviations, ISO 639 Language Codes, ISO 3166 Country Codes, and ISO 4217 Currency Codes. Each of these standards include rigorously defined "codes" that represent allowable data values for a U.S. state, a language, a country, and a currency. Traditional database applications compare code values to standard reference tables or in some cases may incorporate lists of standards code values that are internal to program logic (e.g., "88" levels of a COBOL program).

Enumeration facets describe a list or set of allowable data values for an XML element or attribute. The enumeration capabilities of W3C XML Schemas go well beyond reference tables (Fig. 5.4). As a side note, a limitation of DTD types of schemas is that only attribute containers may be constrained to use enumerated values, whereas a W3C XML Schema can support enumerated values for elements and attributes. In a scenario in which enterprise integration transactions cross many autonomous systems, an application program

Figure 5.4

Enumeration (allowable and valid values) facets.

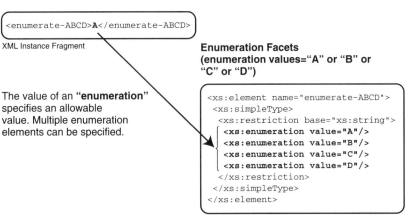

```
<enumerate-ABCD>A</enumerate-ABCD>
```
XML Instance Fragment

The value of an **"enumeration"** specifies an allowable value. Multiple enumeration elements can be specified.

**Enumeration Facets
(enumeration values="A" or "B" or "C" or "D")**

```
<xs:element name="enumerate-ABCD">
 <xs:simpleType>
  <xs:restriction base="xs:string">
   <xs:enumeration value="A"/>
   <xs:enumeration value="B"/>
   <xs:enumeration value="C"/>
   <xs:enumeration value="D"/>
  </xs:restriction>
 </xs:simpleType>
</xs:element>
```
W3C XML Schema Fragment

functioning in one system may not have access to a database reference table of allowable values maintained in another system. As transactions are exchanged, this prohibits the source system from ensuring that the data values sent in a transaction are recognized as allowable values in a target or receiving system. This scenario can be further extended to consider B2B e-commerce applications, in which a transaction moves between systems that are external to the enterprise. In this case, data may originate and be exchanged with many collaborators and trading partners. The ability to access a single common repository of valid values is not efficient or practical. Similarly, attempting to synchronize reference tables among the many sources and targets of an exchange is also not realistic.

Like the transaction itself, a source system could also include the W3C XML Schema (or a component subschema). The source would define standard code values using enumeration facets and include them in the W3C XML Schema. With this technique, the target or receiving system is ensured that any data values it encounters (or that it creates for response transactions) will conform to the list of allowable values provided in the schema.

Technique:

Enumeration facets (a list of allowable values) can be used to describe data standards such as code sets (e.g., country code, currency code, and U.S. state code). However, caution is advised when enumeration lists are defined internally to multiple schemas rather than as external, referenced subset schemas.

An area of controversy in the use of enumeration lists is the frequency of change. Interestingly, the standard code values for countries and currencies are at times subject to modification. Although they do not occur daily or even monthly, such changes are readily evident. When allowable values are defined to static lists, there is an implied need for timely modifications. If the lists are directly embedded within several W3C XML Schemas (e.g., as replicated copies), each of those schemas would need to be tracked and then maintained. In addition to the ongoing maintenance costs, such techniques are also prone to error. The use of enumeration lists that are intrinsically defined (e.g., repeatedly "hard coded") within multiple schemas is not recommended. A more effective approach is to leverage the component subschema capabilities of W3C XML Schemas, in which enumeration lists of allowable values are defined to a single external component subschema and then are reused by referencing from other schemas as necessary (we will discuss this topic further in Chapter 8 [W3C XML Schemas and Reuse]).

Although enumeration lists are a powerful capability, caution is advised. A degree of reasonableness should be applied during the design

Technique:

Although powerful, enumeration lists are not always the best architectural technique for validating allowable values when the list is of excessive length (as a rule of thumb greater than 200 entries) or when it is subject to frequent modification (as a rule of thumb when modifications are required more often than once or twice a month).

Technique:

Pattern facets can be used to constrain the characters and character position within a data value (similar to presentation format). However, similar to enumeration lists, patterns should be externalized as referenced subset schemas to avoid a proliferation of ongoing schema maintenance activities.

and engineering of each W3C XML Schema. The previous technique implied that W3C XML Schemas would in many cases be included with an XML formatted transaction to ensure that the source and target "agreed" on validation rules and in particular on enumeration lists of allowable values. Although generally effective, this technique can be impractical in some scenarios. If the enumeration list is of excessive length or is subject to frequent modification, performance can suffer and maintenance can become costly. In this case, the use of other architectural techniques may be warranted.

Patterns

Patterns facets constrain the expression or form of a data value (not to be confused with architecture or object patterns). Patterns can be defined to describe the allowable characters within a data value, the position at which those characters may be placed, the number of similar characters within a logical group, and embedded literals. As described earlier, a common example in the United States is a Social Security number (Fig. 5.5). Other potential uses for W3C XML Schema-based pattern facets are descriptions of postal code formats, telephone numbers, or any other data value for which a format must be constrained.

The data architect's traditional view of patterns is that they represent data with embedded intelligence or possibly denormalized data. If the pattern-constrained data were directly persisted in a database, this perspective would be accurate. Storage of data with presentation or expressive characteristics (e.g., embedded literal characters) is generally not recommended. However, given the context of global e-commerce or enterprise integration transactions, the ability to prescribe and validate expressive patterns of data can be invaluable. As one example of a global e-commerce scenario, it may be necessary to support varying postal code formats. Postal codes required for international postal addresses can exhibit several forms of intelligence, sequence, and patterns. A W3C XML Schema could include a pattern for each country in which variations in postal code were evident.

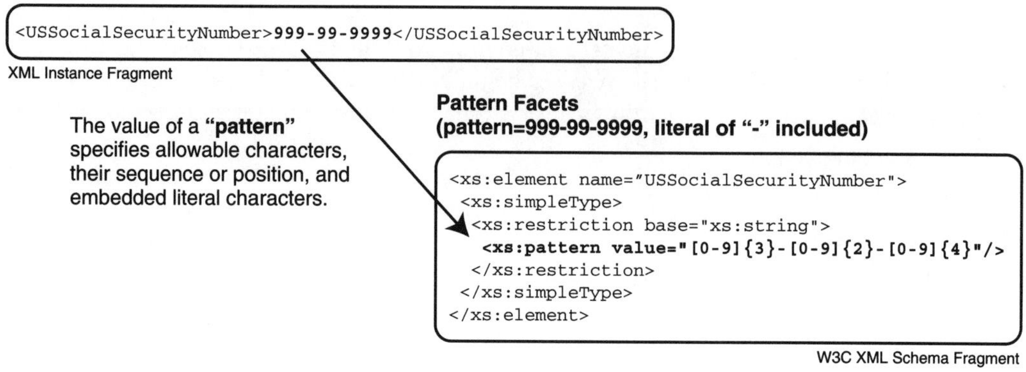

```
<USSocialSecurityNumber>999-99-9999</USSocialSecurityNumber>
```

XML Instance Fragment

The value of a **"pattern"**
specifies allowable characters,
their sequence or position, and
embedded literal characters.

Pattern Facets
(pattern=999-99-9999, literal of "-" included)

```
<xs:element name="USSocialSecurityNumber">
 <xs:simpleType>
 <xs:restriction base="xs:string">
  <xs:pattern value="[0-9]{3}-[0-9]{2}-[0-9]{4}"/>
 </xs:restriction>
 </xs:simpleType>
</xs:element>
```

W3C XML Schema Fragment

Figure 5.5

Pattern facets.

White Space

Recommendation:

Unless the content of the XML document is primarily "document-oriented," use of white space facets should be avoided. Depending upon the parser and validation process, white space facets may result in extracted data at the target of the exchange that no longer matches the originating source XML content.

The term *white space* can be confusing. A schema definition is that white space is simply a space (i.e., a "blank"), carriage return, line feed, or tab character within a string. The use of string- or character-based content that is from primarily document-oriented transactions may introduce the need to restrict or constrain the use of white space characters. As one example, the data content of an element might be a paragraph of text that includes embedded tabs for positioning and alignment of data. However, a receiving system may not be able to recognize or correctly process tab characters. W3C XML Schemas support a white space facet that describes three different options (Fig. 5.6).

When the white space facet has been defined, the "preserve" value will note that all white space characters (i.e., carriage returns, line feeds, and tabs) should be preserved or remain in their encoded form. The "replace" value instructs the parser to replace white space characters (i.e., carriage returns, line feeds, and tabs) with a space character. Lastly, the "collapse" value indicates that all white space characters (i.e., carriage returns, line feeds, tabs, and leading and trailing spaces) should be collapsed or removed. In all cases, it is important to note that specific parser support and application usage may vary.

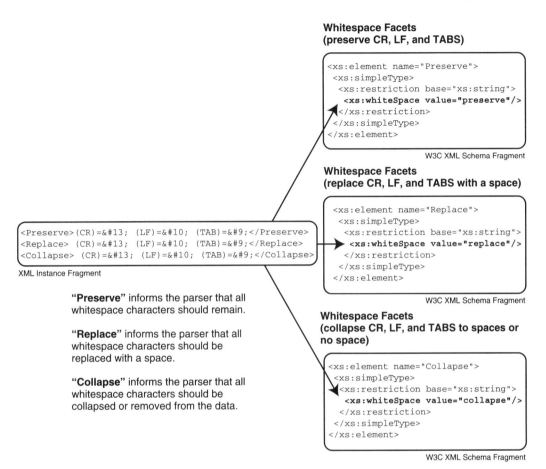

Figure 5.6

White space facets.

The responsibility for data types and their constraining facets should be fundamental to the role of the data architect. The data architect is also responsible for defining data elements, assembling them into groups, and specifying relationships between groups. In many respects these activities are part of the data modeling process. Although XML is not a data model, as we will see in the next chapter there are a number of similar activities that can be applied to XML.

6

Structure Models

A data model is a collection of defined and related information facts and metadata. The data model describes metadata structures, containers, and their characteristics but does not include actual data values. Most data models are aligned with either relational or object relational database architectures in which an entity or table may have relationships with other entities. Different from the most common data models, the structure of an XML document is hierarchical, and relationships are often defined by element location or position. An XML element nested within another element implies a relationship of "parent to child" (e.g., child, parent, grandparent, great grandparent, and so on). The differences between these representational structures are important but do not prohibit transition.

Data models are often represented graphically as an entity relationship diagram (ERD), in which entities are portrayed as boxes, attributes are listed within each entity, and relationships are described by lines between entities. An XML document is a data instance (e.g., a collection of data containers and their contained data values), represented as a hierarchy. Although more of a syntactical or literal form rather than graphically represented, an XML document in prototype form can represent a model of a target implementation.

As a hierarchy, the structure of an XML document or transaction flows top-down and left-to-right. The traditional hierarchy is composed of a *parent*, which may have *children*. Multiple children occurring at the same level within a parent are also known as *siblings*. Children may also contain other children, therefore making them parents as well as children (Fig. 6.1).

The hierarchical structure of an XML document is obvious. However, there are a few basic concepts and rules that need to be understood. First, an XML document is an instance. That is, an XML document is usually created, valued, processed, and maintained by an application program. An XML document contains data values. Alternatively, a W3C XML Schema is a set of rules and constraints that describe an XML document. These concepts are roughly analogous to a relational database. The database tables and columns contain data values. Most often, the data values are processed and maintained by application programs. The "system catalog" of a relational database describes the structure (tables, columns, and relationships), and rules of the database.

Beyond the basic differences between an XML document or "instance" of data and a W3C XML Schema or set of rules and constraints, there are also several structural and syntactic rules. As we have learned previously, the top-most element container of an XML document is known as the root element (of which there is always only one per XML document or transaction). Within the root element, there may be many occurrences of other elements and groups of elements. The containing of elements by other elements presents the concept of nesting. Each layer of nesting results in another hierarchical level (similar to parent–child). Elements may also include attributes. Some elements may also be defined intentionally to remain empty where they may contain nothing. Elements may also repeat, which is a rudimentary form of cardinality or multiplicity (Fig. 6.2).

Figure 6.1

Basic hierarchical structure.

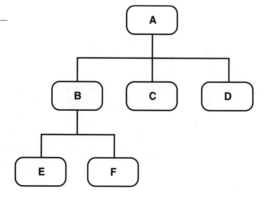

A is the "parent" of B, C, and D.

B, C, and D are "children" of A.

B, C, and D are "siblings."

B is the "parent" of E and F.

E and F are "children" of B.

E and F are "siblings."

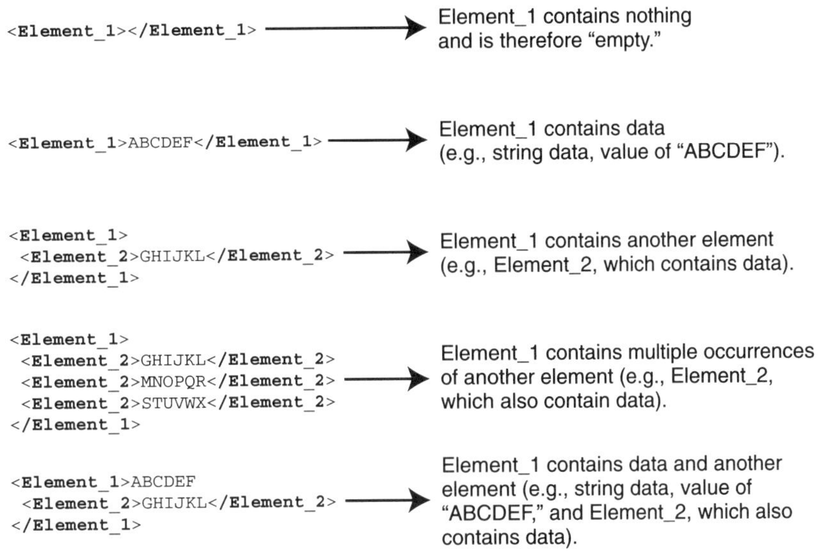

Figure 6.2

Element containers.

```
<Element_1></Element_1>
```
⟶ Element_1 contains nothing and is therefore "empty."

```
<Element_1>ABCDEF</Element_1>
```
⟶ Element_1 contains data (e.g., string data, value of "ABCDEF").

```
<Element_1>
  <Element_2>GHIJKL</Element_2>
</Element_1>
```
⟶ Element_1 contains another element (e.g., Element_2, which contains data).

```
<Element_1>
  <Element_2>GHIJKL</Element_2>
  <Element_2>MNOPQR</Element_2>
  <Element_2>STUVWX</Element_2>
</Element_1>
```
⟶ Element_1 contains multiple occurrences of another element (e.g., Element_2, which also contain data).

```
<Element_1>ABCDEF
  <Element_2>GHIJKL</Element_2>
</Element_1>
```
⟶ Element_1 contains data and another element (e.g., string data, value of "ABCDEF," and Element_2, which also contains data).

XML attributes are a somewhat different type of container. Attributes must be defined to an element (i.e., they may not exist on their own). Both elements and attributes may contain data values, or they may be defined to remain empty. The syntax of an XML attribute is like that of an HTML attribute. XML attributes are defined using a "attribute–value pair" scheme (Fig. 6.3). Also, an attribute may not contain other attributes, and attributes do not exhibit cardinality or multiplicity. When multiple attributes are defined to an element, they may not repeat using the same attribute name.

Similar to traditional metadata representations (e.g., data models and object class diagrams), XML documents and transactions can also represent models. As prototypes, XML documents populated with sample data can provide a simple visual method of modeling the structure of an XML document. When an XML document or transaction is represented as a prototype structure, the number and types of containers (e.g., elements and attributes) become indicative of the structure model. The prototype structure can then be used as a template by the data architect for engineering a corresponding schema and by the developer to begin engineering application code.

Some XML documents use only elements. Others use attributes primarily. Still others combine element and attribute containers. Although

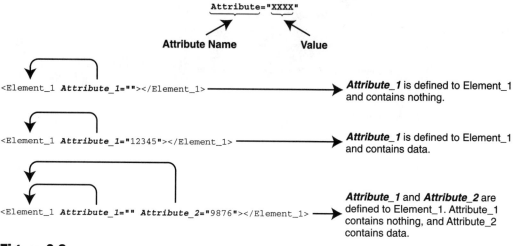

Figure 6.3

Attribute containers.

there may be several variations, the most common XML structure models include the following:

- Vertical
- Horizontal
- Component
- Hybrid

Vertical Models

Vertical models are generally the most common structure applied to XML transactions and messages, and they exhibit significant use of XML element containers. Element containers that are similar or related can be organized according to logical groupings. The term *vertical* describes the hierarchical structure evident in most all XML documents and transactions (i.e., top-down and left-to-right). When combined with nested groups of element containers, vertical models are generally the most intuitive (Fig. 6.4).

Figure 6.4

Vertical XML structure
model.

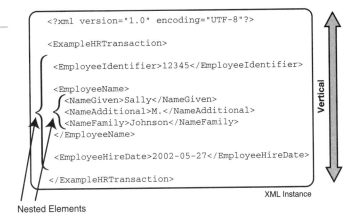

```
<?xml version="1.0" encoding="UTF-8"?>

<ExampleHRTransaction>

   <EmployeeIdentifier>12345</EmployeeIdentifier>

   <EmployeeName>
      <NameGiven>Sally</NameGiven>
      <NameAdditional>M.</NameAdditional>
      <NameFamily>Johnson</NameFamily>
   </EmployeeName>

   <EmployeeHireDate>2002-05-27</EmployeeHireDate>

</ExampleHRTransaction>
```

Vertical

XML Instance

Nested Elements

Another characteristic of vertical structure models is flexibility (e.g., the structure can be designed to dynamically expand or contract to fit the context of the contained data). The concept of flexibility is highly advantageous when the contained data exhibits variability as to the parent–child relationships between containers combined with cardinality. A common example of variable data is global e-commerce data. Consider that the street address lines and other components of an international postal address can vary significantly from country to country. In North America, a common postal address contains one or two street address lines, combined with a city, state or province, and a postal code. Alternatively, international postal addresses vary considerably and may require from one up to four street address lines, a city, multiple regional subdivisions (e.g., district, township, county, or region), a country, and a postal code. The ability of a vertical structure model to contain and describe international postal addresses can be of great advantage for global e-commerce transactions (Fig. 6.5).

When additional instances of an element container are required, they can be inserted into the appropriate parent element group. Considering the example of an international address, if the address structure dictates the need for fourth street address line, an additional "<StreetAddressLine>" element could be appended within the Street Address Lines group element. This type of structural modification can usually be implemented with minimal impact on constraining schemas and potentially

Fact:

Vertical structure models are primarily composed of element containers. When combined with repeating elements (e.g., element cardinality or multiplicity), vertical XML structure models are the most flexible. They can dynamically expand or contract to fit the characteristics of the contained data.

Figure 6.5

International postal
address structure using
a vertical structure
model.

```
<?xml version="1.0" encoding="UTF-8"?>
<ExampleAddress>
 <Address AddressType="Customer-Employment">
  <AddressTo>Dr. Sally M. Johnson</AddressTo>
  <StreetAddressLines>
   <StreetAddressLine>Hamilton Medical Center</StreetAddressLine>
   <StreetAddressLine>654321 N. Wildwind Circle</StreetAddressLine>
   <StreetAddressLine>Hamilton Square</StreetAddressLine>
  </StreetAddressLines>
  <City>London</City>
  <PostalCode>EC1Y 8SY</PostalCode>
  <Region></Region>
  <Country>England, United Kingdom</Country>
 </Address>
</ExampleAddress>
```

Vertical

XML Instance

"Repeating" Street Address Line
elements exhibit cardinality.
The structure can expand or contract
to fit varying address formats.

Recommendation:

Depending upon the number of
element containers, the
volumetrics of the contained
data, and the taxonomy used to
name the elements, vertical
structure models can be overly
verbose and of excessive size.
When application performance
is of significant concern or
bandwidth for transmitting the
XML document is limited, the
data architect may need to
consider compression, evaluate
alternative structure models, or
take a different architectural
approach.

on application logic. From a traditional data modeling
perspective, flexibility is often exhibited by a one-to-many
relationship between entities, in which instances of the
dependent entity may repeat (Fig. 6.6).

One potential disadvantage of vertical structure
models is indirectly related to the use of element containers. Given that all element containers must be represented with both a begin and an end tag (or with the
abbreviated tag syntax if the element does not contain any
data), a vertical structure model tends to be more verbose
than other models. The additional characters of each
element tag can add to the overall size of the XML transaction. If the total size of the transaction is excessive or
bandwidth for the transaction exchange is limited, the data
architect may need to recommend some form of transaction compression, evaluate other structure models, or take
a different architectural approach.

Horizontal Models

Horizontal structure models are somewhat less common
than vertical models. Horizontal models primarily use attributes rather

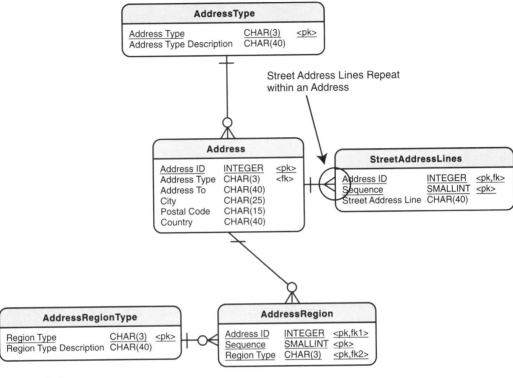

Figure 6.6

Traditional data model with repeating cardinality.

than elements to contain data. Given that horizontal structure models utilize a significant number of attribute containers, the lack of end tags allows them to be less verbose. The resulting structure of the document is horizontal or "flat" (Fig. 6.7). The greatest advantages of a horizontal structure models are that the resulting XML documents are smaller in overall size than vertical models and they closely represent simple relational database extracts.

Horizontal structure models are most often applied when the total XML document or transaction size is excessive or when bandwidth for exchanging the transaction is significantly limited. One potential use of XML transactions that are structured as horizontal models is for the transfer of data from operational systems to a data ware-

Fact:

Horizontal structure models utilize a significant number of attributes. As such, they tend to be "flat" rather than vertical.

Figure 6.7

Horizontal XML
structure model.

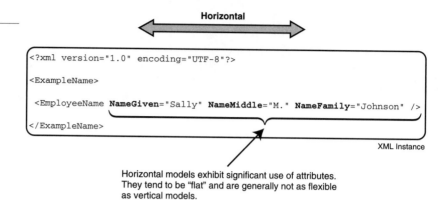

Horizontal models exhibit significant use of attributes.
They tend to be "flat" and are generally not as flexible
as vertical models.

house or similar decision support architecture. In this application, the volumes of data tend to be significant and reduction of file size would be of advantage.

Recommendation:

Horizontal structure models may provide a potential advantage when the total size of the XML document or transaction is excessively large or when bandwidth for transmitting the XML document is limited.

Few differences are seen when a vertical or horizontal XML structure is compared with a traditional data model. The most obvious is that repeating elements of the same name exhibited as cardinality or multiplicity in a data model are not supported by horizontal models. If the data model included entities and attributes to represent the parts of an individual's name, one modeling technique would be to model the individual name particles as a name entity with a one-to-many relationship to another dependent entity of repeating name part instances.

In the scenario in which a data architect must engineer a horizontal XML structure to contain data extracted from a relational model with repeating rows or instances of like-named data, each instance would need to be contained by a uniquely named attribute container. A translation of repeating elements classified by each possible type or context to uniquely named attribute containers of the same intended content would need to take place (Fig. 6.8).

A disadvantage of horizontal XML structure models is their lack of flexibility. Given that attributes may not repeat by name within the context of the element container to which they are defined, attributes must be defined as a set of known and uniquely described containers. Additional instances of like-named attributes cannot be dynamically inserted within the XML document. If additional data are required,

```
<?xml version="1.0" encoding="UTF-8"?>

<ExampleName>

 <EmployeeName NameGiven="Sally" NameAdditional="M." NameFamily="Johnson" />

</ExampleName>
```

XML Instance

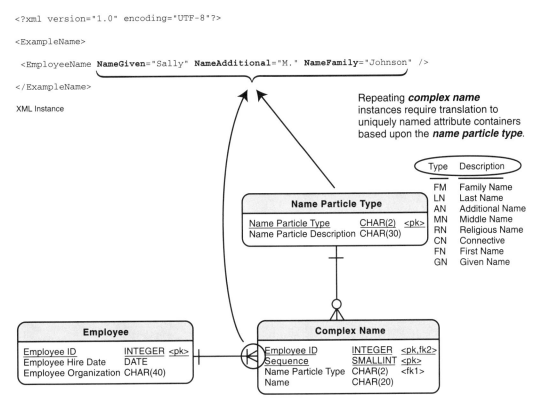

Repeating *complex name* instances require translation to uniquely named attribute containers based upon the *name particle type*.

Type	Description
FM	Family Name
LN	Last Name
AN	Additional Name
MN	Middle Name
RN	Religious Name
CN	Connective
FN	First Name
GN	Given Name

Name Particle Type

Name Particle Type	CHAR(2)	<pk>
Name Particle Description	CHAR(30)	

Employee

Employee ID	INTEGER	<pk>
Employee Hire Date	DATE	
Employee Organization	CHAR(40)	

Complex Name

Employee ID	INTEGER	<pk,fk2>
Sequence	SMALLINT	<pk>
Name Particle Type	CHAR(2)	<fk1>
Name	CHAR(20)	

Figure 6.8

Translation of data model entity with repeating cardinality to a horizontal XML structure model.

one or more new uniquely named attributes would need to be defined to the XML document as well as to any referenced schemas. There is the potential that new attributes might also result in the need for residual application changes.

Component Models

One of the greatest challenges presented to a data architect is reusing a data model or metadata structure. In many cases, a data model is composed of numerous entities, and reuse implies adding a relationship to or from another new entity. In the case of broad-scale reuse, this technique requires relationships to entities in other models (Fig. 6.9). The result is that the structure represented by that entity can be reused but primarily from the perspective of implementation and forward engineering (e.g., generation of syntax such as DDL for a database implementation).

The ability to reuse a data concept or entity in other data models and other data structures is often limited by the data modeling or design

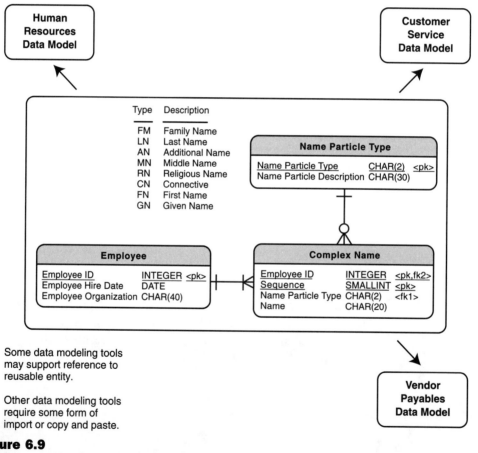

Figure 6.9

Reuse of data model entity by other models and contexts.

tool. Some data modeling tools support reference to or import of entity structures from other models. However, many other data modeling tools do not support this capability, and the process of reuse might be as cumbersome as copying and pasting of the entity. The use of copy and paste processes is minimally effective at best and results in a proliferation of duplicate entities, rather than an enterprise standard metadata definition and structure that are defined once, maintained in one location, and reused by reference.

As an alternative to copy and paste processes, W3C XML Schemas provide extensive reuse capability in the form of component structure models. Component structure models exploit the concept of reuse. The intent of a component structure model is that an XML document is composed of modular groups or collections of related data containers (Fig. 6.10). At an abstract level, each of the modular groups of data

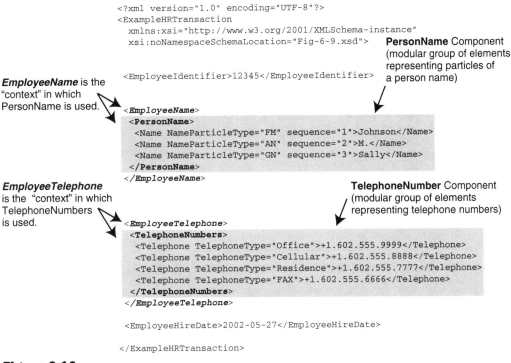

Figure 6.10

Modular groups of related data containers.

containers is then defined by a separate schema. Depending upon the level of abstraction applied to the XML element and attribute names, it may be possible to reuse the schema definitions for each modular group of containers in many other contexts. As an example, a schema describing a modular group of elements for a "person name" might be applied in contexts of employee name, customer name, or vendor contact name. The advantages are design and engineering savings (as new schema development cost avoidance) for each reuse of the standard structure.

When reusable component schemas are used, the W3C XML Schema that describes the overall XML document references each of the modular subschemas. The parser validation process resolves the references to the modular schemas and includes the referenced containers, types, etc. The overall or *master* W3C XML Schema is therefore assembled from the modular subschemas. The advantage of this XML structure model is the ability to define highly standardized and modular XML structures that can be reused in different contexts by other XML schemas.

Although similar methods of referencing externally defined structures are supported by most schema types, W3C XML Schemas provide several options. The XML schema syntax for "include" is perhaps the most simple, because it includes referenced containers and structures (Fig. 6.11). The use of the XML schema include syntax is fundamental to reuse and will be described further in Chapter 8 (W3C Schemas and Reuse).

Fact:

Component structure models provide the greatest advantage in the area of reuse. Highly standardized and modular groups of containers can be defined to externally referenced subschemas that are then reused by other schemas.

Recommendation:

As a general recommendation, the most effective uses of XML attributes are as containers for ordinal sequences of repeating elements and as a method of descriptive classification for an element, standard code values, function or activity, and decomposed parts of element contained data.

Hybrid Models

Hybrid models are the preferred method for modeling the structure of most transaction-oriented data. As implied by their name, hybrid models combine the most advantageous characteristics of the three other structure models (i.e., vertical, horizontal, and component). Vertical models imply an emphasis on element containers and a flexible

```
<?xml version="1.0" encoding="UTF-8"?>
<xs:schema xmlns:xs="http://www.w3.org/2001/XMLSchema">

<xs:include schemaLocation="STD-Name.xsd"/>
<xs:include schemaLocation="STD-Telephone.xsd"/>

 <xs:element name="ExampleHRTransaction">
  <xs:complexType>
   <xs:sequence>
    <xs:element ref="EmployeeIdentifier"/>
    <xs:element ref="EmployeeName"/>
    <xs:element ref="EmployeeTelephone"/>
    <xs:element ref="EmployeeHireDate"/>
   </xs:sequence>
  </xs:complexType>
 </xs:element>

 <xs:element name="EmployeeIdentifier" type="xs:int"/>

 <xs:element name="EmployeeName">
  <xs:complexType>
   <xs:sequence>
    <xs:element ref="PersonName"/>
   </xs:sequence>
  </xs:complexType>
 </xs:element>

 <xs:element name="EmployeeTelephone">
  <xs:complexType>
   <xs:sequence>
    <xs:element ref="TelephoneNumbers"/>
   </xs:sequence>
  </xs:complexType>
 </xs:element>

 <xs:element name="EmployeeHireDate" type="xs:date"/>

</xs:schema>
```

STD-Name.xsd

STD-Name is defined as an external reusable subschema.

STD-Telephone.xsd

STD-Telephone is defined as an external reusable subschema.

PersonName is a "referenced" element structure defined to the **STD-Name** subschema.

TelephoneNumbers is a "referenced" element structure defined to the **STD-Telephone** subschema.

W3C XML Schema

Figure 6.11

Component XML structure model applied to a W3C XML schema.

architecture. Horizontal models utilize attributes to describe the characteristics of the contained data in a less verbose manner, and component models focus on modularization of corresponding subschemas with the intent of reuse (Fig. 6.12).

Like the vertical structure model, a hybrid structure model utilizes elements as data containers. Hybrid models also include effective use of attribute containers. The use of attributes is limited to describing the

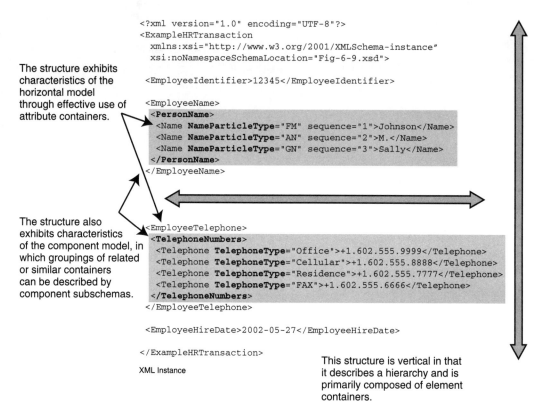

The structure exhibits characteristics of the horizontal model through effective use of attribute containers.

The structure also exhibits characteristics of the component model, in which groupings of related or similar containers can be described by component subschemas.

XML Instance

This structure is vertical in that it describes a hierarchy and is primarily composed of element containers.

Figure 6.12

Hybrid model applied to an XML transaction.

order of repeating elements (e.g., a "sequence," "line," "number," or similarly named attribute) as a classification method for elements (e.g., a "type" or "class" attribute), and as a representative function or activity (for transaction functions such as "add" or "delete"). In some cases attributes are also used to represent decomposed parts of a data value (e.g., attributes used to contain the given, middle, and family name parts of a complete person name). Attributes can also be useful for holding standard code values (Fig. 6.13).

Hybrid models are the recommended structure models for most XML documents and transactions. The

```
<?xml version="1.0" encoding="UTF-8"?>
<ExampleHRTransaction
  xmlns:xsi="http://www.w3.org/2001/XMLSchema-instance"
  xsi:noNamespaceSchemaLocation="Fig-6-9.xsd">

 <EmployeeIdentifier>12345</EmployeeIdentifier>

 <EmployeeName>
  <PersonName>
   <Name NameParticleType="FM" sequence="1">Johnson</Name>
   <Name NameParticleType="AN" sequence="2">M.</Name>
   <Name NameParticleType="GN" sequence="3">Sally</Name>
  </PersonName>
 </EmployeeName>

 <EmployeeTelephone>
  <TelephoneNumbers>
   <Telephone TelephoneType="Office">+1.602.555.9999</Telephone>
   <Telephone TelephoneType="Cellular">+1.602.555.8888</Telephone>
   <Telephone TelephoneType="Residence">+1.602.555.7777</Telephone>
   <Telephone TelephoneType="FAX">+1.602.555.6666</Telephone>
  </TelephoneNumbers>
 </EmployeeTelephone>

 <EmployeeHireDate>2002-05-27</EmployeeHireDate>

</ExampleHRTransaction>
```

NameParticleType is an attribute of the Name element that describes an enterprise standard code value for each name instance.

sequence is an attribute of the repeating Name element that describes the intended order of each instance.

TelephoneType is an attribute of the Telephone element that describes a classification or type for each instance.

Figure 6.13

Examples of uses of attribute containers.

relative strengths of the other models are leveraged, and the limitations are avoided. Although structure models are generally applied to proto-type XML documents, effective engineering of a corresponding schema requires the application of a metadata pattern. In the case of XML, patterns are exhibited as architectural container forms.

7

Architectural Container Forms

An *architectural container form* is the adaptation of an observable and repeatable pattern that is applied to a structure model. Patterns are a somewhat controversial topic. *Patterns* are observable templates or structures that can be applied and repeated in their original form or as a variation. Conceptually, patterns applied to XML and other information technologies have similarities to patterns applied to the architecture of a building. As a simple example of building architecture and structural engineering, a door can be considered as a pattern. Doors are a fundamental part of almost any building. In their most basic form, a door is a simple passage that allows entry and exit of people, animals, items, air, and light and exhibits two mutually exclusive states (either open or closed). As part of a building structure, this definition of a door serves well.

In addition, the application or intended purpose of a door may vary. In a residence, a door might be hinged with a left-to-right and inward method of opening and located at ground level. Alternatively, in a storage warehouse, a door might be roll-up, opening bottom-to-top, with larger dimensions, and located at dock height. As you can imagine, there are many possible variations. The pattern exhibited by a door is observable and can be repeated in different contexts. Each context suggests a new application of the pattern as an architectural form.

With the application of XML, architectural container forms present a similar analogy. The XML structure models described in the previous chapter (i.e., vertical, horizontal, component, and hybrid) are all models of transaction structures. The development of a prototype XML document will initially be aligned with one or more of those XML structure models. When combined with the characteristics of the data that will be contained in and the intended use or purpose of the XML document, architectural container forms extend the document or transaction structure model to fit one or more contexts.

As an example, a prototype XML document that describes delivery address data for orders might also be used for mailing of marketing materials. The elements in which the address data are contained and the intended processing of the address data could vary between applications. In many ways, the adaptation of architectural container forms is similar to the traditional design and analysis processes that extend a simple data model into highly standardized and potentially reusable data architecture.

There are three basic architectural container forms that can be applied to an XML document:

- Rigid

- Abstract

- Hybrid

Each form exhibits one or more desirable characteristics, and in the case of the hybrid form, these characteristics are combined. The challenge for the data architect is to determine which of the architectural container forms to apply to an XML structure model. The adaptation of an architectural container form to an XML structure model is a process that requires an architectural approach rather than a textbook set of steps. Returning to the earlier analogy of a door, the building architect must determine the characteristics of the building, the way the door will be used (both currently and in the future), applicable construction standards and building codes, and the possibility that future structural changes might be required. Similarly, the data architect must think beyond the initial use of the XML transaction or traditional design of database tables. To apply a container form, the data architect must assess a number of important criteria:

- The degree to which the resulting XML document addresses the current information requirements

- The manner in which the XML document might evolve over time (with the potential for ongoing maintenance)

- The variability of the contained data

- The complexity of the XML document (e.g., uniform nesting, number of nested elements, depth of nesting, and containers with derived or aggregate data)

- Alignment with international, industry, and enterprise standards

- Alignment and integration with source and target data architectures

- Potential variations in use, processing, volumetrics, and performance

- Navigational simplicity of the XML document

- The potential for reuse in the current as well as other contexts

Each of the criteria listed can have a significant impact on how well the XML document or transaction will meet immediate and future requirements. It is the application of architectural container forms that extends the XML structure model (initially expressed as a prototype XML document) as a template for engineering a highly standardized, yet flexible, extensible and reusable W3C XML Schema.

Rigid Container Forms

As described by its name, a rigid container form is adapted from a pattern that is generally static or fixed. When a rigid container form is adapted, element containers are named in a manner that implies a strictly enforced and specific taxonomy. Element containers should not be named in the abstract and will generally not repeat (e.g., limited application of cardinality). By using the example of a person's name and adapting a rigid container form to a vertical structure model, each element container would be specifically and uniquely named with the intent to only contain data values of a very specific context (Listing 7.1).

The example in Listing 7.1 is a prototype XML document that adapts a rigid container form to a vertical structure model. The XML structure is primarily composed of element containers that flow top-to-

Listing 7.1

Application of the rigid container form.

```
<?xml version="1.0" encoding="UTF-8"?>
<PersonName>
    <NameGiven>Sally</NameGiven>
    <NameMiddle>M.</NameMiddle>
    <NameFamily>Smith</NameFamily>
</PersonName>
```

bottom (e.g., vertical model). Each element container is explicitly named according to its intended data content (hence the name "rigid"). In the example, the parent element of "<PersonName>" provides a general classification or context for elements that are nested within its bounds. As implied by the parent element tag name, child elements represent the components for a person's name. The child element of "<NameGiven>" is intended to contain a person's given name, first name, or surname. Similarly, the child element of "<NameFamily>" is intended to contain a person's family or last name.

Recommendation:

Rigid architectural container forms are recommended for application to XML documents exchanged between collaborative groups that exist external to the enterprise and for defining a Web Service interface. To avoid misinterpretation, external entities will usually require a rigidly enforced and descriptive taxonomy.

The person name document is a very strict application of taxonomy to element names. One advantage of the rigid form is that the containers are named in a highly descriptive manner that aligns well with the intended data content. Similar to the attributes of a single data model entity or columns of a relational database table, each data element is uniquely named. There should be little question as to the data content of each element. Also, no element will occur twice as a child within the same parent element. When a rigid container form has been applied to a vertical model, the structure is simple and intuitive (Fig. 7.1).

Rigid container forms can be easily applied to any of the XML structure models (e.g., vertical, horizontal, hybrid, or component) and are advantageous for transaction exchanges between external collaborative groups. The use of XML by collaborative groups such as a collection of business trading partners implies the need for an agreed upon vocabulary. XML transactions exchanged between the participants of these collaborative groups will contain data values that meet the expectations of both the sender and recipient. Rigid container forms with explicit and descriptively named element containers are often used to avoid ambiguity and the potential for error.

Figure 7.1

Example of a data
model similar to a rigid
container form.

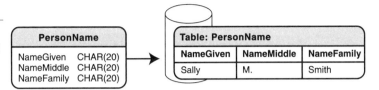

Rigid container forms are also advantageous for defining the inter-face for a Web Service. With well-defined Web Services, the interface is explicitly described by a minivocabulary. This minivocabulary can be expressed using Web Services Description Language (WSDL) and like the collaborative group scenario, a rigid container form avoids potential misinterpretation. The requester of the Web Service relies upon the context and the schema of the service interface to determine what data values are required to request the service and also the structure of the response. We will learn more about Web Services in Chapter 10 (Web Services—An Introduction to the Future).

Fact:

Rigid container architectural forms may simplify the navigation and processing of an XML document structure.

Another advantage of rigid container forms is align-ment with the navigational methods of most parsers. Remember that an XML document is a hierarchical struc-ture. Each XML element container is exposed by the parser as a *node* of the hierarchy (there are several other node types, but element nodes are important for this discussion). XML parsers provide intrinsic *methods*, which are program functions or APIs, that help an applica-tion program navigate and move through the structure of the XML document.

When a rigid container form has been applied to an XML docu-ment, the explicit container names can simplify XML document navigation. Most DOM parsers support a "getElementsByTagName" ("tagNameArgument") method. When invoked, this method can return a list of all elements in an XML document or a list of specific elements that match the tagNameArgument. The application program can "look for" specific elements by element name, rather than walking through the entire XML document and examining each element to determine whether it should be processed. Navigation of the XML document is simplified, because the application program can target specifically named elements for processing. Given that each element is uniquely named with no repetition, additional logic to navigate and evaluate repeating child–sibling elements of the same name is not required.

Although a SAX parser navigates an XML document as individual node events, the "DocumentHandler" interface also provides a similar method of acquiring nodes by name.

A W3C XML Schema for a rigid container form is fairly straightforward. Elements are declared with explicit names, and these elements do not repeat within their parent elements. When the rigid container form has been applied to a horizontal or hybrid structure model, attributes are also defined. Data types for each element or attribute are assigned either by using the W3C XML Schema "type" attribute or by applying a "simpleType" (Fig. 7.2).

Rigid container forms also have disadvantages. A rigid container form rarely uses repeating elements of the same name with defined cardinality. As a result, XML documents with applied rigid container forms are not flexible. They cannot dynamically contract or expand to support element cardinality. When an additional element is required, a new specifically named element container will have to be added. Residual modifications will also be required for any corresponding XML schemas and potentially for the application programs that process the XML document.

Fact:

Rigid container architectural forms are generally inflexible. Addition of new uniquely named data containers will usually require modification of the XML document structure, corresponding schemas, and potentially the application programs that process the XML document.

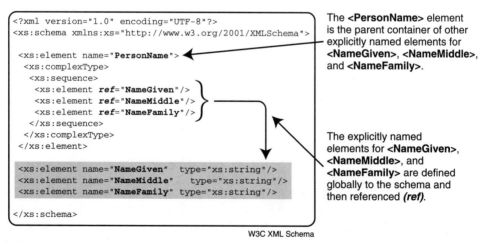

W3C XML Schema

Figure 7.2

Simple W3C XML Schema for an adapted rigid container form.

Abstract Container Forms

Abstract container forms are adapted from a pattern that includes variable and repeating data. This pattern is observable when a set of data elements is applied multiple times in the same or similar context (i.e., cardinality). An example of this pattern is a postal address with multiple street address lines. There are numerous international address formats, each of which may require a different number of street address lines in addition to other variable address components. For global e-commerce, this particular example is often observed and can also be somewhat complex.

Some data architects might argue that a rigid container form could be applied to the international address example. However, consider the fact that international address formats require from one to four street address lines. Adapting a rigid container form would require the definition of four uniquely named street address line containers (e.g., <StreetAddressLine1>, <StreetAddressLine2>, <StreetAddressLine3>, and so on). Also, given that the number of address lines required by different international addresses can vary, each address line element would need to be defined with the modality of optional rather than required. This would avoid carrying extra empty element containers in the XML document when they are not needed (Listing 7.2).

Recommendation:

Abstract container forms are recommended for structures that exhibit a pattern of data that repeats in the same or similar context (e.g., postal address street lines, component parts of a person's name, and telephone numbers of different types).

Listing 7.2

Application of a rigid container form to a postal address.

```
<?xml version="1.0" encoding="UTF-8"?>
<PostalAddress>
    <AddressTo>Sally M. Smith</AddressTo>
    <StreetAddressLine1>Harcourt House</StreetAddressLine1>
    <StreetAddressLine2>50 Sheffield Place</StreetAddressLine2>
    <AddressCity>London</AddressCity>
    <AddressPostalCode>EC3Y-9SY</AddressPostalCode>
    <AddressCountry>England, United Kingdom</AddressCountry>
</PostalAddress>
```

Similar to a single database table containing columns for an address, an XML document of this type would present an architectural form that is largely inflexible when it comes to populating the same structure with different international address formats. A database table defined in this manner would need to include all four possible instances of the street address lines, even though some would be populated while others would remain empty or "null" (Fig. 7.3). The application would need to identify, map, and insert data into individual instances by element name or some similar method. If the architect did not know that up to four address lines may be required for an international address and had only allowed for two or three address line elements in the original structure, adding a fourth address line element would require additional modification to the application logic used to populate the address line elements and to any constraining schemas.

Fact:

Abstract container forms exploit the concepts of repeating elements and cardinality.

An abstract container form presents a far more flexible approach to adapting patterns of repeating data. An abstract container form exploits the ability of XML to support repeating element containers and cardinality. Rather than representing an international postal address as a set of uniquely named elements for an international postal address, the structure would include a group of

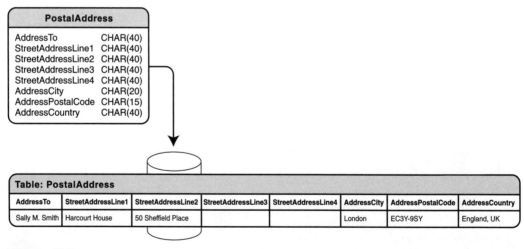

Figure 7.3

Example of a data model for a single address table similar to a rigid container form.

Technique:

Abstract container forms utilize element names that are to some degree named in the abstract. One of the guiding principles of an abstract container form is that element names must be described well enough to identify the intended content of the element yet be abstract enough to allow repetition. When there is a question as to the intended content of repeating elements, the parent element of the repeating group must provide additional context.

repeating elements for street address lines that are of the same name (Listing 7.3). When this address structure requires additional address lines to support other international postal address formats, the XML document can dynamically expand with little or no impact to existing schema definitions or application logic.

With the abstract container form a degree of specificity is removed from the repeating element names (hence the term "abstract"). Some data architects may argue that abstract naming violates the concept of a rigorous taxonomy and would result in the proliferation of XML documents that are prone to misinterpretation and error. If the element naming process remained without guidance or restriction, then this argument might be valid. However, one of the requisite principles of the abstract container form is that although abstract, a container name should be defined to a degree of specificity that a person could readily identify the intended content of the element. Names that are too abstract violate the premise of being self-describing. Names that are too specific significantly reduce the potential for reuse.

If additional context is required (such as roles or classifications), the parent element of the group must provide the necessary perspective. As an example, a repeating element that was named

Listing 7.3

Application of an abstract container form to a postal address.

```
<?xml version="1.0" encoding="UTF-8"?>
<PostalAddress>
    <AddressTo>Sally M. Smith</AddressTo>
    <AddressLines>
        <StreetAddressLine>Harcourt House</StreetAddressLine>
        <StreetAddressLine>50 Sheffield Place</StreetAddressLine>
    </AddressLines>
    <AddressCity>London</AddressCity>
    <AddressPostalCode>EC3Y-9SY</AddressPostalCode>
    <AddressCountry>England, United Kingdom</AddressCountry>
</PostalAddress>
```

"<Line>" rather than "<StreetAddressLine>" would be far too abstract for an international postal address example. Based upon the name, a <Line>element would imply almost any allowable data content. An application developer reading the element name could easily misinterpret the intended content and incorporate program logic that incorrectly processed the element.

Fact:

Abstract container forms often incorporate attributes to describe ordinal sequence of repeating elements.

Recommendation:

With the exception of horizontal structure models, it is recommended that attributes be used only for specification of ordinal sequence, type or classification, standard encoding, intended function or activity, and decomposed parts of a data value.

Another important aspect of the abstract container form is the use of attributes. Abstractly named repeating elements may introduce ambiguity. Additional characteristics of the element are required to resolve important characteristics such as the ordinal sequence of each repeating element. When applied to a vertical structure model combined with an abstract container form, attributes are often used to describe the order or sequence of repeating elements. As we will see later, attributes also apply quite well to the hybrid container form. Regardless, the use of attributes should be limited to descriptions of the following characteristics:

- Ordinal sequence
- Type or classification
- Standard encoding
- Intended function or activity type
- Decomposed parts of a data value

Repeating elements logically occur in the order implied by the hierarchy (top-down and left-to-right), and when validated to a schema by a compositor of a group or complexType. However, there may be occasions for which the order of instantiation in the hierarchy is not that of intended use or only selected instances of repeating elements are to be processed (rather than processing of all of the repeating elements). A "sequence" attribute (e.g., sequence, order, or line number) that describes the intended order could be added to the definition of the repeating elements and populated accordingly (Fig 7.4). The processing application would need to interrogate the sequence attribute and determine what ordinal or selective processing might be necessary.

Although a logical data model is not a pure representation of an XML structure, there are similarities to an abstract container form

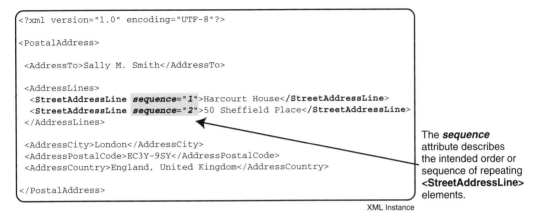

The **sequence** attribute describes the intended order or sequence of repeating **<StreetAddressLine>** elements.

XML Instance

Figure 7.4

Abstract container form with attribute for the ordinal sequence.

Figure 7.5

Data model representing an abstract container form with attribute for the ordinal sequence.

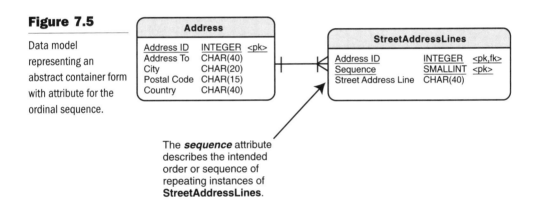

The **sequence** attribute describes the intended order or sequence of repeating instances of **StreetAddressLines**.

(Fig. 7.5). Entities are similar to parent or group element containers. Repeating elements would be defined with cardinality represented as "one-to-many." One difference is that logical data models only support uniquely named attributes within an entity.

A schema for the abstract container form would be aligned with either a vertical or hybrid structure model that is primarily composed of elements. Repeating elements would be defined as children of a parent element group. The W3C XML Schema syntax for declaring cardinality of repeating elements uses the minOccurs and maxOccurs attributes (Fig. 7.6). Conceptually, the *degree* of cardinality describes minimum

```
<?xml version="1.0" encoding="UTF-8"?>
<xs:schema xmlns:xs="http://www.w3.org/2001/XMLSchema">
 <xs:element name="PostalAddress">
  <xs:complexType>
   <xs:sequence>
    <xs:element ref="AddressTo"/>
    <xs:element ref="AddressLines"/>
    <xs:element ref="AddressCity"/>
    <xs:element ref="AddressPostalCode"/>
    <xs:element ref="AddressCountry"/>
   </xs:sequence>
  </xs:complexType>
 </xs:element>

 <xs:element name="AddressTo" type="xs:string"/>

 <xs:element name="AddressLines">
  <xs:complexType>
   <xs:sequence>
    <xs:element ref="StreetAddressLine" minOccurs="1" maxOccurs="4"/>
   </xs:sequence>
  </xs:complexType>
 </xs:element>

 <xs:element name="AddressCity" type="xs:string"/>
 <xs:element name="AddressPostalCode" type="xs:string"/>
 <xs:element name="AddressCountry" type="xs:string"/>

 <xs:element name="StreetAddressLine">
  <xs:complexType>
   <xs:simpleContent>
    <xs:extension base="xs:string">
     <xs:attribute name="sequence" use="required" type="xs:byte"/>
    </xs:extension>
   </xs:simpleContent>
  </xs:complexType>
 </xs:element>
</xs:schema>
```

The degree of cardinality for the repeating **<StreetAddressLine>** element is specified by the **minOccurs** and **maxOccurs** attributes.

The **sequence** attribute describes the intended order or sequence of repeating **<StreetAddressLine>** elements.

W3C XML Schema

Figure 7.6

W3C XML Schema for a simple abstract container form.

and maximum thresholds for the number of instances of repeating data. If the degree of cardinality is unknown or cannot be determined, the minimum and maximum boundaries are infinite. When defined to a W3C XML Schema, the minOccurs attribute would be valued at zero and the maxOccurs attribute would be valued as "unbounded" (i.e., minOccurs = "0" and maxOccurs = "unbounded").

When the minimum and maximum degree of cardinality must be defined with a specific limit or threshold, those values are syntactically

Technique:

When properly applied, specific values for the minOccurs and maxOccurs attributes of repeating elements are a powerful capability of W3C XML Schemas to specify the degree of cardinality. However, caution is advised if the cardinality or characteristics of the repeating elements would be subject to change. Such changes would require modification to the W3C XML Schemas.

Fact:

Abstract container architectural forms may add complexity to the navigation and processing of an XML document structure. Additional application logic may be required for interrogation of attribute characteristics.

defined using the W3C XML Schema minOccurs and maxOccurs attributes. Caution is advised when specific values are applied to the minOccurs and maxOccurs attributes of repeating elements. Such values are limiting constraints that will require modification of the schema if the characteristics of the repeating element changes. Where applicable, an ordinal sequence attribute should also be defined to repeating elements. The attribute should be defined as an integer data type (depending upon the possible number of instances, "byte," "short," "int," "long," or "integer" may apply). This attribute could be evaluated by the processing application to identify the intended order of repeating elements or the position within a group of repeating elements.

Abstractly named repeating elements and attributes to describe intended sequence of repeating elements are required for the abstract container form. Depending upon the complexity of the structure and the level of abstraction, abstract container forms can also introduce navigational complexity. When there are repeating groups of elements, parser methods such as "getElementsByTag-Name" do not expose specific uniqueness of each returned element. To identify uniqueness or process one specific instance of the repeating elements, the application requires additional logic to evaluate the sequence attributes.

Hybrid Container Forms

Hybrid container forms leverage the most advantageous characteristics of both the rigid and abstract forms. A hybrid container form will also include element containers that are specifically and uniquely named. In addition, repeating groups of abstractly named elements will be strategically placed within the structure to allow for variable instances of data. Attributes are included to further describe characteristics such as ordinal sequence (Fig. 7.7).

With a hybrid container form, attributes are also used to describe additional characteristics of a repeating element such as a descriptive type or classification. When an application program requires additional information to resolve ambiguity, a solution is to provide a

Figure 7.7

Hybrid container form.

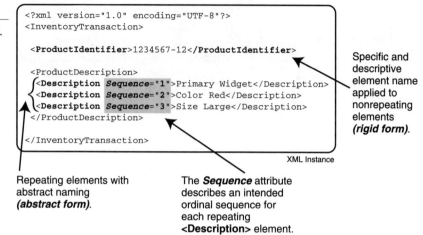

Specific and descriptive element name applied to nonrepeating elements *(rigid form)*.

Repeating elements with abstract naming *(abstract form)*.

The *Sequence* attribute describes an intended ordinal sequence for each repeating **<Description>** element.

Figure 7.8

Hybrid container form with attribute for type.

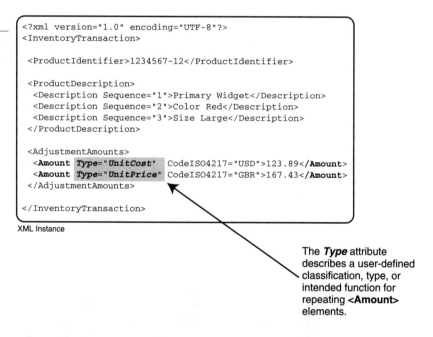

The *Type* attribute describes a user-defined classification, type, or intended function for repeating **<Amount>** elements.

user-defined type or classification attribute that further describes the context or use of the element (Fig. 7.8). The processing application would need to interrogate the "type" attribute and apply program logic accordingly.

Another use of attributes in a hybrid container form is to represent standard code values. This technique is most effective when the primary content of the element container can be further described by one or more codes. Consider an element that contains a monetary amount. The amount value is numeric and may include fractional decimal positions. In addition, the currency type is described by an attribute defined to the element (Fig. 7.9). This technique provides characteristic intelligence to an element container.

Hybrid container forms also use attributes to describe an intended function or activity. This is especially important when the XML document contains transaction-oriented content. Transactions such as an inventory adjustment imply the need to describe characteristics of the adjustment as well as how the adjustment should be applied or processed. Traditional enterprise applications often process transaction files that include a transaction code or type. Similar characteristics can be defined to an XML transaction serving the same purpose. Although the intended function or activity could be described by either an element or attribute, when applied to a vertical structure model and hybrid container form, a descriptive attribute works quite well (Fig. 7.10).

Another effective use of attribute containers is to describe individual decomposed parts of a data value. In some respects, this implies

Figure 7.9

Hybrid container form with attribute for standard code values.

```xml
<?xml version="1.0" encoding="UTF-8"?>
<InventoryTransaction>

 <ProductIdentifier>1234567-12</ProductIdentifier>

 <ProductDescription>
  <Description Sequence="1">Primary Widget</Description>
  <Description Sequence="2">Color Red</Description>
  <Description Sequence="3">Size Large</Description>
 </ProductDescription>

 <AdjustmentAmounts>
  <Amount Type="UnitCost" CodeISO4217="USD">123.89</Amount>
  <Amount Type="UnitPrice" CodeISO4217="GBR">167.43</Amount>
 </AdjustmentAmounts>

</InventoryTransaction>
```

XML Instance

The *CodeISO4217* attribute describes a standard code (encoding) value for the **<Amount>** elements.

```
<?xml version="1.0" encoding="UTF-8"?>
<InventoryTransaction>

 <ProductIdentifier>1234567-12</ProductIdentifier>

 <ProductDescription>
  <Description Sequence="1">Primary Widget</Description>
  <Description Sequence="2">Color Red</Description>
  <Description Sequence="3">Size Large</Description>
 </ProductDescription>

 <AdjustmentQuantities>
  <Quantity Type="Add" Location="AC1" UnitOfMeasure="EA">100</Quantity>
  <Quantity Type="Sub" Location="DE6" UnitOfMeasure="EA">100</Quantity>
 </AdjustmentQuantities>

 <AdjustmentAmounts>
  <Amount Type="UnitCost"  CodeISO4217="USD">123.89</Amount>
  <Amount Type="UnitPrice" CodeISO4217="GBR">167.43</Amount>
 </AdjustmentAmounts>

</InventoryTransaction>
```

XML Instance

For the **<Quantity>** elements,
the *Type* attribute describes
an intended function.

carrying redundant data within the XML transaction (e.g., both the complete data value and the decomposed parts). When the fact that an XML transaction may be designed for several purposes is considered, this technique can be of great advantage. A common example is a person name. An XML document or transaction that contains a person's name might be consumed by applications that will produce mailing lists, form letters, and similar correspondence. A complete person name is usually sufficient for processing by these types of applications. Other applications may require sorting, grouping, and selecting data by person name parts (e.g., sort a list of customers by family name or last name and then first name). A technique to address varied data granularity and processing is to contain the complete person name as element data and also define the individual parts of the person name as attributes within that element (Fig. 7.11). Although this technique results in a highly reusable XML structure, it will also increase the overall size of the transaction, and additional program logic will be required to determine when the element content should be processed vs the attribute content.

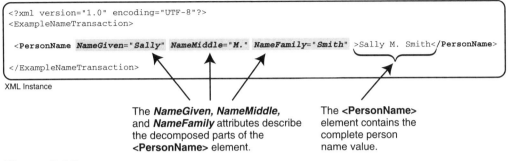

```
<?xml version="1.0" encoding="UTF-8"?>
<ExampleNameTransaction>

 <PersonName NameGiven="Sally" NameMiddle="M." NameFamily="Smith" >Sally M. Smith</PersonName>

</ExampleNameTransaction>
```

XML Instance

The *NameGiven, NameMiddle,*
and *NameFamily* attributes describe
the decomposed parts of the
<PersonName> element.

The **<PersonName>**
element contains the
complete person
name value.

Figure 7.11

Use of attributes for decomposed element data.

In summary, the hybrid container form incorporates explicitly named elements as well as abstractly named repeating elements with defined cardinality. To avoid ambiguity and provide additional context, user-defined attributes are applied for ordinal sequence, type or classification, standard encodings, and intended function or activity. The actual names applied to these elements and attributes are determined by the data architect and follow enterprise and XML naming standards. Data types are assigned either by using the W3C XML Schema "type" attribute or by applying custom defined "simpleTypes." Extended data type facets are also applied where appropriate (Listing 7.4).

Recommendation:

With few exceptions, hybrid container forms are the recommended architectural adaptation for an XML transaction structure.

Advantages of the hybrid container form are the rigorous application of naming practices that result in an intuitive taxonomy, combined with groups of repeating elements that dynamically expand and contract as necessary to meet the characteristics of those data concepts. The hybrid container form exhibits similarities to a robust logical data model that has been constructed to support repeating data instances (e.g., relationships and cardinality) and descriptive characteristics (Fig. 7.12). When applied to an XML transaction, the disadvantages of the hybrid container form are few. Similar to the abstract container form, there may be some implicit navigational complexity for the repeating elements and the need for additional attribute logic. Hybrid container forms can be readily adapted with vertical, component, and hybrid structure models. Some adaptation may be possible with horizontal structure models

Listing 7.4

Example of an XML schema for an adapted hybrid container form.

```xml
<?xml version="1.0" encoding="UTF-8"?>
<xs:schema xmlns:xs="http://www.w3.org/2001/XMLSchema">

    <xs:element name="InventoryTransaction">
      <xs:complexType>
        <xs:sequence>
          <xs:element ref="ProductIdentifier"/>
          <xs:element ref="ProductDescription"/>
          <xs:element ref="AdjustmentQuantities"/>
          <xs:element ref="AdjustmentAmounts"/>
        </xs:sequence>
      </xs:complexType>
    </xs:element>

    <xs:element name="ProductIdentifier" type="xs:string"/>

    <xs:element name="ProductDescription">
      <xs:complexType>
        <xs:sequence>
          <xs:element ref="Description" minOccurs="1"
          maxOccurs="unbounded"/>
        </xs:sequence>
      </xs:complexType>
    </xs:element>

    <xs:element name="AdjustmentQuantities">
      <xs:complexType>
        <xs:sequence>
          <xs:element ref="Quantity" minOccurs="1"
          maxOccurs="unbounded"/>
        </xs:sequence>
      </xs:complexType>
    </xs:element>

    <xs:element name="AdjustmentAmounts">
      <xs:complexType>
        <xs:sequence>
          <xs:element ref="Amount" minOccurs="1"
          maxOccurs="unbounded"/>
```

Listing 7.4 *Continued*

```
        </xs:sequence>
    </xs:complexType>
</xs:element>

<xs:element name="Description">
    <xs:complexType>
        <xs:simpleContent>
            <xs:extension base="xs:string">
                <xs:attribute name="Sequence" use="required"
                type="xs:byte"/>
            </xs:extension>
        </xs:simpleContent>
    </xs:complexType>
</xs:element>

<xs:element name="Quantity">
    <xs:complexType>
        <xs:simpleContent>
            <xs:extension base="xs:integer">
                <xs:attribute name="Type" use="required">
                    <xs:simpleType>
                        <xs:restriction base="xs:string">
                            <xs:enumeration value="Add"/>
                            <xs:enumeration value="Sub"/>
                        </xs:restriction>
                    </xs:simpleType>
                </xs:attribute>
                <xs:attribute name="Location" use="required"
                type="xs:string"/>
                <xs:attribute name="UnitOfMeasure" use="required">
                    <xs:simpleType>
                        <xs:restriction base="xs:string">
                            <xs:enumeration value="EA"/>
                            <xs:enumeration value="DZ"/>
                            <xs:enumeration value="GR"/>
                        </xs:restriction>
                    </xs:simpleType>
                </xs:attribute>
            </xs:extension>
        </xs:simpleContent>
```

Continued

Listing 7.4 *Continued*

```
        </xs:complexType>
    </xs:element>

    <xs:element name="Amount">
      <xs:complexType>
        <xs:simpleContent>
          <xs:extension base="AmountSimpleType">
            <xs:attribute name="Type" use="required">
              <xs:simpleType>
                <xs:restriction base="xs:string">
                  <xs:enumeration value="UnitCost"/>
                  <xs:enumeration value="UnitPrice"/>
                </xs:restriction>
              </xs:simpleType>
            </xs:attribute>
            <xs:attribute name="CodeISO4217" use="required">
              <xs:simpleType>
                <xs:restriction base="xs:string">
                  <xs:enumeration value="GBR"/>
                  <xs:enumeration value="USD"/>
                </xs:restriction>
              </xs:simpleType>
            </xs:attribute>
          </xs:extension>
        </xs:simpleContent>
      </xs:complexType>
    </xs:element>

    <xs:simpleType name="AmountSimpleType">
      <xs:restriction base="xs:decimal">
        <xs:totalDigits value="7"/>
        <xs:fractionDigits value="2"/>
      </xs:restriction>
    </xs:simpleType>

</xs:schema>
```

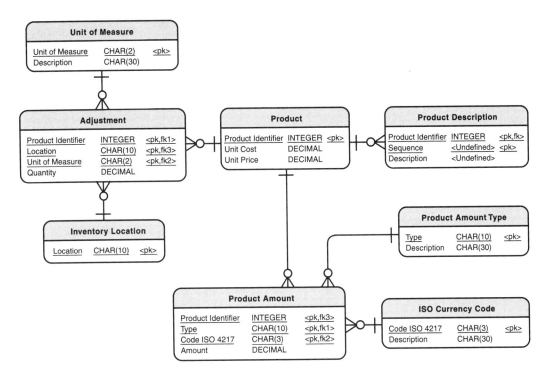

Figure 7.12

Simple data model representing a hybrid container form.

(those that are primarily composed of attributes), but the inability of attributes to repeat are a significant limitation. As a general recommendation, the use of carefully constructed hybrid container forms that meet the requirements of a project, utilize an effective taxonomy, and allow for variable data is the recommended approach.

As we have learned, there are numerous similarities and synergies between traditional data modeling and XML structure modeling. Additionally, observable and repeatable data patterns can be applied with the application of architectural container forms. These activities fit well with the role and responsibilities of the data architect. Yet, there are additional opportunities for the data architect to leverage W3C XML Schemas. Reuse is one.

8

W3C XML Schemas and Reuse

Reuse is one of the most misunderstood concepts in information technology. Many technology executives assume that anything in their inventory (e.g., models, designs, application programs, databases, interfaces, and transactions) can be reused to advantage. They desire the economic benefits intuitive to the concept of reuse but may be unaware of the tactical costs required to achieve these benefits. Technology managers are challenged with aggressive deadlines and limited budgets and often avoid the modifications to their development methodology that are required to achieve effective reuse. Technology practitioners are rewarded for rapid delivery and the number of tested lines of code they develop. In other words, the goals that drive development of new applications are different from those that support reuse. However, all is not lost. The syntactical and functional capabilities afforded by W3C XML Schemas provide tremendous support and opportunities for metadata reuse. The first challenge is to develop a fundamental understanding of what reuse is all about.

From the perspective of information technology, *reuse* is a two-part process that first targets the engineering of information assets with the intent of being able to use these assets more than once and then harvesting these reusable technology assets:

- Reuse engineering
- Reuse harvesting

Fact:

XML schema reuse engineering is the set of practices, techniques, and activities required to engineer a W3C XML Schema or schema component with the specific intent of reuse.

Reuse engineering is the set of practices and techniques required to construct, engineer, and describe a technology asset with the specific intent to be reused. To engineer something for reuse, the data architect must consider how the information asset will be used initially as well as in the future. Reuse engineering includes an architectural approach in which development is not limited to meeting the initial objectives and requirements of a project. Also of importance is the determination whether there is a repeatable pattern exhibited by the technology asset that would support reuse in its current context (also known as *within-domain* or *domain-specific reuse*) and in other contexts (also known as *cross-domain reuse*).[1]

Both within-domain and cross-domain reuse are of value. The benefits of within-domain reuse are generally observed with the number of repeated reuse instances within that specific context. As a representative vocabulary, a W3C XML Schema provides a context (e.g., schemas representing a customer order transaction, a purchase order transaction, or a human resources payroll transaction). Within-domain reuse tends to limit the scope of the technology asset and therefore results in a somewhat less significant development effort. An example would be the initial use and then the further reuse of a defined data type for monetary amounts within a single W3C XML Schema vocabulary (Fig. 8.1).

Cross-domain reuse considers greater degrees of abstraction and generalization to allow for broad scale reuse and can result in a more significant development effort. Given that cross-domain reuse implies reuse opportunities in other contexts, the potential benefits can be greater than those of within-domain reuse. Cross-domain reuse of a W3C XML Schema also infers that the schema is defined as an external subschema that can then be referenced by and from within other W3C XML Schemas. Each of the referencing schemas represents a specific context (Fig. 8.2).

Fact:

XML schema reuse harvesting is a process that includes activities for identification, validation, and implementation of reusable W3C XML Schemas, subschemas, or schema components.

Reuse harvesting is a set of processes that focus on identifying opportunities for reuse, finding an information asset that is a candidate for reuse, validating the fit of that asset to the reuse opportunity (i.e., similar to pattern matching), and incorporating or referencing the reusable

---

[1] Karlsson, E.-V. Software Reuse—A Holistic Approach. John Wiley & Sons, New York, 1995.

Figure 8.1

Within-domain reuse
(internal to a schema).

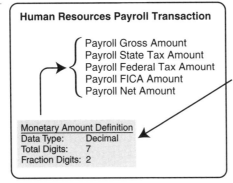

HR Transaction.xsd

Human Resources Payroll Transaction

Payroll Gross Amount
Payroll State Tax Amount
Payroll Federal Tax Amount
Payroll FICA Amount
Payroll Net Amount

Monetary Amount Definition
Data Type: Decimal
Total Digits: 7
Fraction Digits: 2

- Monetary Amount Data Type is not exposed outside the context of the HR Transaction schema.

- Therefore, it cannot be directly reused outside the given context provided by the HR Transaction vocabulary.

Figure 8.2

Cross-domain reuse
(external to a schema).

HR Transaction.xsd

Human Resources Payroll Transaction

Payroll Gross Amount
Payroll State Tax Amount
Payroll Federal Tax Amount
Payroll FICA Amount
Payroll Net Amount

Customer Order.xsd

Customer Order Transaction

Item Unit Price
Item Total Price
Order Total Price

Enterprise Standard TYPES.xsd

Enterprise Standard Types

Monetary Amount Definition
Data Type: Decimal
Total Digits: 7
Fraction Digits: 2

- Monetary Amount Data Type is defined to an enterprise standard subschema.

- This subschema and its contents are then reused by reference from within other schemas.

Purchase Order.xsd

Purchase Order Transaction

Item Unit Cost
Item Total Cost
Purchase Order Total Cost

information asset (e.g., engineering via reference and assembly rather than new development). The majority of initial reuse costs are attributed to reuse engineering. However, there are also some additional costs associated with reuse harvesting processes. Reuse harvesting costs are attributed to the additional effort required to identify a reusable asset, validating that the asset meets the project requirements, and implementing the reusable asset.

With each repeated instance of a harvested information asset the benefits of reuse become evident. The costs associated with the development and unit testing of the reusable information asset are to some degree offset by each reuse instance (e.g., future development cost avoidance as a result of reusing an information asset avoids having to redevelop and unit test a "new" asset many times). Reuse engineering is the initial part of the reuse process and where most development costs are incurred. Reuse harvesting is where reuse benefits are exploited and measured.

W3C XML Schemas present several types of reuse opportunities. The most fundamental reuse opportunities are aligned with the concept of within-domain reuse. A *domain* is a particular application system, set of related business functions, or a defined context. A W3C XML Schema-based vocabulary is a set of containers that represent a domain or some part of a domain. Containers (e.g., XML elements and attributes), groups of containers, and types (e.g., metadata characteristics and custom data types) can also be defined for reuse within a single W3C XML Schema vocabulary. Enterprise standard containers, structures, and metadata definitions can be engineered as subschemas. W3C XML Schemas can also be engineered as assemblies of other externally defined W3C XML Schemas and schema components. A data architect can engineer a W3C XML Schema vocabulary to reference the standard subschemas, rather than individually coding them.

Internal W3C XML Schema Reuse

Reuse within a W3C XML Schema can take several forms. Within a W3C XML Schema, elements can be either locally or globally defined. Locally defined element containers are defined by name at the point in the schema where they are declared (Fig. 8.3). These locally defined elements and attributes are generally not reusable outside of their point of declaration. Alternatively, globally defined elements represent a funda-

Example of a W3C XML Schema

This example of an XML document representing a simple transaction is constrained by the referenced W3C XML Schema.

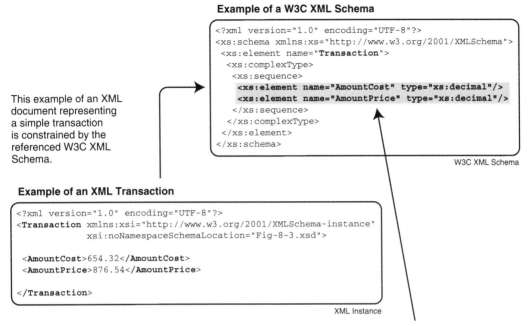

```
<?xml version="1.0" encoding="UTF-8"?>
<xs:schema xmlns:xs="http://www.w3.org/2001/XMLSchema">
 <xs:element name="Transaction">
  <xs:complexType>
   <xs:sequence>
    <xs:element name="AmountCost" type="xs:decimal"/>
    <xs:element name="AmountPrice" type="xs:decimal"/>
   </xs:sequence>
  </xs:complexType>
 </xs:element>
</xs:schema>
```
W3C XML Schema

Example of an XML Transaction

```
<?xml version="1.0" encoding="UTF-8"?>
<Transaction xmlns:xsi="http://www.w3.org/2001/XMLSchema-instance"
             xsi:noNamespaceSchemaLocation="Fig-8-3.xsd">

 <AmountCost>654.32</AmountCost>
 <AmountPrice>876.54</AmountPrice>

</Transaction>
```
XML Instance

- The **<Transaction>** element is a parent element container of other elements defined by name as **<AmountCost>** and **<AmountPrice>**.

- Both elements are locally defined at their point of occurrence, which is within the parent **<Transaction>**.

- As a result, these two elements could not be reused again by reference from elsewhere within this schema.

- If **<AmountCost>** and **<AmountPrice>** elements were also required elsewhere, they would need to be defined again.

Figure 8.3

Local W3C XML Schema element definitions.

mental form of reuse. They are defined to the overall schema rather than at a specific point of occurrence. Globally defined elements are containers that can be defined with the intent of being reused by reference from other places in the schema (Fig. 8.4).

It may be advantageous or necessary to define and reference a collection of similar or related elements rather than individual elements. This can be accomplished using the W3C XML Schemas syntax for

Example of a W3C XML Schema

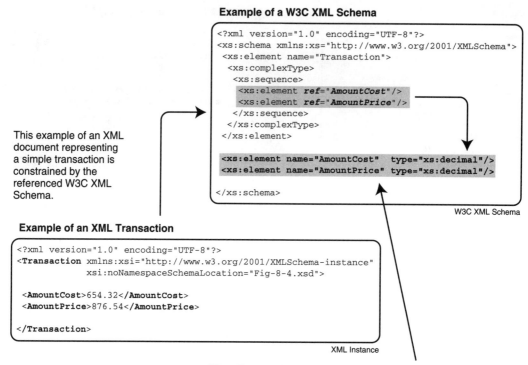

```
<?xml version="1.0" encoding="UTF-8"?>
<xs:schema xmlns:xs="http://www.w3.org/2001/XMLSchema">
 <xs:element name="Transaction">
  <xs:complexType>
   <xs:sequence>
    <xs:element ref="AmountCost"/>
    <xs:element ref="AmountPrice"/>
   </xs:sequence>
  </xs:complexType>
 </xs:element>

 <xs:element name="AmountCost"  type="xs:decimal"/>
 <xs:element name="AmountPrice" type="xs:decimal"/>

</xs:schema>
```

W3C XML Schema

This example of an XML document representing a simple transaction is constrained by the referenced W3C XML Schema.

Example of an XML Transaction

```
<?xml version="1.0" encoding="UTF-8"?>
<Transaction xmlns:xsi="http://www.w3.org/2001/XMLSchema-instance"
             xsi:noNamespaceSchemaLocation="Fig-8-4.xsd">

 <AmountCost>654.32</AmountCost>
 <AmountPrice>876.54</AmountPrice>

</Transaction>
```

XML Instance

- The **<Transaction>** element is a parent element container of other elements *referenced* as **<AmountCost>** and **<AmountPrice>**.

- Both elements are globally defined to the schema (i.e., outside their point of occurrence).

- As a result, these two elements are reusable by reference from elsewhere within this schema.

- If **<AmountCost>** and **<AmountPrice>** elements were also required elsewhere, they would not need to be defined again.

Figure 8.4

Global W3C XML Schema element definitions.

either a "complexType" or a "group." A *complexType* is a defined set of element containers that when named may be reused by reference (using the "extension" syntax within an element). Similarly, a W3C XML Schema *group* is a defined set of containers (also known as an element model group) that are specifically defined with intent of being reused.

Recommendation:

Unless intentionally prohibited from being reused, all XML element containers should be defined globally, allowing for reuse by reference.

Recommendation:

Unless there are obvious advantages to using global "complexTypes," collections of related element containers intentionally targeted for reuse should be globally defined as "groups."

The previous example of two globally defined amount elements could be defined and reused as a single collection of elements rather than as two individual element references. A complexType can be defined globally to the schema and then referenced by name as the extension of an element (Fig. 8.5).

Like a complexType, a group is also a collection of element containers. The concept of a group is similar to that of a complexType, but a slightly different syntax is used. A group is defined with the specific intent of being reused by reference. While a complexType can be defined to be reused as an extension, it can also be defined locally and excluded from reuse. The content of a group can include a list of elements or complexTypes (Fig. 8.6).

Both a complexType and a group allow for a compositor. A *compositor* specifies the sequence and selective occurrence of the containers defined within a complexType or a group. Compositors include sequence, all, and choice (Table 8.1). The *sequence* compositor declares that the individual elements defined within a complexType or a group must occur in the same order in the corresponding XML document. The *all* compositor declares that all of the elements contained within the complexType or group must be present in the corresponding XML document, but may occur in any order. The *choice* compositor states that only one of the elements defined to a complexType or group may occur in the corresponding XML document.

In addition to a compositor, most elements defined or referenced by complexTypes and groups may repeat. The degree of cardinality can be specified for repeating elements using the minOccurs and maxOccurs attributes. The *minOccurs* attribute defines the minimum degree of cardinality or the minimum number of occurrences for a referenced repeating element. A minOccurs attribute with a value of zero (i.e., "0") denotes that the element is optional. The *maxOccurs* attribute defines the maximum degree of cardinality or the maximum number of occurrences for the referenced element. Both the minimum and maximum degree of cardinality can be specific (e.g., a specific value such as "3" or "200"). The maximum degree of cardinality may also be defined as infinite (i.e., a value of "unbounded"). It is important to note that in some cases, the rules of the compositor may constrain cardinality and repeating elements (e.g., the "all" compositor does not allow for repeating elements).

Example of a W3C XML Schema

```
<?xml version="1.0" encoding="UTF-8"?>
<xs:schema xmlns:xs="http://www.w3.org/2001/XMLSchema">
 <xs:element name="Transaction">
  <xs:complexType>
   <xs:complexContent>
    <xs:extension base="AmountGroup" /> ────┐
   </xs:complexContent>                      │
  </xs:complexType>                          │
 </xs:element>                               ▼

 <xs:complexType name="AmountGroup">
  <xs:sequence>
   <xs:element name="AmountCost"  type="xs:decimal"/>
   <xs:element name="AmountPrice" type="xs:decimal"/>
  </xs:sequence>
 </xs:complexType>

</xs:schema>
```

W3C XML Schema

This example of an XML document representing a simple transaction is constrained by the referenced W3C XML Schema.

Example of an XML Transaction

```
<?xml version="1.0" encoding="UTF-8"?>
<Transaction xmlns:xsi="http://www.w3.org/2001/XMLSchema-instance"
             xsi:noNamespaceSchemaLocation="Fig-8-5.xsd">

 <AmountCost>654.32</AmountCost>
 <AmountPrice>876.54</AmountPrice>

</Transaction>
```

XML Instance

- The **<Transaction>** element is a parent element container of a complexType that *references* the **AmountGroup** complexType.

- The complexType is defined globally to the schema (i.e., outside its point of occurrence).

- As a result, this complexType, which also contains two elements, is reusable by reference from elsewhere within this schema.

Figure 8.5

Global W3C XML Schema complexType definition.

As described in Chapter 4 (W3C XML Schema Types vs Database Data Types), W3C XML Schemas provide extensive data type support, including numerous built-in and derived data types that can be applied as a constraint to any element or attribute. Custom data types can also be defined by creating a simpleType with one of the supported

Example of a W3C XML Schema

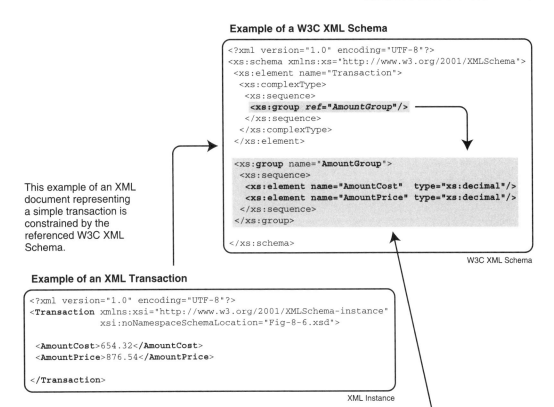

```
<?xml version="1.0" encoding="UTF-8"?>
<xs:schema xmlns:xs="http://www.w3.org/2001/XMLSchema">
 <xs:element name="Transaction">
  <xs:complexType>
   <xs:sequence>
    <xs:group ref="AmountGroup"/>
   </xs:sequence>
  </xs:complexType>
 </xs:element>

 <xs:group name="AmountGroup">
  <xs:sequence>
   <xs:element name="AmountCost"  type="xs:decimal"/>
   <xs:element name="AmountPrice" type="xs:decimal"/>
  </xs:sequence>
 </xs:group>

</xs:schema>
```

W3C XML Schema

This example of an XML document representing a simple transaction is constrained by the referenced W3C XML Schema.

Example of an XML Transaction

```
<?xml version="1.0" encoding="UTF-8"?>
<Transaction xmlns:xsi="http://www.w3.org/2001/XMLSchema-instance"
             xsi:noNamespaceSchemaLocation="Fig-8-6.xsd">

 <AmountCost>654.32</AmountCost>
 <AmountPrice>876.54</AmountPrice>

</Transaction>
```

XML Instance

- The **<Transaction>** element is a parent element container of complexType that includes an element group.

- The element group ***AmountGroup*** contains two elements *referenced* as **<AmountCost>** and **<AmountPrice>**.

- The group and its contents are reusable by reference from elsewhere within this schema.

- If **<AmountCost>** and **<AmountPrice>** elements were also required elsewhere as a group of elements, they would not need to be defined again.

Figure 8.6

Global W3C XML Schema group definition.

Table 8.1   Compositors

Compositor type	Description
sequence	Child elements must occur in the corresponding XML document in the listed order. Specified cardinality of child elements may determine whether a specific child element must occur or may occur and the degree to which it repeats.
all	All child elements must occur in the corresponding XML document. They may occur in any order but cannot repeat (i.e., a degree of cardinality of maxOccurs greater than one cannot be specified).
Choice	Any one (but only one) of the child elements may occur.

Technique:

W3C XML Schema simpleTypes present a powerful method for defining enterprise standard data types and allowable value constraints for element and attribute containers.

data types as a base and adding constraining facets. The ability to define custom data types is a powerful form of reuse. Many organizations have a set of enterprise standard data element definitions. When new data elements of the same type are defined, the data architect is required to apply the enterprise standard metadata characteristics (e.g., data type, length, decimalization, and allowable values).

Common examples of enterprise standard data elements include those for monetary amounts, identifiers (e.g., as in primary key or unique identifiers), text descriptions, and standard code values. These same enterprise standards can be defined as custom data types and implemented as W3C XML Schema simpleTypes. Similar to an element, a *simpleType* can be defined locally and referenced by an element or attribute, or it can be defined globally to the schema with the intent of being reused by reference. When a custom data type is defined using a simpleType, it will include a declared W3C XML Schema data type and any applicable facets (Fig. 8.7). The examples of monetary amount custom data types are defined as a decimal data type, with totalDigits and fractionDigits facets. A simpleType is not limited to monetary amounts or decimal data types. Any of the supported W3C XML Schema data types and facets can be applied.

Reuse of elements, groups of elements, and data types within a single W3C XML Schema is a powerful capability. However, reuse of these internal constructs outside the context of the defining W3C XML

Example of a W3C XML Schema

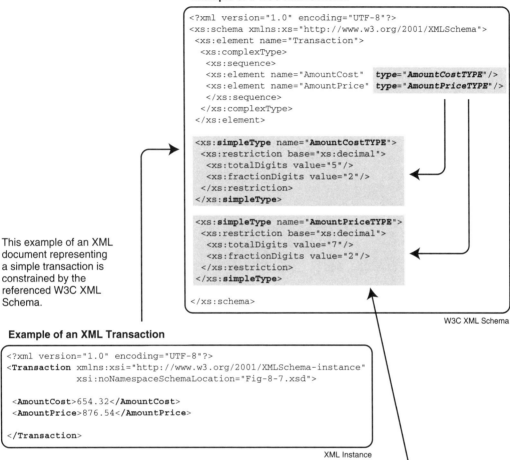

```
<?xml version="1.0" encoding="UTF-8"?>
<xs:schema xmlns:xs="http://www.w3.org/2001/XMLSchema">
 <xs:element name="Transaction">
  <xs:complexType>
   <xs:sequence>
    <xs:element name="AmountCost"   type="AmountCostTYPE"/>
    <xs:element name="AmountPrice"  type="AmountPriceTYPE"/>
   </xs:sequence>
  </xs:complexType>
 </xs:element>

 <xs:simpleType name="AmountCostTYPE">
  <xs:restriction base="xs:decimal">
   <xs:totalDigits value="5"/>
   <xs:fractionDigits value="2"/>
  </xs:restriction>
 </xs:simpleType>

 <xs:simpleType name="AmountPriceTYPE">
  <xs:restriction base="xs:decimal">
   <xs:totalDigits value="7"/>
   <xs:fractionDigits value="2"/>
  </xs:restriction>
 </xs:simpleType>

</xs:schema>
```

W3C XML Schema

This example of an XML document representing a simple transaction is constrained by the referenced W3C XML Schema.

Example of an XML Transaction

```
<?xml version="1.0" encoding="UTF-8"?>
<Transaction xmlns:xsi="http://www.w3.org/2001/XMLSchema-instance"
             xsi:noNamespaceSchemaLocation="Fig-8-7.xsd">

 <AmountCost>654.32</AmountCost>
 <AmountPrice>876.54</AmountPrice>

</Transaction>
```

XML Instance

- The enterprise standards for cost and price monetary amounts include data types, total length, and decimal scale.

- The **<AmountCost>** and **<AmountPrice>** elements reference the enterprise standard types (simpleTypes).

- These simpleTypes are globally defined and may be reused by reference elsewhere in the schema.

Figure 8.7

Global W3C XML Schema simpleType definitions.

Schema may be complex and in some cases not possible. An attempt to reuse these same elements, groups, and types within other schemas would probably require repetition of the W3C XML Schema syntax in each of the other schemas (as a form of copy and paste). Although there is some advantage to this approach, there are also increased costs and risks. The obvious advantage is that enterprise standard elements and data types are to some degree proliferated and reused. However, the cost of maintaining each of these schemas will escalate. Also, the potential for errors resulting from future modifications that are not synchronized to all copies increases over time. Reuse of externally defined W3C XML Schemas presents a more effective approach.

External W3C XML Schema Reuse (Component Subschemas)

From the perspective of reuse harvesting, W3C XML Schemas also provide extensive capabilities in the area of cross-domain reuse. Leveraging W3C XML Schemas for cross-domain reuse implies that a schema (or subschema) can represent a repeatable pattern, and it can be used in different contexts and by different applications. The method of implementation is to define modular W3C XML Schemas as external subschemas. Other W3C XML Schemas (potentially of varying contexts) can then reference and reuse the elements, groups, and data types of the subschemas. The referencing schema vocabularies only need to define the containers, structures, and types exclusive to their specific context. As a form of development by assembly, reused elements, groups, and data types defined to the subschemas are then "referenced" (Fig. 8.8).

Fact:

Reuse of a W3C XML Schema or subschema is a conceptual form of development by assembly. The primary W3C XML Schema is assembled by including references to the contents of other externally defined W3C XML subschemas.

Schema reuse engineering is the process of developing W3C XML Schemas (or subschemas) with the intent of reuse. Each of the external subschemas must be defined in a manner that promotes broad-scale reuse, yet ensures adherence to enterprise structures and metadata standards, which is where the data architect plays a significant role. The identification of candidate data elements, structures, and data types is similar to traditional data architecture practices. The most common opportunities for engineering reusable subschemas include the following patterns:

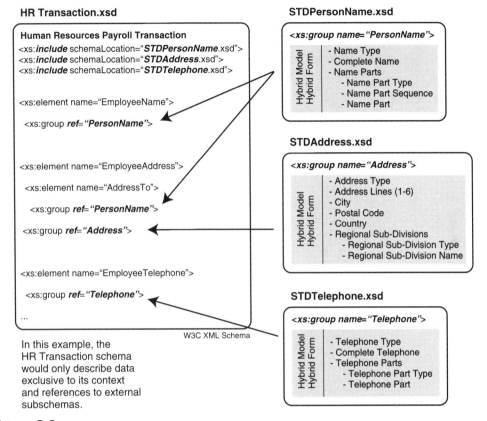

Figure 8.8

W3C XML Schema reuse by reference (e.g., "assembly").

- Highly standardized data structures (e.g., person name, postal address, telephone number, product family structures, and geographic structures)
- Standard codes and allowable values
  - Enumeration lists of internal enterprise standard code values
  - Enumeration lists of international and industry-related encoding standards (e.g., U.S. state abbreviations, country codes, and currency codes)
- Standard data types (e.g., enterprise standard data types for monetary amounts, text descriptions, and identifiers)

The W3C XML Schema syntax allows for subschemas to
define elements, groups, complexTypes, and simpleTypes
that can be included and referenced by other W3C XML
Schemas. The concept is roughly analogous to the concept
of a COBOL Copybook "include," in which data structures and file definitions are defined according to enterprise standards and are then included by reference from
within other COBOL source programs. This helps to
ensure that not only is there a high degree of reuse (resulting in development cost avoidance) but also enterprise structures and
metadata standards are supported.

One of the greatest challenges for today's business enterprise is the
diversity of data resulting from global e-commerce. When varied international cultures and locales are considered, a customer's name presents
an interesting problem. As an integration transaction technology, XML
can be used to exchange person name information between tactical
enterprise systems such as human resources, order processing, and customer service. Similar name information can be exchanged with and
imported into strategic systems such as marketing, customer relationship management, and the data warehouse. Functional uses of person
name data imply repeatable patterns. However, the granularity and data
formats for person name can vary from system to system. Cultural variations of person name introduce even greater complexity.

In the United States, a common format for person name is simply
the combination of first, middle, and last names. However, these name
parts support international and cultural variations minimally (if at all).
In many countries the descriptive data element names of first, middle,
and last are not applicable. Variations may include given name, surname, family name, and additional name.[2] Also, the order or sequence
of name parts may differ (e.g., in some cultures the family or last name
precedes the given or first name). Also, many person names are not
limited to three name parts and may also include connectives (e.g., "von"
or "de").

Another important aspect of a person's name is how it will be used
or processed. Application programs that generate correspondence, mail-
ings, and delivery labels may only require a single complete name that
is composed of all name parts in the desired sequence of the individual.

---

[2] Bean J. XML Globalization and Best Practices. Active Education, Colorado, U.S., 2001.

Alternatively, other applications such as marketing, global customer relationship management, and data warehousing may require the granular parts of an individual's name for the purposes of sorting and grouping. A highly reusable name structure will support multiple uses of person name data.[3]

A W3C XML Schema describing the structure and format of a person name can be engineered with the intent of broad scale reuse. Other W3C XML Schemas can then reference and reuse the person name schema as a subschema, rather than including individually coded name structures parochial to their own processing. Strategic applications such as global customer relationship management (G-CRM) often act as a point of integration for customer information. In this case, the ability to accept, validate, import, and process international customer names and name parts becomes critical to success. Engineering a modular person name subschema requires that the structure can support varied processing and multiple data formats and still apply standards and constraints as necessary (Fig. 8.9).

A person name schema designed for broad scale, cross-domain reuse must support different forms of processing, as well as different structural formats (Fig. 8.10). When XML is used to describe data that will be imported into a database structure, the format, granularity, and taxonomy of that structure become important. If the data will be exchanged between systems that have different functions and purposes or the structure, form, and content of the data are variable, a flexible architecture is of value. Determination of the intended use, potential future use, variability, and granularity of the data requires an architectural perspective. To engineer a reusable schema for person name, the data architect must determine how the data will be used, structured, identified, and described.

An Architectural Approach to Reuse Engineering

W3C XML Schema reuse engineering includes activities specific to the design and development of highly reusable schemas. In this regard, the data architect can play a significant role. To ensure that a W3C XML

---

[3] Bean J. Engineering Global E-Commerce Sites. Morgan Kaufmann, San Francisco, 2003.

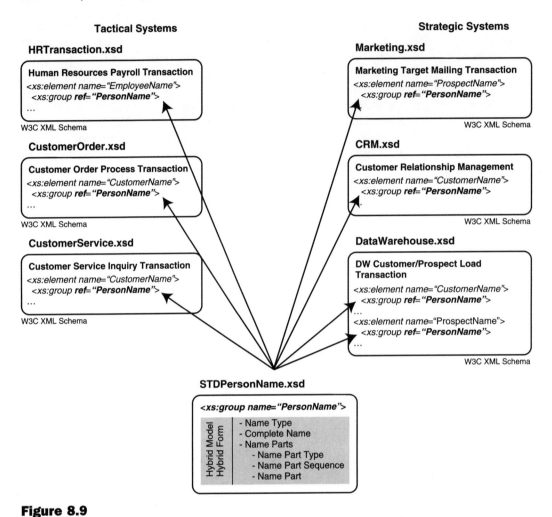

Figure 8.9

Varying use of an enterprise standard subschema for person name.

Schema is intended for broad-scale, cross-domain reuse, the data architect must apply an architectural perspective. This perspective must include several important architecture requirements:

- Schema identification (a file name allowing for later "reuse harvesting")

Figure 8.10

Broad-scale, cross-domain reuse of subschema for person name.

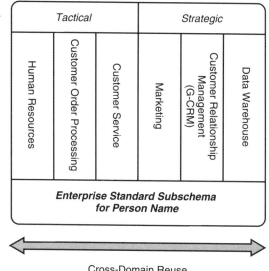

Cross-Domain Reuse

- Version management
- Variable use and processing (e.g., how the XML document and content will be "consumed")
- Application of structure models
- Adaptation of architecture container forms

Recommendation:

The external file name of a reusable W3C XML Schema (or subschema) should be intuitive, be of reasonable specificity, be of mixed character case or camel case, eliminate spaces, and be a maximum of 32 characters in length.

Identification and naming of a schema is critical to reuse. The externally defined W3C XML Schema must be named in a manner that is intuitive and simplifies the identification and harvesting of reusable schemas. The name should also align with enterprise naming standards. Similar to the taxonomy techniques applied to individual XML container names (e.g., elements and attributes), the external file name of the entire W3C XML Schema is important. Even though the schema name might be descriptive, if it is too specific or limited to a particular system, application, or process, reuse potential will be limited. Alternatively, a schema name that is too abstract can be misleading and result in inaccurate identification of reuse candidates. A schema name of "Name" is far too abstract. Name might imply a person's name or might imply a business name, place name, trade name, or a similar form of naming. However, a schema name of "PersonName" is descriptive, depicts a context, and is generally intuitive.

At the physical level, a W3C XML Schema is a Unicode-encoded text file (most often as UTF-8 or an ASCII text file). The external name of that file must conform to the constraints of the file management and operating system (e.g., maximum character length, exclusion of special characters, character case, and support for white space). As a general guideline, file names should be no longer than 32 characters. Although somewhat arbitrary, a file name length of 32 characters is supported by most server-based operating systems (such as Windows). If the platform on which the subschema will be stored has a more restrictive maximum length, it should be used.

As to white space, some operating systems allow blanks or spaces within a file name. However, it is recommended that all white space should be removed. Also, where possible the file name should use mixed-case characters (e.g., applied in the form of camel case as described for element and attribute taxonomy). When combined, these naming techniques will result in descriptive and intuitive file names for W3C XML Schemas.

Recommendation:

The external file name of a reusable W3C XML Schema (subschema) should include a version. The version may be prefixed or suffixed depending upon enterprise standards.

Recommendation:

Reusable W3C XML subschemas should include some form of classification or type in the name (e.g., "STD," "CODES," or "TYPES").

Version management is rarely the responsibility of the data architect. However, it plays a significant role in reuse engineering as part of the schema name (the external file name). As with any technology asset, evolution and change will be experienced. Although the intent of reuse engineering is to develop a reusable schema structure that is also an enterprise standard, over time, modifications will be required. Being able to identify different versions from the external file name becomes critical. During the reuse harvesting process the developer or data architect will need to easily determine the current version of a candidate schema. Including version identification as part of the external schema name is of significant value. The scheme used for versioning (e.g., numbers, characters, and combinations of version and release) should adhere to enterprise standards. The version should be included as part of the external file name (usually as a prefix or suffix).

In addition to the version and the schema name, it may be valuable to describe the schema by a classification or type. The most common types of reusable W3C XML

Schemas are either standard structures, sets of code values, or data types. The ability to identify the type of reusable schema can simplify the reuse harvesting process. As examples, each of the different schema types could be classified as one of the following:

- STD—representing enterprise standard structures

- CODES—representing enumeration lists of standard code values

- TYPES—representing enterprise standard data types

The classification for each schema type should be included in the schema external file name. When developers or data architects are searching for reusable schemas, they can limit their search to a specific type. Terminating the W3C XML Schema file name is the file type or extension (when supported by the file management and operating system). The recommended file type or extension for a W3C XML Schema is "xsd" (Fig. 8.11).

Unlike traditional data modeling, XML transactions used for data exchanges between systems can include denormalized data, abstract data element names, and even duplicate data. When the objectives of the transaction are a combination of data exchange between disparate systems and enterprise integration, the ability to describe the transaction content in different forms, by different names, and with a structure

Figure 8.11

Example of a format for (external) W3C XML Schema file names.

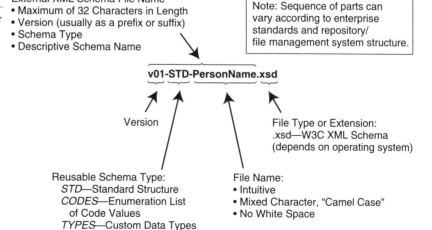

External XML Schema File Name
- Maximum of 32 Characters in Length
- Version (usually as a prefix or suffix)
- Schema Type
- Descriptive Schema Name

Note: Sequence of parts can vary according to enterprise standards and repository/file management system structure.

v01-STD-PersonName.xsd

Version

File Type or Extension:
.xsd—W3C XML Schema
(depends on operating system)

Reusable Schema Type:
STD—Standard Structure
CODES—Enumeration List
of Code Values
TYPES—Custom Data Types

File Name:
- Intuitive
- Mixed Character, "Camel Case"
- No White Space

that can be easily transformed into different formats is requisite. An example is when data of the same general context will be exchanged between different systems but with variation in how those data will be used and processed. To support the varied use and processing of these target applications, it may be necessary to describe multiple structures or formats for the same data. The data architect is challenged with extending traditional data architecture skills to address this paradigm.

Consider a transaction carrying a customer's name. The person name data used by an order processing system and a customer relationship management system may need to support different structures and processes. The order processing system may require a customer's complete name (i.e., the concatenated set of all name parts). Typical uses of this data structure include order correspondence and documentation, the "Address To" line of the order delivery information, and use for customer contact. Alternatively, a G-CRM or marketing application may require a highly variable structure to utilize individual parts of the customer's name as well as the complete name. This type of processing can include sorting and grouping of customer data according to a sequenced set of name parts (Fig. 8.12).

Recommendation:

When used to describe a transaction for data exchange or enterprise integration, a reusable W3C XML Schema should incorporate several different structures and formats to address the potential for varied use and different application processes.

To address both types of person name processing, a single reusable W3C XML Schema should be engineered to incorporate two different name structures. One structure defined to the schema is a single data element for a complete person name. The other is a decomposed, flexible structure of individual data elements for the parts of a globally diverse name. If both structures are defined as optional rather than mandatory, this single schema can be used to describe and constrain different XML documents and transactions (Listing 8.1).

Listing 8.1

W3C XML Schema for different forms of person name data.

```
<?xml version="1.0" encoding="UTF-8"?>
<xs:schema xmlns:xs="http://www.w3.org/2001/XMLSchema">

    <xs:element name="CustomerData">
      <xs:complexType>
```

Listing 8.1 *Continued*

```
      <xs:sequence>
        <xs:element ref="CustomerName"/>
      </xs:sequence>
    </xs:complexType>
  </xs:element>

  <xs:element name="CustomerName">
    <xs:complexType>
      <xs:sequence>
        <xs:element ref="PersonNameComplete" minOccurs="0"
        maxOccurs="1"/>
        <xs:group ref="PersonNameParts" minOccurs="0"
        maxOccurs="1"/>
      </xs:sequence>
    </xs:complexType>
  </xs:element>

  <xs:element name="PersonNameComplete"
  type="PersonNameCompleteTYPE"/>

  <xs:group name="PersonNameParts">
    <xs:sequence>
      <xs:element name="PersonNamePrefix" type="PersonNamePartTYPE"
      minOccurs="0"/>
      <xs:element ref="PersonNamePart" minOccurs="1"
      maxOccurs="unbounded"/>
      <xs:element name="PersonNameSuffix" type="PersonNamePartTYPE"
      minOccurs="0"/>
    </xs:sequence>
  </xs:group>

  <xs:element name="PersonNamePart">
    <xs:complexType>
      <xs:simpleContent>
        <xs:extension base="PersonNamePartTYPE">
          <xs:attribute name="sequence" use="required"
          type="xs:byte"/>
          <xs:attribute name="type" type="PersonNamePartTypeCODE"/>
        </xs:extension>
      </xs:simpleContent>
    </xs:complexType>
  </xs:element>
```

Listing 8.1 *Continued*

```
<xs:simpleType name="PersonNameCompleteTYPE">
  <xs:restriction base="xs:string">
    <xs:maxLength value="80"/>
  </xs:restriction>
</xs:simpleType>

<xs:simpleType name="PersonNamePartTYPE">
  <xs:restriction base="xs:string">
    <xs:maxLength value="20"/>
  </xs:restriction>
</xs:simpleType>

<xs:simpleType name="PersonNamePartTypeCODE">
  <xs:restriction base="xs:string">
    <xs:enumeration value="Family"/>
    <xs:enumeration value="Last"/>
    <xs:enumeration value="Given"/>
    <xs:enumeration value="First"/>
    <xs:enumeration value="Surname"/>
    <xs:enumeration value="Additional"/>
    <xs:enumeration value="Middle"/>
    <xs:enumeration value="Religious"/>
    <xs:enumeration value="Other"/>
  </xs:restriction>
</xs:simpleType>

</xs:schema>
```

When combined with a prototype XML document, the potential for varied use and different types of application processing can also help to identify applicable XML structure models and architectural container forms. The element used to contain the complete name combined with the set of name part elements is a good fit for a vertical structure model. Name part elements should also include attributes for sequence (the preferred order in which name parts should occur), as well as a type for each name part, which implies a horizontal structure model. The ability to reuse a person name structure in different contexts (e.g., customer order processing, employee, and customer contact) infers that this W3C XML Schema is a good fit for a component structure model. Additionally, the data types and allowable values of the name elements could also

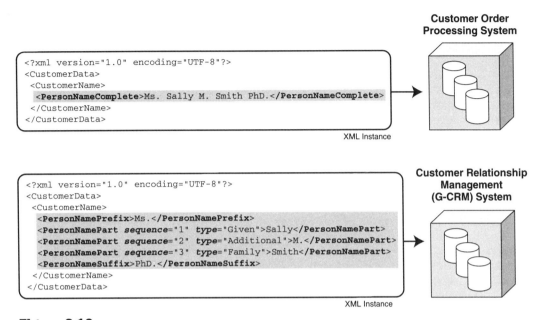

Figure 8.12

Different XML transactions containing person name data.

become enterprise metadata standards that are implemented as other modular component structure models. When considered in total, the person name schema is an excellent candidate for a hybrid structure model, which incorporates advantageous characteristics of the other model types.

Customer relationship management applications will often need to sort, group, and select from customer data by customer name. Because full names may be specified in varied form, using a complete person name element is largely inadequate for this type of processing. Name prefixes and suffixes are rarely used for sorting and may complicate grouping of like names. As a result, prefixes and suffixes are a good fit for specifically named rigid container forms. Individual name parts present an effective use of name data for sort, group, and select processes. Processing names of international customers, for which the number, sequence, and type of name parts can vary widely, requires an abstract container form that can dynamically expand and contract to fit culturally diverse name formats (Fig. 8.13).

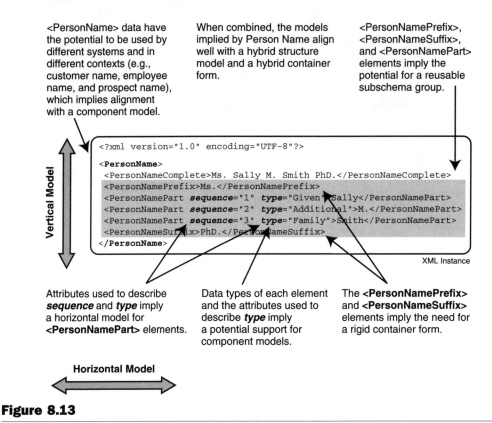

<PersonName> data have the potential to be used by different systems and in different contexts (e.g., customer name, employee name, and prospect name), which implies alignment with a component model.

When combined, the models implied by Person Name align well with a hybrid structure model and a hybrid container form.

<PersonNamePrefix>, <PersonNameSuffix>, and <PersonNamePart> elements imply the potential for a reusable subschema group.

```
<?xml version="1.0" encoding="UTF-8"?>

<PersonName>
 <PersonNameComplete>Ms. Sally M. Smith PhD.</PersonNameComplete>
 <PersonNamePrefix>Ms.</PersonNamePrefix>
 <PersonNamePart sequence="1" type="Given">Sally</PersonNamePart>
 <PersonNamePart sequence="2" type="Additional">M.</PersonNamePart>
 <PersonNamePart sequence="3" type="Family">Smith</PersonNamePart>
 <PersonNameSuffix>PhD.</PersonNameSuffix>
</PersonName>
```

Vertical Model

XML Instance

Attributes used to describe *sequence* and *type* imply a horizontal model for <PersonNamePart> elements.

Data types of each element and the attributes used to describe *type* imply a potential support for component models.

The **<PersonNamePrefix>** and **<PersonNameSuffix>** elements imply the need for a rigid container form.

Horizontal Model

Figure 8.13

Structure models and container forms implied by person name data.

Custom data types and enumerated lists of standard code values also present the opportunity to further decompose the person name schema. Subschemas to represent the enterprise standard person name structure, data types specific to person name data, and applicable standard code values (e.g., Person Name Part "types"), are all excellent candidates for reuse (Fig. 8.14).

The <PersonNameComplete> element is defined by a string data type with a maximum allowable length. The <PersonNamePrefix>, <PersonNamePart>, and <PersonNameSuffix> elements are also defined by a string data type but with a shorter maximum length. Both types are declared as simpleTypes and are included in a subschema that contains all data types for person name data. Similarly, the "type" attribute of the <PersonNamePart> element is described by a set of

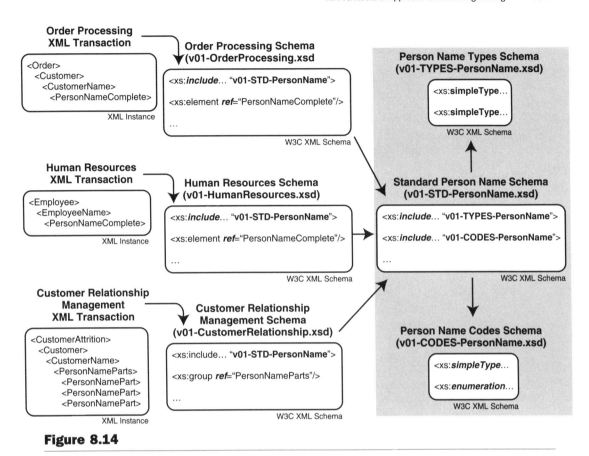

Figure 8.14

Reference of component subschemas.

standard code values. These values are declared as an enumeration list and are defined to a subschema containing all codes and allowable values for person name data. The result is a set of three component schemas. The Person Name Standard Structure Schema references and uses both the Person Name Types and Person Name Codes schemas. Each of the schemas can be reused in whole or in part:

- Person name structure schema (Listing 8.2)
- Person name types schema (Listing 8.3)
- Person name codes schema (Listing 8.4)

Listing 8.2

W3C XML Schema for a person name structure.

```xml
<?xml version="1.0" encoding="UTF-8"?>
<xs:schema xmlns:xs="http://www.w3.org/2001/XMLSchema">

    <xs:include schemaLocation="v01-TYPES-PersonName.xsd"/>
    <xs:include schemaLocation="v01-CODES-PersonName.xsd"/>

    <xs:element name="PersonNameComplete"
    type="PersonNameCompleteTYPE"/>
    <xs:element name="PersonNameParts">
      <xs:complexType>
        <xs:sequence>
          <xs:group ref="PersonNamePartsGroup"/>
        </xs:sequence>
      </xs:complexType>
    </xs:element>

    <xs:group name="PersonNamePartsGroup">
      <xs:sequence>
        <xs:element name="PersonNamePrefix"
        type="PersonNamePartTYPE" minOccurs="0"/>
        <xs:element ref="PersonNamePart" minOccurs="1"
        maxOccurs="unbounded"/>
        <xs:element name="PersonNameSuffix"
        type="PersonNamePartTYPE" minOccurs="0"/>
      </xs:sequence>
    </xs:group>

    <xs:element name="PersonNamePart">
      <xs:complexType>
        <xs:simpleContent>
          <xs:extension base="PersonNamePartTYPE">
            <xs:attribute name="sequence"
            use="required" type="xs:byte"/>
            <xs:attribute name="type" type="PersonNamePartTypeCODE"/>
          </xs:extension>
        </xs:simpleContent>
      </xs:complexType>
    </xs:element>

</xs:schema>
```

Listing 8.3

W3C XML Schema for
person name types.

```xml
<?xml version="1.0" encoding="UTF-8"?>
<xs:schema
xmlns:xs="http://www.w3.org/2001/XMLSchema">

    <xs:simpleType name="PersonNameCompleteTYPE">
      <xs:restriction base="xs:string">
        <xs:maxLength value="80"/>
      </xs:restriction>
    </xs:simpleType>

    <xs:simpleType name="PersonNamePartTYPE">
      <xs:restriction base="xs:string">
        <xs:maxLength value="20"/>
      </xs:restriction>
    </xs:simpleType>

</xs:schema>
```

Listing 8.4

W3C XML Schema for
descriptive person
name codes.

```xml
<?xml version="1.0" encoding="UTF-8"?>
<xs:schema xmlns:xs=
"http://www.w3.org/2001/XMLSchema">

    <xs:simpleType name="PersonNamePartTypeCODE">
      <xs:restriction base="xs:string">
        <xs:enumeration value="Family"/>
        <xs:enumeration value="Last"/>
        <xs:enumeration value="Given"/>
        <xs:enumeration value="First"/>
        <xs:enumeration value="Surname"/>
        <xs:enumeration value="Additional"/>
        <xs:enumeration value="Middle"/>
        <xs:enumeration value="Religious"/>
        <xs:enumeration value="Other"/>
      </xs:restriction>
    </xs:simpleType>

</xs:schema>
```

Syntax for Referencing a Component W3C XML Schema

For a W3C XML Schema to be reused, it must be referenced by another schema. As previously described, the process of referencing a schema is conceptually similar to the COBOL Copybook include syntax. When the primary W3C XML Schema is validated during the parsing process, the parser will locate referenced subschemas as resources, include the declarations of the referenced subschemas, and then resolve referenced constructs. Subschema references are not limited to a single nesting layer or reference. A subschema can reference another subschema, which can reference another subschema, and so on. There is no specifically documented limit to the number of nested schema references, but caution is advised. Significant nesting has the potential to slow the parsing process. The W3C XML Schema syntax for referencing one schema (e.g., a subschema) from within another can take on any of three syntactical forms:

- Include

- Redefine

- Import

Recommendation:

When the primary or referencing W3C XML Schema is of a single context (e.g., namespace), the "include" syntax is the desired form for referencing an externally defined subschema.

When the primary W3C XML Schema is representative of a single context, the preferred method of referencing a subschema is to use the "include" syntax. In this case, the included schema becomes part of the overall namespace of the primary or referencing schema (e.g., the "master" schema). When the primary W3C XML Schema is composed of several contexts and the desired subschema reference must match one of those contexts, the "import" syntax may be a better fit. The import syntax targets a specific context using a namespace to provide uniqueness. The "redefine" syntax is similar to the include syntax (e.g., targeting a single context and namespace). However, the redefine syntax includes a referenced subschema and allows for modification of referenced constructs. Regardless of the chosen syntax, references to desired subschema constructs must be made and resolved.

The include syntax incorporates both a reference to the name and location of the desired subschema and one or more internal references to components declared in the subschema (Fig. 8.15). The W3C XML Schema syntax for a schema include is simple and intuitive. The primary

The **<include>** element informs the parser of a requirement to include another externally defined subschema.

The **schemaLocation** attribute of the **<include>** element names the subschema and optionally identifies the location (the default is a relative reference to the subschema as a resource in the same location).

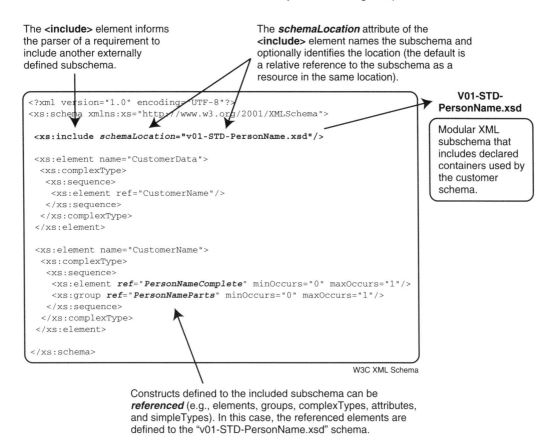

V01-STD-PersonName.xsd

Modular XML subschema that includes declared containers used by the customer schema.

```
<?xml version="1.0" encoding="UTF-8"?>
<xs:schema xmlns:xs="http://www.w3.org/2001/XMLSchema">

 <xs:include schemaLocation="v01-STD-PersonName.xsd"/>

 <xs:element name="CustomerData">
  <xs:complexType>
   <xs:sequence>
    <xs:element ref="CustomerName"/>
   </xs:sequence>
  </xs:complexType>
 </xs:element>

 <xs:element name="CustomerName">
  <xs:complexType>
   <xs:sequence>
    <xs:element ref="PersonNameComplete" minOccurs="0" maxOccurs="1"/>
    <xs:group ref="PersonNameParts" minOccurs="0" maxOccurs="1"/>
   </xs:sequence>
  </xs:complexType>
 </xs:element>

</xs:schema>
```

W3C XML Schema

Constructs defined to the included subschema can be **referenced** (e.g., elements, groups, complexTypes, attributes, and simpleTypes). In this case, the referenced elements are defined to the "v01-STD-PersonName.xsd" schema.

Figure 8.15

W3C XML Schema include syntax.

XML Schema uses an "include" element in the primary or referencing schema (e.g., <xs:include>). The "schemaLocation" attribute of the include element is valued with the name and location of a referenced subschema. The value of the schemaLocation attribute can be a relative resource location or an absolute resource location. A *relative resource location* requires that the referenced subschema is located in the same place or directory as the primary or referencing schema. An *absolute resource location* not only names the referenced subschema as a resource but also identifies a specific location for the subschema (e.g., the server, the directory, the node path, or a similar location of the referenced

Figure 8.16

W3C XML Schema import and redefine syntax.

XML Schema "Import" Syntax

```
<?xml version="1.0" encoding="UTF-8"?>
<xs:schema xmlns:xs="http://www.w3.org/2001/XMLSchema">

   <xs:import schemaLocation="schema-location-goes-here"
        namespace="namespace-goes-here"/>


</xs:schema>
```
W3C XML Schema

XML Schema "Redefine" Syntax

```
<?xml version="1.0" encoding="UTF-8"?>
<xs:schema xmlns:xs="http://www.w3.org/2001/XMLSchema">

   <xs:redefine schemaLocation="schema-location-goes-here">

   ... revised complexTypes, simpleTypes, groups go here
   ...
   ...

   </xs:redefine>

</xs:schema>
```
W3C XML Schema

subschema). During the validation process, the parser identifies the include element, interrogates the schemaLocation attribute, searches for the named resource, and includes or brings in the referenced schema content.

Although the W3C XML Schema include syntax is an effective method for reusing other W3C XML Schemas by reference, caution is advised. If the content and context of the referenced subschema are unknown, there is the potential to include constructs of the referenced schema that are not applicable. Also, a referenced W3C XML Schema may reference and include other W3C XML Schemas and so on. This could introduce an inefficient assembly and processing chain for the parser.

The W3C XML Schema syntax for import and redefine are somewhat similar to include, although the resulting methods of reference are different. The import syntax requires an import element being defined to the primary schema (e.g., <xs:import>). Additionally, schemaLocation and namespace attributes are included. The schemaLocation attribute identifies the location of the referenced subschema. The namespace attribute defines the context. The redefine syntax includes a "redefine" element (e.g., <xs:redefine>) and a schemaLocation attribute. Like the include and import syntax, the schemaLocation attribute identifies the location and name of the referenced subschema. Additionally, the redefine syntax allows specific containers and constructs to be defined differently (Fig. 8.16).

So far, the important data architecture and metadata activities required to engineer flexible, extensible, and reusable W3C XML Schemas have been described. Next we will identify how data architects can leverage their roles, and how these activities will be integrated with the application development process.

9

Design and Engineering for the Data Architect

To this point, the focus has been on applying modeling and architecture principles to XML prototypes and more importantly their representative W3C XML Schemas. In addition to these techniques, a process for schema design and engineering is needed. Given the rapid adoption of XML by the development community, the design and engineering of W3C XML Schemas has to date been somewhat ad hoc. When the decision to use XML has been made, the resulting structures and constraining schemas are often generated from an object-oriented model such as a class diagram. However, the development community may not have the expertise or the time to incorporate rigorous metadata characteristics or to apply critical data standards. Also, the responsibility for schema design and engineering may not have been formally defined, leading to a lack of rigorous metadata and related architectural practices.

The fundamental definition and capabilities of XML need to be considered with any design and engineering process. To repeat, XML is a descriptive metadata language and W3C XML Schemas provide a method of constraining XML content according to structure, organization, and metadata rules. What should be obvious to any practitioner is that effective engineering of a schema requires expertise with metadata and related data architecture disciplines. Without a metadata and data architecture focus, the broad proliferation of nonstandard and ad hoc XML transactions and schemas will be seen, resulting in increased data disparity, integration complexity, and a failure to reduce related technology costs.

Alternatively, the data architect must also recognize that an XML document (e.g., an "instance" that contains data values) is both created and consumed by application programs. The hierarchical nature of an XML document requires a level of development expertise for navigation and processing. This expertise generally lies outside the realm of the data architect and should remain with the development community. Further, there are potential complications associated with the capabilities and strengths of XML. As described earlier, the application of a rich taxonomy can significantly increase the size of an XML document (remember that the "tags" are carried along with the data values in an XML document). Although XML-related technologies will continue to improve over time, the application of XML transactions and processes to mission-critical enterprise applications requires reasonable performance. An effective schema design and engineering process must borrow from traditional development methodologies, adopt best practices from more recent processes (e.g., object-oriented and iterative), and provide for collaboration between technology practitioners rather than distinct separation of responsibilities. Both the data architect and the development community can provide much needed expertise to ensure acceptable performance.

The Design and Engineering Process

The XML design and engineering process incorporates several tasks that borrow from traditional development processes. Initially the schema design process appears to progress through a set of defined steps that are similar to a waterfall methodology. However, to gain acceptance from both the business and technology communities of the enterprise, the process also incorporates rapid application development, with a focus on prototyping, iterative revision, and validation (Fig. 9.1).

Initial XML design and engineering tasks include the identification of data and functional requirements. The activities of identifying, documenting, and validating requirements are fundamentally the same processes used for other application development projects. Also of importance are the identification of data sources and targets. It is the combination of requirements and identification of data sources and targets that guide the initial development of a prototype XML document.

Given that XML will often be used to describe a document, transaction, or message, the "exchange" or "movement" of information

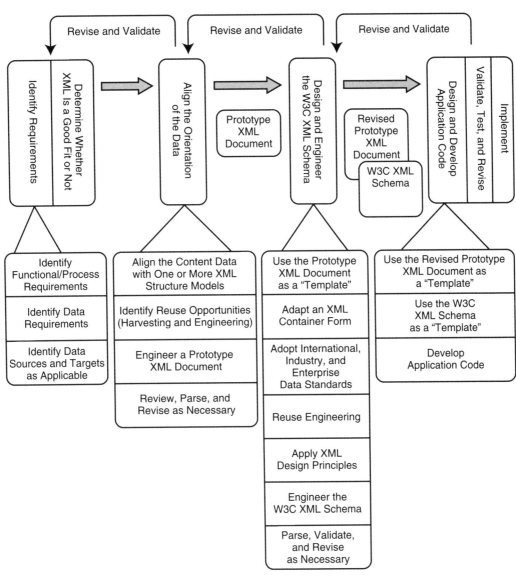

Figure 9.1

The XML design tasks and process.

between a source or origin and one or more destinations or targets is implied. The data sources for an XML transaction can include user key entry, database extracts, application logic, triggered events, or other transactions. The targets of an XML transaction are most often application programs that process or consume the transaction data, application programs that publish or distribute the transaction data, application programs that render or present the transaction data for consumption by an individual, or applications that persist (store) the transaction data.

When the target of an XML transaction and contained data is a persisted data architecture (e.g., in a database or file management system), there are several important considerations. Depending upon the intended use of the transaction, the contained data can be persisted in XML form and syntax. The storage medium for data persisted using XML syntax (e.g., including descriptive containers and following the hierarchical structure of XML) is usually a simple file, a database specifically designed to store XML, or an XML "enabled" database. When the XML structure and the contained data values are not subject to frequent modification, storing data using XML syntax can be an acceptable technique. However, given the current state of database technologies and XML extensions, these situations warrant careful evaluation. It may be more advantageous to leverage the traditional data capabilities and strengths of a database that also includes XML support and extensions for extraction of data values rather than to store the data as an XML-formatted structure. It is expected that like any technology, over time, XML-specific databases and data access utilities will provide many of the same benefits as those of today's relational and object relational databases. However, for now caution is advised.

One obvious difference with traditional development methodologies is the early identification of XML as the best technology choice for describing transaction data. Although XML is a powerful and effective metadata language, there are scenarios in which XML may not be the best technology choice. Traditional methodologies do not usually identify specific technologies until late in the process. Characteristics such as volumetrics, performance, use and type of application processing, and the frequency of an exchange can all introduce complexity. As a result, there should be some method of early validation to determine if XML is a reasonable candidate for application to a project. XML can be validated as a good-fit technology with a criteria checklist or a more rigorous set of evaluation criteria.

Perhaps the most valuable aspect of the XML engineering process is the development of a prototype XML document.[1] In many ways, the process of prototyping is similar to the development of a data model. A prototype can be easily constructed, populated with sample data, and represented in a visual form that is easily understood by project participants. Key activities of the XML prototype development effort include the following:

- Evaluating the data requirements of the project

- Aligning the data requirements with the functional requirements

- Aligning the data requirements with an XML structure model

- Identifying opportunities for reuse (both within and outside the project or system)

- Engineering the prototype structure

- Populating the prototype structure with sample data that closely resembles the final implementation

- Reviewing and revising

A prototype XML document presents a reasonable facsimile of the structure that will be implemented, and it becomes the "template" for engineering a corresponding schema. As part of the prototyping process, a structure model and an architectural container form will be applied. The characteristics of the contained data combined with the intended processing of the XML transaction will guide the selection of the most appropriate container form. Application of architectural container forms promotes architecture principles of flexibility and reuse. Also of importance are alignment with data standards and reuse engineering. Where applicable, the rigorous application of data standards will help to ensure a high level of data quality and a limitation in the number of transformations or translations of the transaction.

To recognize and exploit reuse, enterprise standard component W3C XML Schemas that describe data required by the project should

---

[1] Bean J. XML Globalization and Best Practices. Active Education, Colorado, U.S., 2001.

be incorporated by reference (reuse harvesting). This activity not only promotes the proliferation of standards by using common schemas, but also reduces development costs by avoiding redevelopment of new schemas. As new W3C XML Schemas are engineered, opportunities to externalize constraints and structures as other reusable subschemas are also valuable (reuse engineering).

W3C XML Schemas are then "verified" by validation to the prototype XML document. Schemas also require review with the development community to ensure that they are intuitive, flexible, and navigable. Although the most flexible design techniques can be applied to a schema, they are of little benefit if the XML document cannot be readily processed and consumed. Revisions are reapplied to the structure of the prototype XML document to ensure that the originating data and functional requirements are effectively resolved. Upon acceptance, the prototype XML document, resulting W3C XML Schemas, and the functional requirements drive the development of application logic.

Absent from the described XML process are the traditional activities of data modeling, database design, and object modeling. These activities have not been intentionally eliminated and are addressed through conventional development tasks. As described in previous chapters, there are a number of synergies between traditional data architecture practices and the design and engineering of W3C XML Schemas. Data modeling and database design processes accommodate requirements related to the extraction of data from and storage in database architectures. Process and object models formalize the function to data relationship and facilitate the development of application logic. As defined, the XML process includes a number of tasks. The challenge is determining how to effectively apply enterprise resources and expertise to complete these tasks.

Responsibilities of the Data Architect

One controversial and largely unresolved topic in XML applications is differentiation of the responsibilities of the data architect vs those of the developer. The premise of this book is that XML and W3C XML Schemas are fundamentally data and the metadata that describe them. An XML document is a file that contains data values. The file represents a document, transaction, or message that is created and processed by an application program or similar utility process. A W3C XML Schema describes the rules and constraints that are applied to a referencing XML document. Similarly, a database contains data values and is populated and processed by one or more application programs. The metadata characteristics and rules of the database are defined by the model from which it was generated and the managing system catalog of the implemented data architecture. In both cases, there is an obvious focus on data and metadata, which are traditional responsibilities of the data architect.

Historically, most organizations give the responsibility for data modeling and database design to the data architect. The development community is responsible for the engineering of application logic to extract, insert, modify, delete, exchange, and process data. The design and engineering of W3C XML Schemas are similar processes, but a more effective process incorporates a collaborative approach. When the process has been completed and the technology is implemented, the XML documents implemented as "production" are created, maintained, and processed by one or more applications.

Some organizations may elect to specifically assign development of a prototype XML document to the development community. In some cases, this may be an effective practice. However, a prototype XML document also incorporates two forms of metadata: taxonomy and structure. A taxonomy is applied to the formalization of XML element and attribute tag names, whereas the structure represents the organization of data containers and their relationships.

Recommendation:

It is recommended that the W3C XML Schema design and engineering process should be a collaborative effort. The data architect and the developer should both participate in the development of a prototype XML document and the corresponding W3C XML Schemas.

It is therefore proposed that the development of a prototype XML document should be a collaborative effort between the data architect and the developer. The data architect will ensure that the necessary data containers are included to meet the data requirements and that these containers align with known data sources and targets. The data architect will also organize collections of related data containers and develop a descriptive tag name for each data container. Additionally, the data architect will identify opportunities to apply previously defined standards (a form of reuse harvesting) and develop new standard structures with the intent of being reusable. The developer will ensure that the prototype XML document is intuitive and navigable by an application program and can be processed in a manner that addresses the functional requirements. The developer will also provide guidance in the areas of performance and complexity, whereas the data architect will focus on flexibility, standards, and reuse.

As the design and engineering process progresses to the development of W3C XML Schemas, the data architect assumes greater responsibility. Of significance is the identification and formalization of metadata characteristics and rules for each data container of the prototype XML document. These rules will be implemented as combinations of data types, facets, and relationships between elements (e.g., complexTypes and groups). To engineer the W3C XML Schema, the data architect also needs a reasonable level of expertise with W3C XML Schema syntax. If the enterprise has adopted the use of XML-enabled design and development tools, it is likely that an initial draft schema can be generated from a software tool or utility (e.g., similar to forward engineering), which provides much of the baseline syntax. The data architect will then enhance, extend, and modify the schema as necessary. The developer will review the metadata rules and constraints to determine the applicable logic required during the parser validation process and actions for resolution of parser violations.

The data architect will also apply architectural principles such as structure models, container forms, and reuse practices. Depending upon the complexity of the schema, the application of an architectural container form could result in residual modifications to the prototype XML document structure. In this case, the developer will provide guidance to ensure that the modified XML document is still intuitive and navigable. In the area of schema reuse, the data architect will incorporate references to applicable standard subschemas. Additionally, the data architect will identify opportunities for reuse engineering and externalize those structures as new subordinate W3C XML Schemas. Schemas and subschemas are initially tested by parser validation to the prototype XML document.

After the W3C XML Schemas are accepted, the developer takes primary responsibility for further development tasks (e.g., development of application logic). The combination of the prototype XML document, W3C XML Schemas, and functional requirements will guide the development of application logic. If during the performance of these tasks additional modifications to either the prototype XML document or the W3C XML Schemas are required, the data architect will participate in review and revision (Fig. 9.2).

In brief, the recommended XML design and engineering process places a greater degree of early design responsibility on the data architect and shifts the role of the developer to a combination of consultant,

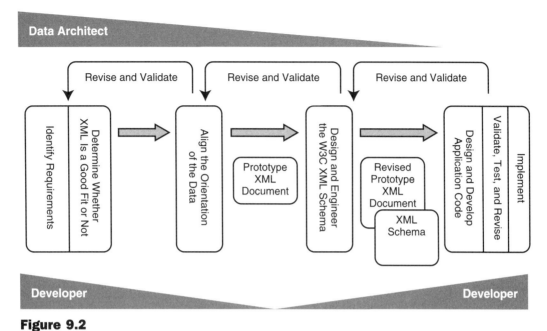

Figure 9.2

Responsibility for XML design tasks and process.

advisor, and user. The responsibility for later design and engineering tasks moves to the developer (especially tasks related to development of application logic). However, both data architects and developers participate through much of the process as collaborators, reviewers, and consultants. This collaboration will help to ensure that the XML document produced by the application program is efficient, interoperable, flexible, reusable, and complete. It will also ensure that the expertise of the data architect was realized in the form of highly standardized and reusable W3C XML Schemas.

The Challenges of Complexity

Regardless of the development methodology or process, there are potential complexities and risks associated with the use of XML. As a metadata practitioner and specialist, the data architect applies best practices to ensure that each XML document (i.e., document, transaction, or message) and schema will resolve the requirements of the project and will be designed in a manner that promotes flexibility, reuse, and standards. Similarly, the application developer will design the business logic and engineer the application program to resolve the functional requirements of the project. The developer's effort is typically focused on functionality, performance, and rapid delivery. Both sets of practices, techniques, and goals are intended to produce the best possible solution for a set of defined requirements. However, the characteristics of an applied technology such as XML can also introduce a level of complexity.

The best designed and engineered XML documents and corresponding W3C XML Schemas are of little value if they cannot be accurately and effectively processed. Alternatively, an XML document and schema that are developed without a focus on flexibility, reuse, and standards will exhibit little if any potential for reuse, will need on-going maintenance, and can result in the proliferation of inaccurately represented data. Given that the most common use of an XML document is to exchange, share, or move data, there is an implicit need to ensure that data architecture best practices should be applied. The W3C XML Schema design and engineering processes should be collaborative, and there are several areas for which the developer can provide much needed advice and guidance.

Structural and Navigational Complexity

One area of complexity and potential risk is the structure of the XML document. Previously, emphasis has been placed on the design and engineering of an XML document that is flexible (i.e., can dynamically expand or contract to meet the characteristics of the contained data). Flexible XML document structures implement combinations of nesting and abstraction (allowing for like-named repeating elements as children of a parent element). Parent element containers provide a form of context or scope for their participating child element containers. Repeating child element containers are named in the abstract and inherit the context of their parent. Depending upon the intended use and processing of the XML transaction combined with the variability of the data, this is an effective architectural approach.

Recommendation:

As a general recommendation, the maximum depth or levels of element nesting for transaction-oriented content should be around 10 levels.

One area of concern is the depth to which XML element containers are nested. Although there may be parser-specific limitations, the XML specification (W3C) does not specify a maximum limit to the number of levels or "depth" for which elements can be nested. As a result, the XML document could be engineered to include parent-to-child nesting of element containers of 20, 30, or more levels. When significant levels of nested elements are allowed, program navigation becomes exceedingly complex. Nesting of repeating XML elements is a powerful technique but should be used within reason. A common sense limit should be applied to the nesting of elements. As a general recommendation, the maximum depth or levels of element nesting for transaction-oriented content should be around 10 levels.

Another area of navigational complexity is that associated with repeating elements. When the context of a repeating element cannot be determined by either its location in the XML document (i.e., its parent element), its taxonomy, or other methods of classification (such as a namespace), the element is subject to processing ambiguity. Also, although the schema can apply cardinality constraints (minOccurs and

Technique:

When the number of repeating elements within a parent element group is important to navigation logic, add an attribute at the level of the parent element to contain a value noting the number of repeating element occurrences. However, be aware that additional application logic to both determine a value and insert it into the attribute as well as logic to later interrogate the attribute will be required.

maxOccurs), there is no intrinsic method for notifying the parsing application of how may repetitions of an element occur in an XML document instance. Consider an XML document that contains several international postal addresses. The number of street address lines within each postal address can vary from one to several. Intrinsic parser functionality such as the "getElementsByTagName" method can be invoked to return all street address lines, but there is no property of that method to describe how many street address line elements exist. Application logic would be required to deal with variations.

One design technique that is useful is to include a user-defined attribute for the parent or owning element of repeating element containers that contains a value for the number of repeating element instances. The parsing application could include logic to interrogate the value of the attribute and determine the maximum boundary before navigating through repeating element instances. In addition, each repeating element could include a user-defined attribute to denote intended sequence or order. The order of elements as found in the XML document should be predetermined. However, there may be processing-specific variations in order or sequence (Fig. 9.3).

The use of user-defined attributes in the previous example is an effective design technique. However, there are potential risks and complexities. First, an attribute describing the number of repeating elements is a form of metadata (i.e., the maximum degree of implemented cardinality). With this technique the parsing application must include logic to identify and interrogate the attribute. Also, carrying a similar attribute with each repeating element adds to the overall size of the document and requires application logic for interrogation and processing. Before adding attributes to the prototype XML document and the W3C XML Schema, consult with the application developer. The developer

Figure 9.3

Using attributes to help resolve navigational complexity.

The **AddressLineCount** attribute of the <AddressLines> parent element contains the maximum number of repeating <AddressLine> elements.

```xml
<?xml version="1.0" encoding="UTF-8"?>
<ExampleCustomers>
 <Customer CustomerID="P123456" CustomerType="Customer-Prospect"
  Source="List 01-02-03">
  <CustomerAddresses>
   <Address AddressType="Residence-Primary" AddressNo="1">
    <AddressLines AddressLineCount="3">
     <AddressLine Sequence="1">62789 N. Shadow Drive</AddressLine>
     <AddressLine Sequence="2">Building 23</AddressLine>
     <AddressLine Sequence="3">Apt. 236</AddressLine>
    </AddressLines>
    <AddressCity>Chicago</AddressCity>
    <AddressRegion>
     <StateUSAAbbrev StateName="Illinois">IL</StateUSAAbbrev>
    </AddressRegion>
    <AddressPostalCode>60699-0001</AddressPostalCode>
    <AddressCountry CountryCode="USA"
     CountryNo="840">USA</AddressCountry>
   </Address>
  </CustomerAddresses>
 </Customer>
</ExampleCustomers>
```

XML Instance

The **Sequence** attribute identifies the intended sequence or order of each repeating <AddressLine> element.

should understand the intended purpose and determine what logic will be necessary to both value and interrogate the attribute.

Another potential area of structural complexity is seen with strictly horizontal structure models. Horizontal structure models are primarily composed of XML attribute containers rather than elements. What should be obvious is that a horizontal model is not completely devoid of elements, given that attributes cannot exist on their own (e.g., an XML attribute container must be defined to an element). When the XML document is parsed, XML attribute containers become child nodes of their owning element. Conceptually, they also contain data describing what should be implied properties of the owning element node. Given the hierarchical nature of an XML document, the attributes defined to an element are logically all "siblings." They exist at the same level of the hierarchy.

Recommendation:

As a general recommendation, try to avoid strictly horizontal structure models unless there is an overall size restriction for the XML document or the XML document represents nothing other than a simple relational database extract.

A limitation of attributes is that they cannot be defined to repeat. As a result, multiple attributes defined to the same owning element must be named uniquely and cannot dynamically expand as new containers are required. Navigating through a large number of sibling attributes can also introduce a degree of complexity. If the parsing application is selectively processing different attributes of an owning element node (rather than all attributes of that node), it must be "aware" of the intended content of each attribute. The name of the attribute acts as a form of identification, and the parsing application must "seek out" attribute nodes that either match those of specific business logic or that map to the attributes of a defining object class.

If a horizontal XML structure model includes a predefined number of attributes for a set of similar or related data values and a new attribute is later required, modifications to the XML document, W3C XML Schema, and the processing application logic will most likely be required. Although each of the attributes could be defined as optional, the structure would not be able to expand based upon the dynamics of the data. Additionally, each of the defined attributes would require a unique name. Methods to expose attributes and attribute data values are provided by most parsers, but these methods do not relieve the processing application from having to individually process (or process by class) the attribute data (Fig. 9.4).

The most valuable overall recommendation for avoiding structural complexity is to design and engineer XML documents and schemas that are simple, intuitive, navigable, flexible, reusable, and standardized.

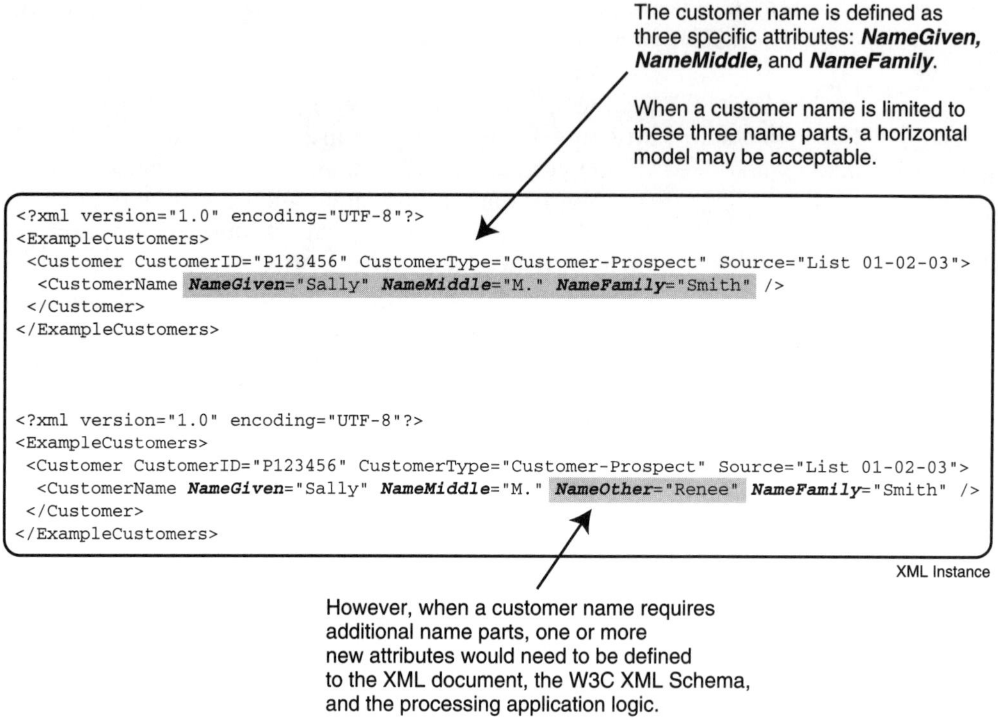

The customer name is defined as three specific attributes: *NameGiven, NameMiddle,* and *NameFamily.*

When a customer name is limited to these three name parts, a horizontal model may be acceptable.

```xml
<?xml version="1.0" encoding="UTF-8"?>
<ExampleCustomers>
 <Customer CustomerID="P123456" CustomerType="Customer-Prospect" Source="List 01-02-03">
  <CustomerName NameGiven="Sally" NameMiddle="M." NameFamily="Smith" />
 </Customer>
</ExampleCustomers>



<?xml version="1.0" encoding="UTF-8"?>
<ExampleCustomers>
 <Customer CustomerID="P123456" CustomerType="Customer-Prospect" Source="List 01-02-03">
  <CustomerName NameGiven="Sally" NameMiddle="M." NameOther="Renee" NameFamily="Smith" />
 </Customer>
</ExampleCustomers>
```

XML Instance

However, when a customer name requires additional name parts, one or more new attributes would need to be defined to the XML document, the W3C XML Schema, and the processing application logic.

Figure 9.4

The dangers of attributes in expanding horizontal models.

Document Size

The size of an XML document presents an interesting challenge. Regardless of form or protocol, most transaction data are exchanged or moved across a network. The performance characteristics of the network can significantly impact the ability to exchange and process large amounts of data. As a transaction increases in overall size (i.e., size as determined by character count or the file size in bytes), the time required to send and receive the transaction also increases.

Another challenge related to the size of an XML document is application of the parsing process. DOM parsers generate an in-memory model of an XML document structure and its contents. As the size of the XML document increases, so does the resulting memory footprint.

If the XML document size exceeds available memory, the parser will resort to alternative memory assignment such as temporary disk paging or in rare cases parsing may fail.

One of the greatest advantages of using XML to describe the content of a document, transaction, or message is the application of self-describing data containers. When combined with a rich and descriptive taxonomy, the contents of an XML document are intuitive. However, the self-describing nature of an XML document comes at a cost. Descriptive element and attribute names (i.e., tags) are carried within the XML document, transaction, or message along with the data values. If the element and attribute names become overly verbose, the overall size of the XML document, transaction, or message increases.

Recommendation:

Overall document size can have an effect on network and parsing application performance. Estimates comparing the character counts of XML document element and attribute tag names to the character counts of contained data values should be evaluated. If the "tag-to-data ratio" exceeds a reasonable limit, the use of XML should be reconsidered.

A limitation to the size of an XML document should not prohibit the application of a rich taxonomy. However, the taxonomy should include reasonable limits for element and attribute name lengths. A technique to compare effective taxonomy vs document size weighs the character count of element and attribute names to the character count of the contained data. When the character counts of the element and attribute names are excessive compared with the character counts of the data values, the transaction is carrying significantly more metadata than data. The effectiveness of XML then comes into question. If the ratio of container name to data value size exceeds a threshold, the use of XML should be evaluated. This comparison is expressed as the "tag-to-data ratio."

Obviously the number of repeating instances within an XML document, the network bandwidth characteristics, and the use of compression technologies can all dramatically affect document size. Also, some character counts are highly variable depending on the nature of the contained data and may not be known until after the XML document and schema have already been engineered. When possible, estimates and averaging using the prototype XML document should be used.

Derived and Redundant Data

Traditional data architecture practices include a significant focus on the process of normalization and as a result definitions of derived and redundant data are avoided. There are several rules that guide the development of a normalized data model or database as well as different interpretations of these rules. The first three normalization rules are those most often referenced and applied. The first normalization rule can be interpreted as "all nonkey attributes should be dependent upon the key." This rule implies that every collection of data should be identified by a unique identifier or primary key. The second normalization rule notes that when the "key" is composed of multiple parts (e.g., a composite or aggregate key), "nonkey attributes should be dependent upon the entire key." The second normalization rule is really self-explanatory. It states that when an identifier or primary key is composed of a combination of data values, reference to or dependence on that identifier must consider all of its component parts. The third normalization rule states that "nonkey attributes should be dependent upon the key, the entire key (i.e., all parts of a composite key), and nothing else." This rule implies that nonkey data should not depend on nonkey data or other types of identifiers other than the primary key.

In simple terms, application of these normalization rules will result in a data structure in which

- Every data element should have a formal dependence on an identifier of some type.

- Multiple data elements representing an identifier are always considered in their entirety.

- Data that repeat within the scope of a particular context will be moved to separate structures with a relationship that incorporates multiple degrees of cardinality.

- Derived data are not easily decomposed and should not be defined by any data element.

As any data architect knows, when data are intended to be persisted (i.e., stored in a database), normalization rules are not only important but also are critical for effective design and processing. There are also technology-specific exceptions to normalization. As you probably know, databases designed to contain a large number of data elements, complex relationships, and very large data structures can also pose potential performance and navigational complexities. Like a database, normalization rules can in many cases also be applied to the structure of a transaction-oriented XML document. There are also potential exceptions. One significant difference between an XML transaction and the storage of data within a database is that transaction-oriented XML documents are primarily used for describing exchanges or movement of data rather than for persisting (storing) data.

The data architect should apply normalization rules when they can be used to advantage. As an example, collections of related data contained in a transaction should also reference an identifier element. When the identifier is composed of several component data elements (e.g., a composite or aggregate identifier), it is of value to carry the individual data elements of those identifier parts. There are also exceptions to rigorous application of normalization rules. When a transaction-oriented data exchange that includes the movement of the transaction data from a source or origin to one or more targets is considered, performance related to network bandwidth and the total size of the transaction become important. However, network bandwidth constraints and document size should not be the only criteria for determining whether normalization rules should be applied to the structure of an XML transaction. In addition, the data architect must assess the overall complexity of the transaction, the way in which the transaction is intended to be used, and the potential risks when normalization rules are violated (e.g., risks related to performance, architecture, reuse, flexibility, or other factors). The data architect must consider the importance of normalization as it applies to each part of the XML transaction rather than to the transaction as a single entity.

Derived data are defined as the application of business rules or logic to one or more data elements. Derived data can be of several forms (e.g., aggregate, decomposition, and derivation). A common method for describing a name is to use person name data that are captured as separate name parts and contained within individual data elements (e.g., family name, given name, and additional name). Alternatively, a complete person name that is the concatenation of separate name parts and stored as a single data element is an example of derived data. Another example of derived data is the total amount of a purchase, in which taxes, shipping, handling, and insurance have been applied to an item price (Fig. 9.5).

In the case of e-commerce, a transaction can be created by the user through some form of Internet or Web interface and moved through a series of applications and processes, with one or more additional transactions and responses flowing between the customer and the business

Technique:

For some processing scenarios, derived data defined to an XML transaction can be of value. However, careful evaluation of overall document size, complexity of the derivations, and the number of granular data elements is warranted.

Figure 9.5

Examples of derived
data.

Derived Complete Person Name

Complete Person Name		Given (First) Name			Additional (Middle) Name			Family (Last) Name
			Blank			Blank		
Sally M. Smith	=	Sally	+ Space	+	M.	+ Space	+	Smith

Derived Item Total Price

Item Price	14.32	
Local Tax	1.43	(* 10%)
Shipping	5.95	
Handling	2.50	
Insurance	3.00	
Total Price	27.20	

enterprise. In the case of enterprise integration, transactions are moved between and processed by one or more applications within the enterprise. Of obvious importance to both examples is performance. Depending upon the granularity, volumetrics, and intended uses of the transaction, it may be of value to incorporate transaction data that are derived. If the derivation can be completed accurately, once, at the source and distributed to multiple targets, the target applications can avoid additional processing and respond in a more expeditious manner.

The advantages of carrying derived data can vary. If multiple collections of data within a single transaction are intended for sequential processing, derived data can be of value. If the same transaction will be consumed by other types of application processes, carrying the more granular data elements comprising the derived data is also advantageous. A common example is an XML transaction containing multiple instances of address data that are targeted for mailing list processing and for sales report processing. If the mailing list application is intended to process high volumes of name and address data, without the application of any business logic (e.g., the process is limited to extracting name and address data and printing mailing labels), then a data element containing a derived "complete" person name would be of significant value. If the same transaction were targeted for reuse by a different application process that sorted and selected groups of customers according to family name, separate person name parts would be required. The intent to reuse the same XML transaction for varied processing implies a requirement to carry both the derived complete person name and the granular person name part data elements (Fig. 9.6).

The example describes a scenario in which derived and redundant data can be defined to a single, reusable XML transaction structure and processed by different types of applications. However, derived and redundant data can also introduce several complexities and risks. As previously noted, an area of concern is the overall size of the XML transaction. By nature of being self-describing, each container has named tags. The character count of each tag contributes to the overall size of the XML transaction document. As a result, carrying additional data elements or attributes that contain what are conceptually redundant data can significantly increase the size of the transaction, which can affect exchange performance and general processing of the XML document. The use of derived data also implies the application of business rules or logic that in some cases may not be decomposable without the more granular data elements and logic from which it originated. As a

Customer Person Name data include both a complete name (assumed to be derived or captured at the point of origin/source) as well as the individual name parts.

```xml
<?xml version="1.0" encoding="UTF-8"?>
<CustomerData>
 <Customer CustomerIdentifier="1234567890">

  <CompletePersonName>Sally M. Smith</CompletePersonName>

  <PersonName Sequence="1" Type="Given">Sally</PersonName>
  <PersonName Sequence="2" Type="Additional">M.</PersonName>
  <PersonName Sequence="3" Type="Family">Smith</PersonName>

 </Customer>

 <Customer CustomerIdentifier="2345678901">

  <CompletePersonName>John S. Johnson</CompletePersonName>

  <PersonName Sequence="1" Type="Given">John</PersonName>
  <PersonName Sequence="2" Type="Additional">S.</PersonName>
  <PersonName Sequence="3" Type="Family">Johnson</PersonName>

 </Customer>
</CustomerData>
```

XML Instance

Figure 9.6

Derived and redundant XML person name data.

result, careful evaluation of the overall document size, the complexity of the derivation, and the number of granular data elements is warranted.

So far, XML has been described in the context of a document or transaction. A recent innovation is the concept of collaborative processing, for which XML can also play a significant role. XML-based Web services is an example worthy of discussion.

10

Web Services—An Introduction to the Future

Web Services are a recent technology innovation for the World Wide Web. Simply put, a *Web Service* is a Web-based application program with a defined interface that accepts and processes requests and returns a response back to the requester. A Web Service is not directly bound to a specific requesting application (e.g., a Web Service is "loosely coupled"). In some respects, a Web Service is similar to a client server model, where the Web Service is a server. However, a Web Service is a platform agnostic program that is accessible from the Web. The characteristics of a Web Service include the following:

- The Web Service supports common methods of invocation.

- The interface for a Web Service is generally platform agnostic.

- The method of internal implementation for a Web Service is generally unknown by the requester (i.e., the client).

- The functionality provided by a Web Service implies a context but is not restricted to use by any single application or application type.

Although not a restriction, a typical (external) Web Service operates across the World Wide Web. Almost any communication protocol or form of messaging can be used for invocation (e.g., a Web Service is interoperable). Currently, the most common protocol is HyperText Transmission Protocol (HTTP), but this is not a restriction. In fact a Web Service could be invoked using File Transfer Protocol (FTP), Remote Procedure Call (RPC), or similar methods. The obvious advantage of interoperability is that applications using HTTP to transport information can be readily adapted to carry the request and response messages of a Web Service.

The Web Service interface is platform agnostic. If the Web Service is defined as public, it has the potential to be used by any type of application, from anywhere on the Web. Because XML is enabled using Unicode character encoding (most often UTF-8 and ASCII), it fits well as a method of describing the Web Service interface and the request sent to the Web Service when invoked. In fact, many fully enabled Web Services utilize XML to describe the Web Service provider, the characteristics of the Service, and the interface for interacting with the Service.

A Web Service can be internally implemented using almost any programming language. In fact a Web Service could be implemented using Visual Basic (VB), Java, C, C#, C++, Perl, or almost any other programming language. The primary constraints that govern the programming languages and technologies that can be used to implement a Web Service include the following:

- Interaction with Web communication protocols
- Processing of input parameters as part of a request
- Return of a response to a requester

The functionality provided by a Web Service is not unlike that of a specialized program, function, method, or subroutine. The idea is to externalize one or more similar functions, with the intent of being used by one or more application programs (i.e., requesters). By virtue of providing specific functionality, the Web Service implies a context. The Web Service can be engineered to provide specific functionality or services within the context as determined by parameters defined to the interface. As examples, coarse-grained consumer-oriented Web Services can be engineered to provide functionality such as

- Stock Market information (for a given market: current market position, historical market activity, market trends, etc.)

- Weather information (for a given location: current temperature, barometer, horizon, wind speed, etc.)

- Consumer quote and purchase (for a given item type: supplying retailers, item availability, item pricing, etc.)

Although the name "Web Services" implies that the service is exposed to the World Wide Web, this also is not a restriction. In fact, Web Services could be defined within the enterprise and exposed over an internal network. In this form the Web Service is really an "enterprise" Web Service. Traditional program subroutines for functionality such as data conversion, currency conversion, data access, cross-system data exchange, and similar activities present tremendous opportunities for enabling internal Web Services. Also, other more fine-grain Web Services can be defined to provide specific functionality to an application program or the communication between application programs.

Opportunity:

Although most Web Services are targeted to consumer and business applications, they present an opportunity to enable enterprise integration and data brokers.

Given the previous examples and the definition of a Web Service, a data architect might question: "Why are these Web Services important to me?" The answer is twofold. First, beyond the typical consumer and business-oriented logic of a Web Service, there are even greater opportunities in the area of enterprise integration. For many business enterprises, information of considerable value is "locked up" in numerous parochial systems. The structure and characteristics that define this information can vary from system to system. Data sharing and XML-defined transaction exchanges are becoming preferred methods for enterprise integration. However, the approach used by these methods is often implemented as direct or "point-to-point" interfaces.

As an alternative to business applications, Web Services can be engineered as the interface to facilitate data access, data transformation, and data exchange requests from system to system. Behind the integration Web Service are one or more data brokers. Data brokers access data sources, extract data, map and transform data, and move data between sources and targets. To effectively transform data from one form to another, the mapping of source and target metadata is critical. When implemented as common and transformable enterprise vocabularies, W3C XML Schemas can be used to facilitate this mapping and provide much needed support for enterprise integration. The data architect plays an essential role in the source and target mapping and in the development of W3C XML Schema-based enterprise vocabularies.

Also of importance is the content of the Web Service request and the response. As noted earlier, a Web Service should be interoperable. As a result, the preferred method for defining the content of a Web Services request and response is XML. Regardless of the context and use for a Web Service, the interface will generally incorporate input (request) and output (response) data elements. The defining characteristics of these interface data elements are metadata. Here again, the participation of the data architect in development of supporting schemas becomes important.

XML and Web Services

To effectively engineer and use a Web Service, there are several important activities that must be completed. Once engineered, the Web Service must be "published" for an intended audience. This audience may be open or public (e.g., exposing the Web Service for use by any application without restriction) or private (e.g., exposing the Web Service for use by one or more identified or trusted applications). In addition, the characteristics of the Web Service must be exposed to potential users. Characteristics of a Web Service may include a description of provided functionality, a description of the interface (e.g., especially the request and response message), and the methods used for invoking the Service (e.g., a resource identifier or similar identification, allowable communication protocols, and specific binding information). For the Web Service to be "found," the Web Service information must be published to a directory that is available to potential users.

When a Web Service has been identified, the requesting application must develop a request that meets the expectations of the Service. Similarly, the requesting application must also prepare for the receipt and processing of a response from the Web Service. The content of the request and the response follow a prescribed structure and will contain data values of a certain type. These activities imply three distinct parts of the Web Service framework:

- A directory where Web Services information is published and made available

- A description of the Web Services interface and method of invocation

- An interaction (request and response) that conforms to the Web Services interface

Each of these component parts comprise a framework from which a Web Service can be described, found, invoked (e.g., binding), and processed (Fig. 10.1).

Figure 10.1

The basic Web Services framework.

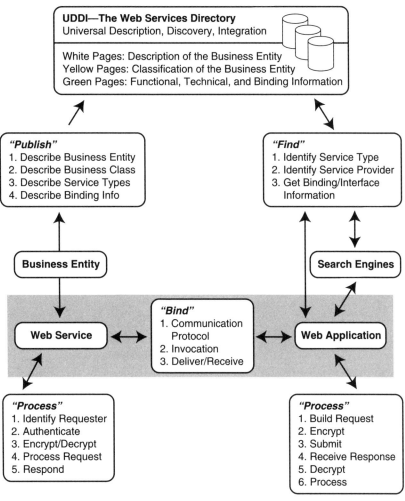

UDDI—Universal Description Discovery and Integration

An important aspect of a Web Service is how it is described and published to the Web. To be used by an application, the identification, functionality, and the interface of Web Service must be available to requesting applications. The UDDI directory describes registered Web Services.[1] When the Service is engineered for broad-scale World Wide Web use, characteristics about the Service provider and the Service are published to the UDDI directory. Applications can query the directory to search for available Web Services. Publishing Web Services information to and accessing Web Services information from the UDDI directory can be accomplished using XML (Fig. 10.2).

When a Web Service is specific to internal enterprise use, there may be restrictions regarding the functionality of and access to the Web Service. As a result, publishing to a more public and World Wide Web accessible UDDI directory may not present the best directory solution. However, potential internal enterprise users must be able to find the Service. In this case, an internally developed directory or a directory such as Lightweight Directory Access Protocol (LDAP) may present a more appropriate solution. The use of an internal directory can be restricted to specific users or applications and may also be customized. However, caution is advised in that customization of the directory or descriptive characteristics can result in additional development efforts.

After the Web Service has been identified as available for use, and the described functionality meets the requirements of the requesting application, the next step is determining how to invoke and interact with the Service.

WSDL—Web Services Definition Language

WSDL provides a method of describing technical information about the Web Service,[2] as well as the interface (e.g., the request and response message). It is important to note that the use of WSDL to describe a

---

[1] Universal Description Discovery and Integration of Web Services. Ariba, International Business Machines, and Microsoft. UDDI, 2000. Available at http://www.uddi.org/.
[2] Web Services Description Language (WSDL) version 1.2. World Wide Web Consortium (W3C), 2002. Available at http://www.w3.org/TR/wsdl12/.

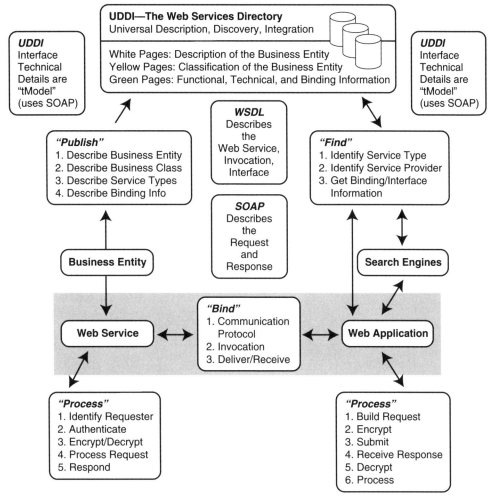

Figure 10.2

Web Services and XML.

Web Service is optional. If the method of invocation and the format of the interface are otherwise formally provided to the requesting application, the value of using WSDL might be of questionable. However, this would also imply that there is some form of proprietary architectural awareness or binding between the requesting application and the Web

Service. As a result, changes to the functionality, interface, or method of invocation for the Service could impact the requester. Although WSDL is technically optional, it is valuable when there is no other form of describing the Web Service interface, and it warrants careful consideration.

There are several parts to WSDL, but given the focus on data architecture, the definition of *types* deserves discussion (Fig. 10.3). The "types" section of the WSDL document describes the metadata characteristics of the Web Services interface. A strength of WSDL is that W3C XML Schemas can be used for this section, which provides strong data type support. Related sections of the WSDL document relate the types to named elements of the message and to the message structure (e.g., input vs output).

After the method of invocation is known and the interface is defined, the Web Service can be used. If the method of invocation includes HTTP, sending the request message to the Web Service is roughly analogous to requesting a Web page. A resource location and identifier are provided and the content of the request is sent. Conceptually, the content of the Web Services request is a set of parameters and data values that must match the expectations of the Web Service. When the request is received, the Web Service authenticates the request (e.g., "Are the request and the requester authorized?") and then verifies that the content of the request is correct. The process of verification can include simple parsing, extraction of request parameter data values, and processing of the request message data, or it may include more extensive validation to a schema to ensure that the message content conforms to a set of metadata rules. Also of significance is the potential need for encryption and decryption. Depending upon the capabilities of the Web Service and the requester and the sensitivity or confidentiality of the interface message data, part of the message content may require encryption.

SOAP—Simple Object Access Protocol

The invocation of a typical Web Service includes a request message that is sent to the Service and a response message that is returned to the requester. Given the need for interoperability, these messages are often defined using a form of XML. SOAP is a dialect or syntax

W3C XML Schema (describing the interface)

```
<?xml version="1.0" encoding="UTF-8"?>
<xs:schema xmlns:xs="http://www.w3.org/2001/XMLSchema">
 <xs:element name="computePriceFromCost">
  <xs:complexType>
   <xs:sequence>
    <xs:element ref="AmountCost"/>
    <xs:element ref="AmountPrice"/>
   </xs:sequence>
  </xs:complexType>
 </xs:element>

 <xs:element name="AmountCost"  type="xs:decimal"/>
 <xs:element name="AmountPrice" type="xs:decimal"/>

</xs:schema>
```
W3C XML Schema

WSDL Document

```
<?xml version="1.0" encoding="utf-8"?>
<definitions xmlns="http://schemas.xmlsoap.org/wsdl/"
     xmlns:soap="http://schemas.xmlsoap.org/wsdl/soap/"
     xmlns:http="http://schemas.xmlsoap.org/wsdl/http/"
     xmlns:soapenc="http://schemas.xmlsoap.org/soap/encoding/"
     xmlns:mime="http://schemas.xmlsoap.org/wsdl/mime/"
     xmlns:y="http://new.webservice.namespace"
     targetNamespace="http://new.webservice.namespace">

 <types>

  <xs:schema>
        ... Schema goes here ....
  </xs:schema>

 </types>

 <message name="computePriceFromCost"/>
 <portType name="typeName"/>
 <binding name="bindingName" type="y:typeName"/>
 <service name="computePrice"/>

</definitions>
```
W3C XML Schema

Figure 10.3

W3C XML Schemas and the WSDL "types" section.

for describing the message that is sent to and received from a Web Service.[3] The SOAP protocol includes three basic parts:

- SOAP envelope
- SOAP header
- SOAP body

Conceptually, the SOAP envelope is the overall set of descriptors and container for message data. Similar to the basic namespace of a W3C XML Schema, the SOAP envelope includes a namespace that references the SOAP version. As SOAP evolves, this version can be important to the Web Service as a method of determining what type of interpretation and processing should be applied. The SOAP envelope also includes two other parts: the SOAP header and the SOAP body.

The SOAP header contains information about the specific message. The header can include information such as identification of the requester, the point of origin or source of the message, authentication information, security and encryption information, and more technical data about how the request should be processed (e.g., in the case of failure). The SOAP header also allows for custom extension if it is necessary for processing by the Web Service.

The SOAP body defines the content of the request. This section of the SOAP message is a set of data containers (often defined by element containers) and data values as contents of those containers. The data values of a SOAP request message are similar to parameters. The structure of the SOAP body depends on the requested Service. The interface required by the Web Service (optionally described by a WSDL document) determines the structure. It is the definition of the SOAP body, for which metadata characteristics become important. If the data elements of the request message as defined to the SOAP body do not conform to an expected structure (e.g., the required element containers, containers ordered in the necessary sequence, and appropriate data types), the Web

Opportunity:

The design of the Web Services interface (specifically the "SOAP body") implies the need for descriptive metadata. Although the development practitioner will take primary responsibility for engineering Web Services, the data architect should participate in the design of the message structure and a schema to describe applicable metadata characteristics.

[3] Simple Object Access Protocol, SOAP Version 1.2. W3C, 2002. Available at http://www.w3.org/TR/soap12-part1/, http://www.w3.org/TR/soap12-part2/, and http://www.w3.org/TR/soap12-af/.

Service will not be able to process the request. The design of the SOAP body is similar to the development of a prototype XML transaction and a constraining schema. Although in this case, the developer would take primary responsibility, it is advantageous to include the data architect as a collaborator in the development of the SOAP body. Additionally, the data architect would also engineer a representative W3C XML Schema. If WSDL is used to describe the interface, "types" from the W3C XML Schema would then become part of the WSDL "type" element group (Fig. 10.4).

Why Would a Company Develop and Publish Web Services?

Some might question why a company would develop and deploy a Web Service for use by others. With the premise that Web Services promote a collaborative business model, the justification for developing Web Services can be difficult to formalize. Currently, there are three basic business models to support the development of most Web Services:

- Altruistic
- Direct revenue generation
    - Per request
    - Period-based license
- Indirect revenue generation
    - Collection and marketing of request data (click stream, topic, and requester)

From a profit perspective, the altruistic model is the most difficult to justify. As implied by the name, the intent is to develop and deploy Web Services for primarily unrestricted use or use without cost to the requester. The result would be Web Services deployed in an open environment, in which the user would not be required to pay a fee for use. There may be variations of this model, in which the intellectual property rights are maintained by the developer and copying of the Web Services interface or functionality is restricted. Most revenue-based enterprises have difficulty with the altruistic model. However, it might be possible to extend justification as a form of "good will," or as a promotional service that leads to other revenue. This business model promotes an "open" Web.

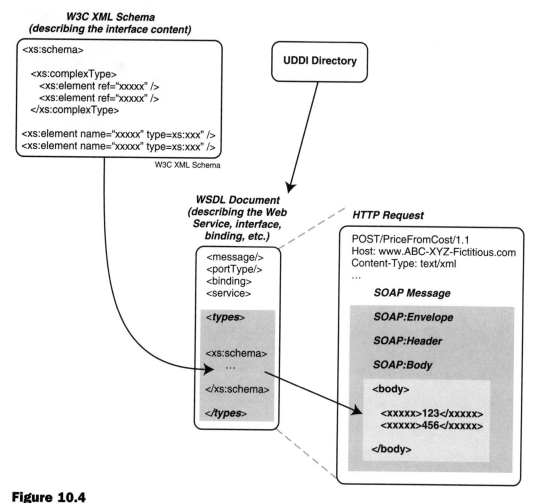

Figure 10.4

The Web Services message using HTTP and SOAP.

A direct revenue-generating model is fairly intuitive and understood by most businesses. The intent behind the Web Service is revenue. Two basic variations of this model are (1) a fee per request and (2) periodic licensing (i.e., a license to use the Web Service for a determined period of time). In this case, there must be a viable market for the Web Service. The emphasis on revenue and fees may be perceived by some as being prohibitive to open and collaborative computing. The Web Service would also need to include logic for authentication of the requester (e.g., to determine if this is a licensed or authorized requester) and some form of logging to count each request.

The third basic Web Services business model is indirect revenue generation. This model is similar to the collection of user ID, e-mail address, and click stream data from Web page visitors for use in determining product and service preferences and potentially for later remarketing. As a point of reference, click stream is similar to the tracking of Web pages and objects of interest that a user visits. Given that a Web Service provides functionality for a purpose or within a context, associating a requester with the type of requested service implies the ability to perform information prospecting. It may be assumed that a requester for a service of a particular type may be interested in similar products and services. Risks associated with this business model are related to privacy regulations and liability associated with exposing requester data.

These business models are primarily focused on Web Services deployed for use over the World Wide Web and potentially by consumers other than the original developer. Justification for internal Web Services (those internal to the enterprise) are usually focused on development cost reduction and reuse. Like a standard subroutine, an internal Web Service could be engineered to provide enterprise functionality in a platform agnostic manner. The Web Service would be deployed for use over an internal network but like an external Web Service, the actual business logic and programming methods would be hidden from the requester. As with any reusable technology asset, there are also development synergies resulting from cost avoidance (e.g., not having to redevelop application logic that already exists) and decreased development time.

Recommendation:

When the Web Services request or response message contains sensitive or confidential information, appropriate security and encryption techniques should be applied.

The development and deployment of Web Services can also introduce challenges and risks. If the Web Service is engineered and deployed over the Web for use by others, there are the costs and challenges associated with technical support and availability. If the Web Service suffers from poor availability or performance or is prone to error, it is doubtful that it will survive as a method of revenue generation. There are also risks associated with unauthorized use, the potential for intrusion, exposure of sensitive information, and similar liability risks, regardless of whether the service is external or internal to the enterprise. Although each of these challenges is important, they are not insurmountable.

The Future of Web Services

As previously described, a Web Service is similar to a subroutine or server function. Clients (which may include users, businesses, or application programs) request the Web Service and then process a resulting response. Alone, this model for application development is not revolutionary. The future of Web Services has yet to be determined, but the direction is toward orchestrated or coordinated combinations of Web Services as intelligent agents. A set of criteria could be submitted in the request to the Web Service, and it would process and return a response with various options. The requesting application is an assembly of component functions that evaluate responses to services, determine appropriate actions, and collaborate. To avoid the complexities that arise with use of different platforms and technologies, collaboration implies rigorous use of XML.

As mentioned earlier, a Web Service could be engineered to act as the primary interface for an enterprise integration data broker. Adding intelligence as a set of collaborative functions could extend the data broker concept to identify the primary source for enterprise data, as well as to provide routing and extraction from alternative data sources if the primary source were unavailable. Data extracted by the broker could also be evaluated for metadata format, quality, and volumetrics. The integration data broker could invoke other Web Services to perform necessary cleansing and transformations. The result is that the primary Web Service targets resolution and response of the data integration request, but, depending upon subordinate processes and responses, many courses of action could be taken. The requester does not need to be notified of these activities unless the resulting response did not meet the expectations of the request.

Other similar applications could also be developed. Extensions to the Web Service that define the enterprise data broker could detect when new data are being "pushed" out to the enterprise. If a profile of these new data (derived from its taxonomy, context, and metadata characteristics) matched that of other decision support requirements, additional cleansing and transformation Web Services could be invoked as preparation for a new data warehouse feed. If the cleansing and transformation logic were available from a source external to the enterprise, those Web Services could also be invoked. Obviously, these example Web Service applications are somewhat theoretical and would require rigorous analysis and design. Additionally, the traditional issues of security, performance, and availability must be resolved. However, potential opportunities for application of Web Services are almost without bound. It is the ability to develop applications programs that collaborate over the Web and in some form apply abstract intelligence resulting from dynamic events and responses that pose the greatest opportunity for Web Services.

Appendix A

Facts, Recommendations, Techniques, and Opportunities

A key feature of this book is the valuable information defined as:

- Facts
- Recommendations
- Techniques
- Opportunities

Facts are based upon available reference or frequent observation. Recommendations are subjective and are the result of my experience and research. Techniques define tactical practices, and opportunities help determine when to apply a technique or avoid a potential pitfall.

In addition to their definition in the chapter text, they are repeated here grouped by topic with page references to supporting context.

Motivation

Fact: XML is self-describing (supports descriptive element and attribute tags). (p. 12)

Fact: XML is generally interoperable (XML is by default encoded as Unicode and UTF-8, supporting basic ASCII characters). (p. 17)

Fact: XML is reusable (W3C XML Schemas can be engineered as modular component schemas). (p. 19)

Fact: XML is flexible (XML structures can be engineered to dynamically expand or contract). (p. 23)

Fact: XML is extensible (XML structures and schemas can be extended or "added to"). (p. 24)

Schema Types

Recommendation: XML Document Type Definitions (DTD) can be an effective method of describing and constraining simple document-oriented content. However, in many cases W3C XML Schemas can be applied equally well. (p. 33)

Recommendation: W3C XML Schemas are generally a very good fit for transaction-oriented content (both internal and external to the enterprise). (p. 42)

Recommendation: W3C XML Schemas are generally a good fit for message-oriented content. (p. 45)

Fact: Depending upon the characteristics of the data content, the intended use, and the number of processing applications, more than one type of schema may be required. (p. 48)

Recommendation: If a single schema type must be used, consider using W3C XML Schemas as the default. (p. 48)

Taxonomy

Opportunity: When existing enterprise data architecture naming standards and processes are descriptive, intuitive, and well received by the enterprise and do not violate XML syntax rules, they may be adapted for application to XML element and attribute names. (p. 50)

Recommendation: An XML element or attribute name should be intuitive (the "intuitive rule"). (p. 50)

Recommendation: Avoid the use of articles, prepositions, pronouns, and proper names as part of an XML tag name. (p. 52)

Recommendation: Avoid the use of acronyms and abbreviations unless they are broadly recognized and accepted. (p. 52)

Recommendation: Use class words only when they are concise and representative of a recognized and clearly defined constraint. (p. 53)

Recommendation: Unless there is an obvious constraint or limitation (e.g., existing technologies and tools only support a specific character case), consider using mixed character case for XML element and attribute names. (p. 55)

Recommendation: Name particle separators should only be used to improve readability of element and attribute names. (p. 56)

Fact: Name particle separators such as an underscore ("_"), dash ("-"), and period (".") can be used in an XML element or attribute name. However, such use will consume a character position with each occurrence. (p. 57)

Recommendation: If the applied character case is camel case, the use of a leading character of upper case for name particles will result in an implied name particle separator. Additional name particle separators such as an underscore ("_"), dash ("-"), and period (".") can then be avoided. (p. 58)

Recommendation: XML element and attribute names should be of reasonable length (not overly verbose and not highly abbreviated). (p. 59)

Recommendation: XML element and attribute name lengths should be rationalized and aligned with the most common data sources and targets. (p. 59)

Opportunity: Abstract XML elements and attributes that exclude internal "roles" or "classifications" from the name and apply the roles as parent elements or descriptive attributes are highly reusable. (p. 60)

Fact: XML element and attribute names that are overly abstract can introduce unnecessary complexity and even the potential for misinterpretation. (p. 61)

Opportunity: The data architect is generally well versed in taxonomy and naming processes and has a tremendous knowledge of enterprise information assets (definition and use). Regardless of the level of abstraction, specificity, or other taxonomy processes applied to XML, there is an obvious opportunity for data architects to participate and apply their skills. (p. 62)

Data Types

Fact: Data types are not always implemented or supported among database products in the same manner regardless of the data type name. (p. 70)

Fact: The most common examples of data carried in a transaction or interface file will have in some form originated from a database and will in some form be persisted in a target database. (p. 71)

Fact: W3C XML Schemas provide extensive date and time data type support (e.g., date, time, duration, time zone, and fractional date particles). However, other than basic date and time data types, database platforms may not provide corresponding ISO 8601 data types. Use of some W3C XML Schema date and time types can require use of character or numeric database types to contain date data and the application of derivation logic. (p. 72)

Fact: W3C XML Schema decimal data types and several of the integer data types are by default not constrained by a minimum or maximum value (i.e., they are "infinite"). However, most database decimal and integer data types have specific minimum and maximum values. Caution is advised when one exchanges numeric data that have the potential to exceed database minimum and maximum limits. (p. 73)

Technique: The syntactical form for applying W3C XML Schema data types is "type="datatype"" where "datatype" is a supported W3C XML Schema type such as "integer," "date," "dateTime," "decimal," or "boolean." (p. 77)

Recommendation: Identifying data that are critical to the processing of an XML transaction or message should be included as an element or attribute and be clearly described by name or location in the document. (p. 84)

Recommendation: The same level of granularity and composition of unique identifiers as defined by the data source or data target should be used in the XML transaction. If the identifier is a combination of separate data elements (e.g., a composite key), similar containers should be defined. (p. 85)

Recommendation: Use of the W3C XML Schema identifier data type (ID) should be limited to data elements and attributes for which uniqueness within a single XML document is required. Owing to limitations of allowable data values, the "ID" data type should not be used to describe database primary keys or similar unique identifiers. Ensuring uniqueness of database identifiers (i.e., primary keys) should be left to the originating database systems. (p. 87)

Facets

Fact: Facets further limit, constrain, or describe a data type. In some cases and depending upon the data type, facets may be combined. (p. 114)

Technique: Character length facets can be used to help resolve differences between metadata characteristics of disparate data sources and targets by constraining the number of character positions to the lowest common denominator. (p. 115)

Technique: The minLength facet can be used to check for a mandatory data value being present for an XML element or attribute. If a minLength value of "1" is defined, a validating parser will check to ensure that the data value contained in the XML document is of at least one character position. If no data value is specified (i.e., similar to a "null"), a validation error will be raised. (p. 117)

Technique: In some cases, value limit facets (minInclusive, maxInclusive, minExclusive, and maxExclusive) can be used to help resolve differences between metadata characteristics of disparate data sources and targets by limiting the range of allowable values to an agreed upon range between systems. (p. 117)

Technique: Digit facets can be used to help resolve differences between metadata characteristics of disparate data sources and targets by limiting the number of digits and character positions to the lowest common denominator. (p. 119)

Technique: Enumeration facets (a list of allowable values) can be used to help enforce standards and in some cases to resolve differences between metadata characteristics of disparate data sources and targets by limiting the allowable values to an agreed upon set for both systems. (p. 121)

Technique: Enumeration facets (a list of allowable values) can be used to describe data standards such as code sets (e.g., country code, currency code, and U.S. state code). However, caution is advised when enumeration lists are defined internally to multiple schemas rather than as external, referenced subset schemas. (p. 122)

Technique: Although powerful, enumeration lists are not always the best architectural technique for validating allowable values when the list is of excessive length (as a rule of thumb greater than 200 entries) or when it is subject to frequent modification (as a rule of thumb when modifications are required more often than once or twice a month). (p. 123)

Technique: Pattern facets can be used to constrain the characters and character position within a data value (similar to presentation format). However, similar to enumeration lists, patterns should be externalized as referenced subset schemas to avoid a proliferation of on-going schema maintenance activities. (p. 123)

Recommendation: Unless the content of the XML document is primarily "document-oriented," use of white space facets should be avoided. Depending upon the parser and validation process, white space facets may result in extracted data at the target of the exchange that no longer matches the originating source XML content. (p. 124)

Structure Models

Fact: All XML structures are by default hierarchical (i.e., top-down and left-to-right). (p. 128)

Fact: Vertical structure models are primarily composed of element containers. When combined with repeating elements (e.g., element cardinality or multiplicity), vertical XML structure models are the most flexible. They can dynamically expand or contract to fit the characteristics of the contained data. (p. 131)

Recommendation: Depending upon the number of element containers, the volumetrics of the contained data, and the taxonomy used to name the elements, vertical structure models can be overly verbose and of excessive size. When application performance is of significant concern or bandwidth for transmitting the XML document is limited, the data architect may need to consider compression, evaluate alternative structure models, or take a different architectural approach. (p. 132)

Fact: Horizontal structure models utilize a significant number of attributes. As such, they tend to be "flat" rather than vertical. (p. 133)

Recommendation: Horizontal structure models may provide a potential advantage when the total size of the XML document or transaction is excessively large or when bandwidth for transmitting the XML document is limited. (p. 134)

Fact: Component structure models provide the greatest advantage in the area of reuse. Highly standardized and modular groups of containers can be defined to externally referenced subschemas that are then reused by other schemas. (p. 138)

Recommendation: As a general recommendation, the most effective uses of XML attributes are as containers of ordinal sequences of repeating elements and as a method of descriptive classification for an element, standard code values, function or activity, and decomposed parts of element contained data. (p. 138)

Fact: Hybrid structure models combine characteristics of the three other structure models (i.e., vertical, horizontal, and component). When properly applied, hybrid models result in flexible, well-defined, and reusable XML structures. (p. 140)

Architectural Container Forms

Recommendation: Rigid architectural container forms are recommended for application to XML documents exchanged between collaborative groups that exist external to the enterprise and for defining a Web Service interface. To avoid misinterpretation, external entities will usually require a rigidly enforced and descriptive taxonomy. (p. 146)

Fact: Rigid container architectural forms may simplify the navigation and processing of an XML document structure. (p. 147)

Fact: Rigid container architectural forms are generally inflexible. Addition of new uniquely named data containers will usually require modification of the XML document structure, corresponding schemas, and potentially the application programs that process the XML document. (p. 148)

Recommendation: Abstract container forms are recommended for structures that exhibit a pattern of data that repeats in the same or similar context (e.g., postal address street lines, component parts of a person's name, and telephone numbers of different types). (p. 149)

Fact: Abstract container forms exploit the concepts of repeating elements and cardinality. (p. 150)

Technique: Abstract container forms utilize element names that are to some degree named in the abstract. One of the guiding principles of an abstract container form is that element names must be described well enough to identify the intended content of the element yet be abstract enough to allow repetition. When there is a question as to the intended content of repeating elements, the parent element of the repeating group must provide additional context. (p. 151)

Fact: Abstract container forms often incorporate attributes to describe ordinal sequence of repeating elements. (p. 152)

Recommendation: With the exception of horizontal structure models, it is recommended that attributes be used only for specification of ordinal sequence, type or classification, standard encoding, intended function or activity, and decomposed parts of a data value. (p. 152)

Technique: When properly applied, specific values for the minOccurs and maxOccurs attributes of repeating elements are a powerful capability of W3C XML Schemas to specify the degree of cardinality. However, caution is advised if the cardinality or characteristics of the repeating elements would be subject to change. Such changes would require modification to the W3C XML Schemas. (p. 155)

Fact: Abstract container architectural forms may add complexity to the navigation and processing of an XML document structure. Additional application logic may be required for interrogation of attribute characteristics. (p. 155)

Recommendation: With few exceptions, hybrid container forms are the recommended architectural adaptation for an XML transaction structure. (p. 159)

Reuse

Fact: XML schema reuse engineering is the set of practices, techniques, and activities required to engineer a W3C XML Schema or schema component with the specific intent of reuse. (p. 166)

Fact: XML schema reuse harvesting is a process that includes activities for identification, validation, and implementation of reusable W3C XML Schemas, subschemas, or schema components. (p. 166)

Recommendation: Unless intentionally prohibited from being reused, all XML element containers should be defined globally, allowing for reuse by reference. (p. 171)

Recommendation: Unless there are obvious advantages to using global "complexTypes," collections of related element containers intentionally targeted for reuse should be globally defined as "groups." (p. 171)

Technique: W3C XML Schema simpleTypes present a powerful method for defining enterprise standard data types and allowable value constraints for element and attribute containers. (p. 174)

Fact: Reuse of a W3C XML Schema or subschema is a conceptual form of development by assembly. The primary W3C XML Schema is assembled by including references to the contents of other externally defined W3C XML subschemas. (p. 176)

Fact: The most common types of reusable subschemas include standard structures, standard codes and allowable values, and custom data types. (p. 178)

Recommendation: The external file name of a reusable W3C XML Schema (or subschema) should be intuitive, be of reasonable specificity, be of mixed character case or camel case, eliminate spaces, and be a maximum of 32 characters in length. (p. 181)

Recommendation: The external file name of a reusable W3C XML Schema (subschema) should include a version. The version may be prefixed or suffixed depending upon enterprise standards. (p. 182)

Recommendation: Reusable W3C XML subschemas should include some form of classification or type in the name (e.g., "STD," "CODES," or "TYPES"). (p. 182)

Recommendation: When used to describe a transaction for data exchange or enterprise integration, a reusable W3C XML Schema should incorporate several different structures and formats to address the potential for varied use and different application processes. (p. 184)

Recommendation: When the primary or referencing W3C XML Schema is of a single context (e.g., namespace), the "include" syntax is the desired form for referencing an externally defined subschema. (p. 192)

Design Techniques

Recommendation: It is recommended that the W3C XML Schema design and engineering process should be a collaborative effort. The data architect and the developer should both participate in the development of a prototype XML document and the corresponding W3C XML Schemas. (p. 203)

Recommendation: As a general recommendation, the maximum depth or levels of element nesting for transaction-oriented content should be around 10 levels. (p. 207)

Technique: When the number of repeating elements within a parent element group is important to navigation logic, add an attribute at the level of the parent element to contain a value noting the number of repeating element occurrences. However, be aware that additional application logic to both determine a value and insert it into the attribute as well as logic to later interrogate the attribute will be required. (p. 207)

Recommendation: As a general recommendation, try to avoid strictly horizontal structure models unless there is an overall size restriction for the XML document or the XML document represents nothing other than a simple relational database extract. (p. 209)

Recommendation: Overall document size can have an effect on network and parsing application performance. Estimates comparing the character counts of XML document element and attribute tag names to the character counts of contained data values should be evaluated. If the "tag-to-data ratio" exceeds a reasonable limit, the use of XML should be reconsidered. (p. 211)

Technique: For some processing scenarios, derived data defined to an XML transaction can be of value. However, careful evaluation of overall document size, complexity of the derivations, and the number of granular data elements is warranted. (p. 213)

Web Services

Opportunity: Although most Web Services are targeted to consumer and business applications, they present an opportunity to enable enterprise integration and data brokers. (p. 219)

Opportunity: The design of the Web Services interface (specifically the "SOAP body") implies the need for descriptive metadata. Although the development practitioner will take primary responsibility for engineering Web Services, the data architect should participate in the design of the message structure and a schema to describe applicable metadata characteristics. (p. 226)

Recommendation: When the Web Services request or response message contains sensitive or confidential information, appropriate security and encryption techniques should be applied. (p. 229)

Appendix B

W3C XML Schema Syntax Examples

W3C XML Schema "element" Syntax (Locally Declared)

(Example of an W3C XML Schema "fragment")

```
<xs:complexType>
    <xs:sequence>
      <xs:element name="ElementName" type="xs:integer"/>
    </xs:sequence>
</xs:complexType>
```

The element is defined at the point at which it is initially declared. Locally declared elements are usually not available for reuse outside the scope of their originating declaration.

W3C XML Schema "complexType" Syntax (Locally Declared)

(Example of an W3C XML Schema "fragment")

```
<xs:element name="ParentofcomplexType">
    <xs:complexType>
      <xs:sequence>
        <xs:element name="ElementName1" type="xs:integer"/>
        <xs:element name="ElementName2" type="xs:integer"/>
      </xs:sequence>
    </xs:complexType>
</xs:element>
```

The complexType is defined at the point at which it is initially declared. A sequence compositor has been applied to the example syntax fragment. Locally declared complexTypes are usually not available for reuse outside the scope of their originating declaration.

W3C XML Schema "element" Syntax (Globally Declared)

(Example of an W3C XML Schema "fragment")

```
<xs:complexType>
    <xs:sequence>
      <xs:element ref="GlobalElementName"/>
    </xs:sequence>
</xs:complexType>

<xs:element name="GlobalElementName" type="xs:integer"/>
```

The named element declaration is defined to the entire schema (hence the term "global"). As defined, this globally declared element can be reused by reference from elsewhere within the W3C XML Schema (in this case referenced from within the bounds of a complexType).

W3C XML Schema "group" Syntax (Globally Declared)

(Example of an W3C XML Schema "fragment")

```
<xs:group ref="GlobalGroupName"/>

<xs:group name="GlobalGroupName">
    <xs:sequence>
      <xs:element name="ElementOneName" type="xs:string"/>
      <xs:element name="ElementTwoName" type="xs:integer"/>
    </xs:sequence>
</xs:group>
```

The named group declaration contains two child elements with an applied sequence compositor. The group is defined to the entire schema (hence the term "global"). As defined, this globally declared group can be reused by reference from elsewhere within the W3C XML Schema.

W3C XML Schema "simpleType" Syntax (Globally Declared Data Type)

(Example of an W3C XML Schema "fragment")

```
<xs:element name="ElementName" type="GlobalsimpleTypeName"/>

<xs:simpleType name="GlobalsimpleTypeName">
    <xs:restriction base="xs:string">
      <xs:minLength value="3"/>
      <xs:maxLength value="10"/>
    </xs:restriction>
</xs:simpleType>
```

The named simpleType declaration represents a custom data type. It is based upon the W3C XML Schema "string" type and includes two constraining facets: minLength and maxLength (other facets could have been included). The simpleType is defined to the entire schema (hence the term "global"). As defined, this globally declared simpleType can be applied and reused by reference from elsewhere within the schema. In this case, the simpleType becomes the applied data type for the referencing element.

W3C XML Schema "simpleType" Syntax (Globally Declared Enumeration List)

(Example of an W3C XML Schema "fragment")

```
<xs:element name="ElementName" type="GlobalsimpleTypeName"/>

<xs:simpleType name="GlobalsimpleTypeName">
    <xs:restriction base="xs:string">
      <xs:enumeration value="ABC"/>
      <xs:enumeration value="DEF"/>
      <xs:enumeration value="GHI"/>
      <xs:enumeration value="JKL"/>
    </xs:restriction>
</xs:simpleType>
```

The named simpleType declaration represents a custom data type. It is based upon the W3C XML Schema "string" type and includes constraining facets for enumeration. Each enumeration facet includes a value. In total, the list of enumeration facets describes the set of allowable values for the simpleType. The simpleType is defined to the entire schema (hence the term "global"). As defined, this globally declared simpleType can be applied and reused by reference from elsewhere within the schema. In this case, the simpleType becomes the applied data type for the referencing element.

Glossary

abstract cardinality   Similar to infinite cardinality, a form of cardinality (e.g., repeating elements) in which the degree or threshold as a maximum number of occurrences is unknown. The value specific for an XML schema maxOccurs attribute would in this case be "unbounded."

abstract container form   An architectural form or pattern of like-named element containers that repeat in a given context. Implied by an abstract container form are element names (e.g., "tag" names) that are to some degree abstract. As an example, elements abstractly named as "<PersonName>" would be used in place of elements specifically named as "<EmployeePersonName>."

architectural container form   The application or adaptation of an observable and repeatable pattern to an XML structure model.

attribute   A named container for data. In the case of XML, an attribute is of a syntax similar to that of HTML (e.g., "name–value pair"). Of importance is the fact that an XML attribute is defined to an element and may not repeat.

binding   The coupling or integration of objects. It is often applied to the concept of data and presentation, for which data are bound to a Web page.

Business-to-Business (B2B)   Describes a type of Web site that is operated by a business and targets other businesses as the primary customers.

Business-to-Consumer (B2C)   Describes a type of Web site that is operated by a business and targets consumers (individuals, persons, or groups).

camel case   A method of applying character case to a phrase, word, or term. Depending upon the source, techniques for applying camel case may vary. A common technique is to apply upper case to the first character of each distinct word, with other characters remaining in lower case.

child element   A child or dependent element of a parent element.

class word   A classification or type that is generally assigned as part of a name. When applied to an element name, the class word is most often intended to describe a selection of valid values, a range of allowable values, or a data type.

click stream   Similar to the path taken by users when they navigate a Web site. Click stream information is sometimes captured by the enterprise and used for Web site marketing analysis.

component   A decomposed part of a larger concept or object. In the example of a postal or delivery address, city is a component. Conceptually, the combination of all directly related components will represent the primary object from which they are decomposed.

component XML structure model   A structure model that incorporates collections of similar or related containers as named and identified groupings. XML schemas that describe these groupings of elements become candidates for reuse as subschemas.

container   In the case of XML, generally an element or attribute. An object that contains or holds data, another container, both, or nothing.

content   The data values contained within an XML document.

context   The definition or applied use of an object, information, collection, or item of data. Context can be explicit (clearly identified and described) or implicit (implied by a set of data elements). In the case of XML, a context is often represented by an XML schema vocabulary or by a parent container.

cross-domain reuse   Broad scale reuse. Reuse of an information asset that crosses application systems or domains.

Customer Relationship Management (CRM)   Customer relationship management combines business functions of marketing, sales, personalization, customer service, customer retention, and analysis. The ability to identify, target, attract, service, capture, grow, and retain customers are the basic objectives of customer relationship management.

data concept   A general classification for a type or collection of data in the abstract. Examples of data concepts include "postal address," "person name," "telephone number," and others.

data concept particle   A defined set of particles, information fragments, or component parts of a data concept. Given name and family name are particles of the person name data concept.

data disparity   Characteristic differences between data concepts, data items, and their metadata characteristics. Data disparity is an observable trait between similar, but not identical, pieces of information. Data disparity must be resolved to achieve data integration.

data particle or part   A particle, fragment, or component part of a data concept. A data particle is often considered to be "atomic" (the data particle is defined at or represents the lowest reasonable level of decomposition).

data standard   A representative and accepted definition, set of encodings, form, structure, or allowable values. Data standards can be applied to a data concept, data concept particle, or data particle.

degree of cardinality   As a defined threshold, the minimum or maximum number of occurrences allowed or prescribed for repeating data elements.

document   In the context of XML, a document, transaction, message, file, or similar overall container for information.

Document Type Definition (DTD)   A type of XML schema that is based upon SGML. The syntax of a document type definition is different than that of XML or a W3C XML Schema.

domain   A scope, context, or collection of similar or related concepts, functions, data structures, applications, or systems.

element   A named container for data. An XML element is of a syntactical form similar to that of HTML (e.g., "<element-name> . . . </element-name>" or "<element-name/>").

enterprise integration   The goal and process for aligning and integrating information assets from different enterprise systems.

enterprise   A business or set of related businesses that operate as a whole. The enterprise includes resources (human and other), processes, information, goals, and strategies.

eXtensible Markup Language (XML)   A language derived as a conforming subset of SGML. XML is often referred to as a self-describing metadata language. XML is gaining in popularity for use in Web applications and to define e-commerce transactions. For additional information, visit the World Wide Web Consortium Web site (www.w3c.org).

eXtensible Stylesheet Language (XSL, XSLT)   An XML technology that allows for navigation of a referencing XML document and the application of presentation format or transformation logic.

flexible   An architectural characteristic where a structure can expand or contract.

Global Customer Relationship Management (G-CRM)   Global customer relationship management extends the concept of customer relationship management to incorporate the global and locale characteristics and preferences of a customer.

horizontal XML structure model   A structure model that is primarily composed of attribute containers to hold data values. Horizontal structure models are also described as "flat."

hybrid container form   An architectural container form that combines the most advantageous characteristics and capabilities of other container forms.

hybrid XML structure model   An XML structure model that combines the most advantageous characteristics and capabilities of other structure models.

HyperText Markup Language (HTML)   An application of SGML. Developed to simplify presentation of information over the Web.

HTML form   HyperText Markup Language form. An extension of HTML that allows for user interaction (data entry, acceptance, limited validation, and submission of data to a Web server or similar application). HTML forms utilize declarative elements (e.g., <INPUT/>, <TEXTAREA/>, and <SELECT/> elements). HTML form elements are also often referred to as "HTML form fields."

HTML form field   Unofficial synonym for an "HTML form element." Used within an HTML form, an HTML form field allows for data entry, acceptance, and limited validation from the Web browser. HTML form fields (elements) include <INPUT/>, <TEXTAREA/>, and <SELECT/>.

instance   An instantiation. In the case of a document instance, the XML document that contains data.

integration   A process that results in the derivation, combination, aggregation, exchange, transformation, and processing of information assets by multiple enterprise systems.

interoperable   The ability to communicate, collaborate, process, or be consumed on or between different operating systems, network environments, databases, or other technologies.

locale   Defined by a combination of characteristics and describing the geography and preferences of an international user. There is no clearly defined standard for a locale. However, most locales can be described as a combination of geography (country, regional area, city, etc.), and preferred language, currency, and unit of measure system.

metadata   The characteristics, form, allowable values, standards, and rules that describe and define data. Often referred to as "data about data."

modality   Describing the concept of optional or mandatory.

parent element   Owning or higher level element of one or more child elements.

parser   In the case of XML, a software utility that checks an XML document for syntax and allows an application to process the document (e.g., navigate, extract data, and insert data).

pattern   An observable form or template that is adaptable and also repeatable.

Relational Database Management System (RDBMS)   A type of database that is founded on matrices, tuples, and relational algebra. The concept of a relational database is most often attributed to the work of E. F. Codd. A relational database not only stores information, but also supports the ability to relate data and view relationships between data.

reuse   The ability to use something more than once. More specifically, the ability to use something more than once that was engineered with the intent of being reused.

reuse engineering   The design, engineering, and development of an information asset with intent of being reused.

reuse harvesting   The identification, validation, and use of a reusable information asset.

rigid container form   An architectural container form that is primarily composed of specifically named elements that are not defined to repeat.

root element   Top-most or overall element of an XML document.

server   A computer device or application process that provides services to a requester. Servers may be of various types (e.g., Web, application, data, and enterprise).

Simple Object Access Protocol (SOAP)   An XML-based protocol used to request Web Services.

specific cardinality   Cardinality defined with specific boundaries or thresholds. The degree of cardinality is defined by a finite value. The XML schema syntax provides minOccurs and maxOccurs attributes that can be valued with a specific number representing the degree of cardinality for repeating elements.

strongly typed data   Data that have been described or defined by granular characteristics such as a data type (e.g., string, integer, and date).

tag   A name applied to a container or structure in XML syntactical form.

taxonomy   A scheme and form of classification that is often extended to the development of names.

Universal Description Discovery and Integration (UDDI)   A repository-based approach to describing Web Services.

user interface   The method of interacting with a person that is implemented by one or more technologies. The user interface defines or resides at the presentation layer.

validation   For XML, a parser process that compares an XML document to a referenced schema. Violations and errors are reported back to the parsing application. This process requires a "validating" parser.

vertical XML structure model   A structure model that is composed primarily of element containers. A vertical structure model can be visualized as flowing from top to bottom.

Web page   A defined set of information (also known as content) identified as a resource on the World Wide Web that is presented to a Web user. A Web page is usually served by a Web server. Many Web pages may be defined to a Web site.

Web server   A type of server. A Web server provides or serves Web pages as resolution of requests that are generally in the form of a universal resource locator (URL).

Web Service   A program, function, or logic identified as a resource on the World Wide Web that may be invoked by a message. A Web Service accepts requests and provides responses.

Web Services Description Language (WSDL)   An XML-based language that can be used to describe a Web Service, its interface, and methods of invocation.

Web site   A collection of Web pages or similar Web resources. A Web site is generally identified by a universal resource locator (URL).

within-domain reuse   Reuse of an information asset within a specific context, application system, or domain.

XML attribute   A type of XML container that is defined to an XML element. An XML attribute may not exist on its own (without a corresponding XML element). An XML attribute may be defined only to contain data or nothing at all. An XML attribute may not be defined to contain other attributes or elements.

XML Data Reduced (XDR)   A type of XML schema that preceded the development of W3C XML Schemas.

XML document   A file, document, transaction, or message defined using the syntax of XML. An overall container of XML data containers and data values.

XML element   The type of XML container most often used. An XML element is defined in the form of a tag name placed between a left angle bracket and a right angle bracket. An XML element container may be defined to contain data, other element containers, both, or nothing. An XML element can also be defined to intentionally remain empty of any value.

XML Schema (also known as a W3C XML Schema)   An XML-based type of schema that includes rules and constraints for a referencing XML document. An XML schema can include an extended set of metadata characteristics (format, structure, rules, and allowable values). As of May 2001, XML Schemas are defined as a "recommendation" of the World Wide Web Consortium (W3C).

XML structure model   A structural model applied to an XML document, transaction, or file.

Bibliography and Recommended Reading

American National Standards Institute (ANSI), X3 Working Group. X3.138 Information Resource Dictionary System. *Data Entity Naming Conventions*, Special Publication 500-149.

Bean J. *Currency Data Concept, Web Globalization Guide Framework*. James Bean ©1996–2002. Available at *http://www.globalwebarch.com/*

Bean J. *Engineering Global E-Commerce Sites*. Morgan Kaufmann, San Francisco, 2003.

Bean J. *XML Globalization and Best Practices*. Active Education, Colorado, U.S., 2001.

Crawford M, Egan D, Jackson A. *Federal Tag Standards for Extensible Markup Language*. GS018T1, p 27. Logistics Management Institute (LMI), June 2001. Available at *http://xml.gov/*

IBM DB2 Universal Database, SQL Reference, Version 71, SC09-2974-01. IBM, 1993, 2001. DB2 Universal Database for OS/390, z/OS, SQL Reference, Version 7, SC26-9944-01. IBM, 1982, 2001. Available at *http://www.ibm.com/*

International Standards Organization (ISO). ISO 3166, Country Codes, TC46 Technical Committee. Available at *http://www.iso.ch/iso/*

en/stdsdevelopment/tc/tclist/TechnicalCommitteeDetailPage. Technical CommitteeDetail?COMMID=1757

International Standards Organization (ISO). ISO 3166, Country Codes, MA Maintenance Agency. Available at *http://www.din.de/gremien/nas/ nabd/iso3166ma/a3ptnorm.html*

International Standards Organization (ISO). ISO 4217, Currency Codes, TC68 Technical Committee. Available at *http://www.iso.ch/ iso/en/stdsdevelopment/tc/tclist/TechnicalCommitteeDetailPage. TechnicalCommitteeDetail?COMMID=2183*

International Standards Organization (ISO). ISO 4217, Currency Codes, UN/ECE United Nations Economic Commission for Europe. Available at *http://www.unece.org/cefact/rec/rec09en.htm*

International Standards Organization (ISO). ISO 8601, Date and Time, TC154 Technical Committee. Available at *http://www.iso.ch/iso/ en/stdsdevelopment/tc/tclist/TechnicalCommitteeDetailPage. Technical-CommitteeDetail?COMMID=3827*

Internet Explorer 6. Microsoft, 1995–2000 (used for various reference images). Available at *http://www.microsoft.com*

Karlsson, E-V. *Software Reuse—A Holistic Approach.* John Wiley & Sons, New York, 1995.

Manual for Data Administration, Special Publication 500-208, InterNational Committee for Information Technology Standards (INCITS). Available at *http://www.x3.org/incits/*

Microsoft SQL Server, Transact-SQL Reference (on-line), Data Types, Updated September 2001. Available at *http://msdn.microsoft.com/ library/default.asp?url=/library/en-us/tsqlref/ts_da-db_7msw.asp*

Object Management Group. OMG Modeling and Metadata Specifications. XML Metadata Interchange (XMI®). Available at *http://www.omg.org/*

Oracle 9i *Applications Developer Guide,* release 1 (9.0.1), part A88876-02. Oracle Corporation, 1996–2001. Available at *http://www.oracle.com/*

PowerDesigner, Data Modeling Tool. Sybase. Available at *http://www.sybase.com*

Simple Object Access Protocol, SOAP Version 1.2. World Wide Web Consortium (W3C), 2002. Available at *http://www.w3.org/TR/soap12-part1/*, *http://www.w3.org/TR/soap12-part2/*, and *http://www.w3.org/TR/soap12-af/*

Sybase Adaptive Server Enterprise 12.5. Transact-SQL, Content ID 1009196, revised Feb. 1, 2002. Sybase Inc., 2002. Available at *http://www.sybase.com/*

Universal Description Discovery and Integration of Web Services. Ariba, International Business Machines, and Microsoft. UDDI, 2000. Available at *http://www.uddi.org/*

Web Services Description Language (WSDL) version 1.2. World Wide Web Consortium (W3C), 2002. Available at *http://www.w3.org/TR/wsdl12/*

World Wide Web Consortium (W3C). eXtensible Markup Language (XML) 1.0, 2nd ed. W3C Recommendation, October 6, 2000. Available at *http://www.w3.org/TR/2000/REC-xml-20001006*

World Wide Web Consortium (W3C). HTML 4.01 Specification. W3C Recommendation, December 24, 2001. Available at *http://www.w3.org/TR/1999/REC-html401-19991224*

World Wide Web Consortium (W3C). XHTML™ 2.0. W3C Working Draft, August 5, 2002. Available at *http://www.w3.org/TR/2002/WD-xhtml2-20020805*

World Wide Web Consortium (W3C). XML-Data (e.g., "XML Data Reduced"). Note, January 5, 1988. Available at *http://www.w3.org/TR/1998/NOTE-XML-data-0105/*

World Wide Web Consortium (W3C). XML Schemas. W3C Recommendation, May 2, 2001. Available at *http://www.w3.org/TR/2001/REC-xmlschema-1-20010502/* (structures); *http://www.w3.org/TR/2001/REC-xmlschema-2-20010502/* (data types).

XML Spy, XML Edit and Development Tool. Altova, Inc. Available at *http://www.xmlspy.com*

Index